# PIRATES OF THE PRAIRIE

*Outlaws and Vigilantes*
*in America's Heartland*

## KEN LIZZIO

Guilford, Connecticut

An imprint of The Rowman & Littlefield Publishing Group, Inc.
4501 Forbes Blvd., Ste. 200
Lanham, MD 20706
www.rowman.com

Distributed by NATIONAL BOOK NETWORK

British Library Cataloguing in Publication Information available

**Library of Congress Cataloging-in-Publication Data available**

ISBN 978-1-4930-3659-2 (hardcover)
ISBN 978-1-4930-3658-5 (e-book)

♾ ™ The paper used in this publication meets the minimum requirements of American National Standard for Information Sciences—Permanence of Paper for Printed Library Materials, ANSI/ NISO Z39.48-1992.

Printed in the United States of America

# Contents

# Acknowledgments

I would like to thank the Ogle County Library and the Library of Southern Illinois University at Carbondale for making available hitherto hard-to-find documents. Thanks also to Roberta Fairburn at the Abraham Lincoln Presidential Library for her invaluable assistance in providing many of the photos that appear in this book.

# Prologue

*Not without thy wondrous story, could be writ the nation's glory, Illinois.*

—C.H. Chamberlin, from *Illinois State Song*

In the spring of 1836, twenty-year-old Eliza Wood Farnham (née Burhans), a feisty feminist and abolitionist from New York who had long wished to see something of "life in the West," set out for Illinois. Traveling by steamboat, she descended the Ohio River to the Mississippi then chugged upriver to Alton. There she boarded a fresh steamer and ascended the Illinois River, turgid and swollen by spring rains, into the heart of the tallgrass prairie. Eliza fell in love with the country at first sight. "I have lived again in the land of my heart," she rhapsodized. "I have seen the grasses wave, and felt the winds, and listened to the birds, and watched the springing flowers, and exulted in something of the old sense of freedom which these conferred upon me."[1]

After some time in the state, Eliza took passage up the Rock River, disembarking at the terminus of Dixon's Ferry, a town established just a few years earlier. As she strolled through the hamlet to a boardinghouse where she planned to spend the night, she took in the natural beauty all around her: verdant parks, copses of stately oaks and sycamore trees along the river bottom, and prairie tallgrass swaying softly on the bluffs above. For the young adventuress, Illinois was an idyllic fairy wilderness, an Arcadia of the soul as well as the senses.

But when she arrived at the boardinghouse she was brought rudely back to reality. At first, it was the rakish proprietor that repulsed her:

*You felt conscious of the presence of a villain; one of those universal prowlers, whose business it is to prey upon society, and who, when it will be most advantageous, prosecute their schemes alone, and when otherwise, surround themselves with a gang of ruffians, whose less disguised vices form a barrier between their leader and public indignation.*[2]

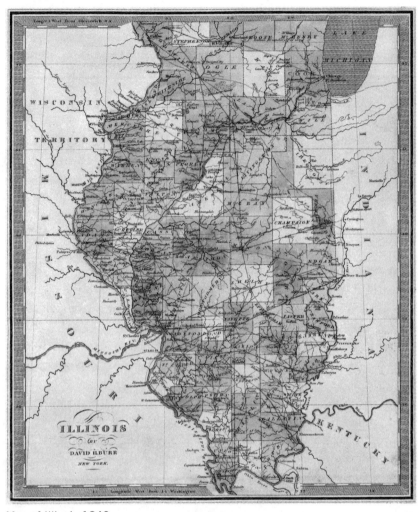

Map of Illinois 1840
*Source: Courtesy David Rumsey Map Collection*

Complaining of the summer heat and the long journey upriver, she asked to be shown a comfortable room with water. The proprietor led her to a room off the parlor but when she entered she noticed a man's hat and boots in the room.

"There appears to be a gentleman in the room," she said.

"Yes, it is occupied by a gentleman, but he's out and won't be here till night," came the casual reply.

With no other rooms available, he offered her use of the parlor for an hour to wash and rest. "A gross creature" brought her some towels and stood annoyingly by until Eliza ordered her to leave. She then barricaded the doors with rifles and a couple of trunks lest someone enter inadvertently. She had not yet finished her toiletries when a man began banging on the door angrily demanding it be opened so he could pass to his room. Flustered but unyielding, Eliza insisted he would have to wait. Muttering curses, the boarder retreated downstairs. A few minutes later, he returned and again pounded on the door. Still Eliza refused to open it. When she finally emerged fifteen minutes later, she recoiled in horror at what she saw:

> *Everything I now saw convinced me that I was in a den of the foulest iniquity; but imagination, stimulated as it was by fear, did not conceive the half of what I afterward learnt to be true of the vile people who consorted there . . . The people who live here are persons whose daily business is the stealing of horses, the manufacture of counterfeit money, et cet.; and such was their strength at the period spoken of, that although the better population of the place, of which I was informed there was a highly respectable body, held them in the abhorrence which their acts merited, they could make no demonstration against them without endangering their own and the lives of their families.*[3]

Readers at the time might have suspected Eliza of embellishing her narrative for the sake of suspense. Even today, the hotel's dodgy boarders seem more like characters out of the Wild West than the wholesome and halcyon heartland of America. Yet long before the American frontier west of the Mississippi came into being, there was an earlier frontier, Illinois.

Nearly four hundred miles long and two hundred miles wide, the prairie state formed a vast portion of what was then the northwestern United States. And at a time it was every bit as wild and lawless as any Dodge City or Tombstone ever was.

Between 1835 and 1850, several hundred outlaws and desperados descended on the Illinois frontier, holding up stagecoaches, robbing homes and individuals, rustling cattle and horses, counterfeiting, murdering, and terrorizing residents with virtual impunity. In the northern prairie, wilderness where most of the outlaws had clustered, they were known as "the banditti of the prairie" or "prairie pirates;" in the dense forests of the south, they were "land pirates," while those who preyed on Ohio River traffic were "river pirates." In a state that was sparsely settled, these outlaws went undetected for years, often masquerading as law-abiding farmers and merchants while preying on isolated settlers and passing emigrants. Although twice before Illinois had been beset by outlaws—in the early 1800s and again in the 1820s—the banditti of mid-century were a scourge unlike anything settlers had seen before or since.

If it was hard to detect the banditti, it was harder still to capture them and bring them to justice. On the American frontier, settlement preceded society so that there were always too few sheriffs to hunt them down and no secure jails to put them in when they did. If tried in a court of law, which was usually a rickety log cabin, the outlaws enlisted their confederates to intimidate witnesses, pack juries, and concoct alibis. Too often, to the exasperation of victimized citizens, the result was acquittal. By suborning the justice system, Illinois's outlaws were able to hold dominion over large portions of the prairie state for fifteen years.

Extraordinary conditions called for extraordinary measures. With law enforcement incapable of checking outlaws, frustrated citizens eventually took matters into their own hands, administering frontier justice, better known as vigilantism.

Scotch-Irish settlers introduced vigilantism in the 1760s, drawing on their own turbulent history and John Locke's ideas of the social contract. A political philosopher, Locke believed that the government had an obligation to serve and protect its people in return for which citizens were obligated to obey the law. But what happened when the government failed, when it was incapable of performing normal functions like policing or justice? According to Locke,

> *Where the laws cannot be executed, it is all one as if there were not Laws . . . If any mischief come in such Cases, it is not to be charged upon him, who defends his own right, but on him, that invades his neighbor.* [my ital.] *Whosoever uses force without Right, as everyone does in Society, who does it without law, puts himself in a State of War, with those, against whom he so uses it, and in that state all former ties are cancelled, all other Rights cease, and everyone has a right to defend himself and to resist the aggressor.*[4]

Whether the aggressor was a criminal or a tyrant, it was not the individual who had the right to undertake action against him but the community.

> *The Power that every individual gave the Society, when he entered into it, can never revert to the individual again, as long as the Society lasts, but will always remain in the community; because without this there can be no Community, no Commonwealth, which is contrary to the original Agreement.*[5]

Locke believed such expediencies were always temporary, relinquished when order was restored or institutions were able to assume their mandate.

America's first vigilantes, the South Carolina Regulators, were organized in 1767 to deal with criminal activity in the backcountry, a task that took two long years.* In 1780, magistrate Charles Lynch put down sporadic outbreaks of Tory violence in Virginia's piedmont. Lynch tried those he captured in his informal court; those found guilty were tied to a walnut tree on his property in Chestnut Hill and whipped. "Lynch Law," as he dubbed his method of summary justice, met with the approval of none other than the state's governor, Thomas Jefferson, who, in a letter to Lynch applauding his methods, nonetheless expressed the hope that Tories would receive a "regular trial." They didn't.

---

*The term Regulator first appeared in England in 1655 and referred to a practice of temporarily deputizing citizens to supplement existing law enforcement. The English Regulator, however, had nothing in common with its American counterpart.

Lynch's unique brand of justice and South Carolina's Regulators became models for subsequent vigilante movements all over the American frontier.[6] Posses were organized, outlaws were hunted down and swept from their lairs or subject to summary judgment. If they were lucky, miscreants got off with a harsh whipping with a promise to leave; if not, they were shot or hanged. Thus did Regulators "regulate" by returning an intolerable situation to the status quo ante.

It is a mistake to think vigilantes were wild mobs acting irrationally. Regulators tended to be collective, socially constructive enterprises with a constitution that mirrored actual laws—or vigilantes' sometimes imperfect understanding of them. Provision was even made for defense of the accused, though the verdict—if not the punishment—was often a foregone conclusion. What often lent legitimacy to these groups was that they often consisted of the most prominent members of the community including judges, sheriffs, constables, and legislators.

Still, more philosophically minded Regulators might have been surprised to know that Locke himself stopped short of endorsing vigilantism. He believed that "[s]elf-love will make men partial to themselves and to their Friends. And on the other side, that Ill Nature, Passion and Revenge will carry them too far in punishing others. And hence nothing but Confusion and Disorder will follow." [7] For Locke, extralegal justice could never be sanctioned for it was invariably personal and unmanageable. Popular tribunals always contained men who had been wronged and, thus, had a particular score to settle. In Locke's view, only the sanctity of the law and formal institutions could assure fairness and impartiality.

That not all vigilante groups in Illinois (or elsewhere for that matter) yielded positive (or just) outcomes confirmed Locke's own worst fears about the tendency of public tribunals to enact personal vendettas that ultimately led to chaos. Indeed, this is just what happened in southern Illinois in the bizarre war between the Flatheads and the Regulators, a protracted conflict so violent and chaotic that it became virtually impossible to distinguish which side was acting in the name of law and order, begging the question, Were Illinois vigilantes justified in their extralegal actions, or was Locke right all along?

On the one hand, pioneers had settled on the frontier in the hope of scratching a better life out of the prairie soil than the one they left behind. Starting with little, they labored mightily only to have their horses stolen, their homes robbed, or their loved ones murdered. Living in isolation or small, vulnerable hamlets, terrified families cowered in fear, not knowing when or where the pirates would strike next. Farmers took to sleeping in their barns with their trusty rifles by their side to protect family and livestock. That law enforcement was powerless to check the outlaws only emboldened them to commit acts of even greater audacity and violence. For helpless settlers seeking peace and stability in their fledgling communities, vigilantism was a method of last resort. It was swift and effective. Best of all, it worked.

On the other hand, vigilantism was a decidedly imperfect form of justice and for the very reasons that concerned Locke. In some cases, the bandits got off too lightly, only to strike, and more viciously, another day. In others, the punishment, meted out as it was by those who had been personally wronged, was far worse than the guilty deserved. One case of vigilantism in southern Illinois sparked a five-year civil war in which countless innocent settlers were murdered, driven from their homes, or dispossessed of their wealth. As Locke rightly anticipated, such were the dangers of going outside the orderly constraints of sacred law.

To be a Regulator or not, vigilantism was a vexing dilemma, to be sure. Still, one cannot help but wonder how Locke might have felt had he been a struggling Illinois pioneer and not a comfy London surgeon.

Consider the remarkable story of the outlaws and vigilantes on the Illinois frontier.

# John Driscoll

*We are great, and rapidly—I was about to say fearfully—growing!*

—JOHN C. CALHOUN, *Debates of Congress*, 1817

As Eliza discovered, frontier Illinois was a Janus-faced land, as civilized as it was untamed. Since gaining statehood in 1818, its population had grown fivefold to 150,000 by 1830. Cities and towns hummed with the same social and political sophistication as any back east. One could find stores selling silk, satin, broadcloth, and other fine fabrics as well as choice wines and liquors. The farmhouse had begun to replace the log cabin, that icon of the American frontier, and the farmer and lawyer were usurping the coarse pioneer and backwoodsman. Men were casting off frontier garb of coonskin hat, linsey shirt, and buckskin breeches for the more civilized look of fur hats, coats, and shoes or boots. Ladies, too, were trading homespun cotton frocks for dresses of silk or linen and dainty straw hats for frumpy bonnets.

Despite the trappings of civilization, Illinois of 1830 was still unmistakably frontier: raw, undeveloped, and predominantly wilderness. Most people in the state had come from the south and settled in the central and southern parts of the state. Apart from several thousand people working the lead mines at Galena, northern Illinois consisted of untrammeled prairie with a sprinkling of communities here and there. Scarcely a single trail or road existed north of Springfield. Indeed, the state's main thoroughfares were still the Illinois and Wabash Rivers and still used by backwoodsmen and traders of the American Fur Company.

And there were Indians to contend with. In eastern Illinois, the Winnebago had been effectively subdued, having signed a treaty turning over most of their land in 1827. The Sac and Fox, however, still contested a large tract of territory in the Rock River Valley. In 1804, five Sac and Fox chiefs had signed a treaty ceding fifty million acres of land in Illinois and surrounding areas after being generously plied with firewater by the territorial governor, William Henry Harrison. The besotted chiefs had no idea what they had signed, nor were the Sac and Fox nations ever consulted about the treaty. Even though successive treaties affirming the 1804 agreement were signed by Black Hawk, an old chief of the Sac, he patently refused to recognize them, arguing, "What do we know of the laws and customs of the white people? They might buy our bodies for dissection, and we would touch the goose quill to confirm it, without knowing what we are doing."[1]

For the Sac, the Rock River Valley was integral to their very souls. Originally from the St. Lawrence River Valley, they were hounded west by the French in a series of bloody skirmishes. When they arrived at the confluence of the Rock and Mississippi Rivers in the 1760s, weary and beleaguered, they felt they had at last found their promised land. The Rock River Valley was as beautiful as it was bountiful. There were lush tall prairie grasses on which they could graze their many horses and a cornucopia of wild edibles like chokecherries, raspberries, plums, strawberries, and crab apples. The prairie teemed with succulent prairie hen and quail, the woods with huge, wild turkeys, pecans, and hickory nuts. Lakes and streams abounded with waterfowl: swans, geese, mallards, and many other kinds of ducks. In the fertile soil, the women cultivated corn, beans, squash, and pumpkins. The Sac thrived and vowed never to leave a land that had become sacred to them.

When white squatters began encroaching on Sac lands in 1830, Black Hawk receded into the Iowa Territory. He believed the move to be temporary, however, especially as his people were unable to scratch a living from the poor soil they had found in Iowa. So in the spring of 1831, Black Hawk and his band crossed back to their old homes on Rock River. Acting on false settler reports of aggressive acts by the Sac, the governor called in six hundred volunteers and ten companies of army regulars. After watching the menacing troops assemble outside his village, Black

Ma-ka-tai-me-she-kia-kiak or Black Hawk, Chief of the Sac
*Source: Courtesy of the Abraham Lincoln Presidential Library and Museum*

Hawk again retreated into Iowa, consenting never to cross east of the Mississippi without the permission of the US government.

But after another harsh winter that left his people near starvation, Black Hawk once again returned to Illinois, this time with four hundred warriors and his entire band of women, children, and the elderly. The Sac chief only wished to cultivate his fields with his friends the Winnebago. Yet, reports that he had met with his old allies, the British, Potawatomi, and Winnebago, led settlers to fear that Black Hawk's intentions were hostile. This time the governor called up 1,600 militias to supplement ten companies of infantry already moving toward Dixon's Ferry. With trigger-happy volunteers itching for a showdown, a clash was inevitable.

After several skirmishes in which both sides lost men, Black Hawk was taken prisoner. Upon his release in June 1833, he returned to the last of his people in Iowa. Mourning his great loss, he said, "Rock River was a beautiful country. I loved my towns, my cornfields, and the home of my people. I fought for it. It is now yours."[2]

With the begrudging departure of the Sac, the trickle of white settlers suddenly surged. Unlike those who had settled in the south, most newcomers were Yankees from Pennsylvania, Ohio, New York, and New England. They also came from England, Ireland, and Scotland. They came as individuals, families, even entire towns. Having sold most of their possessions for the arduous trek, they borrowed what additional money they needed from friends and family. They came across the prairie over rutted trails in horse-drawn flatbed wagons, big-bodied New England carts, Conestoga wagons, and stagecoaches, and in flatboats down the Ohio River with their horses and cattle.

Many went out of a desire to establish themselves as farmers where land was cheap and where they could "grow up with the country." Among these young emigrants were merchants, doctors, lawyers, farmers, and schoolmasters who purchased tracts of land from the government at $1.25 an acre. The poor simply squatted on the land, a practice the young state, anxious to develop, did not discourage. Soldiers who had pursued Black Hawk across the prairie were impressed by the beauty and potential of the land and took advantage of the Military Tract, land set aside from the old Sac lands—some 3.5 million acres—to reimburse them for their service in the War of 1812, each soldier receiving a bounty of 160 acres. Still others bought on speculation, hoping to reap huge profits from the rapid settlement.

The Rock River Valley was the kind of place pioneers dreamed about, a land as beautiful as it was abundant. Although the buffalo had long since faded from Illinois, there were still plenty of elk, deer, and fowl roaming meadows and woods. Rich groves of oak, white pine, stately elm, and sycamore filled the bottomlands and brightly colored parakeets flitted among the trees. Streams snaked through gently rolling tallgrass prairie, and pearl-filled clams studded streambeds. Flowing through the blessed country was the pristine Rock River. When poet William Cullen

The Rock River
*Source: Courtesy of the Abraham Lincoln Presidential Library and Museum*

Bryant passed through in 1832 he described the Rock as "one of the most beautiful of our western streams . . . The current is rapid and the pellucid waters glide over a bottom of sand and pebbles."[3] One young man from the east paid homage to the land's beauty with a poem:

> I am all in my glory when I think of Peoria,
> That gentle and beautiful lake,
> Where the goose and the swan do the waters adorn,
> There pleasure I mean for to take.
> With a wife by my side down the waters I'll glide
> With a love that shall banish all fear;
> And then we will roam to our cabin, our home,
> Nor dream that an Indian is near.[4]

Most newcomers chose to settle on prairie land along wooded groves, which provided wood for fires and fences as well as protection against the howling prairie winds. To be sure, the prairie sod was devilish to "bust," but once they did, the earth beneath was rich beyond imagination, unlike anything seen back east. Relatives and friends of settlers wrote home extolling the beauty and benefits of the valley. Books and newspaper articles described the lay of the land, the best routes to take, what to bring, and what to expect when they arrived. It was easy to see why Black Hawk had been loathed to give up Rock River country.

Despite the land's bounty, frontier life was demanding. The pioneer needed to know so many things in order to survive in the wilderness: how to track and kill game, to recognize forest plants, to build a cabin and make furniture. If you arrived by boat or wagon, you slept in it until the log cabin was completed. It took about seventy to eighty trees—usually black oak—about ten inches thick to build a cabin. To help with the labor required for construction, neighbors were invited to a "log raising" as much a social event as work with whiskey and food provided by the owner. The finished cabin was a single-story bare-bones affair thirty feet by twenty feet with a dirt floor or with puncheons, logs split into planks. The hearth was made of stone or clay. Windows, if there were any, were small sashes ten inches by twelve inches. For roofing, bark slabs were laid like shingles and held fast with logs. Lastly came the porch, which spanned the entire length of the cabin and was covered with cleft boards. Few houses had locks, though some had simple hatches and were, thus, quite insecure. Farms generally had corn cribs while barns and cow and pig pens tended to be less common. From their first settling, farmers raised some Indian corn, a little wheat and oats, and small produce gardens of turnips, peas, pumpkins, potatoes, cabbage, cucumbers, radishes, and the like. Families kept poultry, pigs, and a small flock of sheep, marked in the ears, primarily as a source of wool, just as geese and ducks were kept for their feathers. Corn was the main staple, roasted or made into a mush. Meat was preserved by salting and smoking. When salt was unavailable, meat was packed in wood ashes, then washed in boiling water and smoked over a fire. Coffee, a luxury, was consumed only on Sunday morning.

By today's standards, it seems like a hard life, but it was, in fact, the very life hardy pioneers had dreamed about when they set out for the frontier.

For John Driscoll, the Rock River Valley was the kind of place he too dreamed about but for altogether different reasons. By the time the fifty-five-year-old escaped convict arrived in 1835, the same year as Eliza, he had spent most of his life following the ever-expanding frontier perfecting the art of horse stealing.

He was born Johnson Driskel (he later changed his name while on the run) to Daniel and Eleanor Driskel on November 15, 1780, in Bedford County, Pennsylvania.[5] Bedford was a frontier community at the foot of the Allegheny Mountains, an area acquired by treaty from the Indians just twelve years earlier, but which morose Indians still contested. Irish by descent, the Driscoll family formed part of a large contingent of Irish that had settled on the Bedford frontier. Daniel was likely a small farmer— or tenant farmer—many of whom, because of the lack of roads, were converting grain crops to easily transportable whiskey or other distilled spirits. When the federal government imposed a tax on distilled spirits to pay the Revolutionary War debt, farmers in western Pennsylvania revolted in 1791 in what became known as the Whiskey Rebellion. It is likely that Daniel Driscoll joined the protest as the fiercest opposition came from western Pennsylvania. After a skirmish between rebels and government forces in which one rebel was wounded, protestors from five counties—including Bedford—declared independence from the United States. Determined to put down the rebellion and assert federal authority, President George Washington called up four state militias in October 1794. It was the only time a sitting American president led troops in the field. When Washington's army marched into western Pennsylvania, the insurrection finally collapsed. In the wake of the defeat, many residents of the area looked to move beyond the long reach of the state. So, too, did the Driscolls.

In his early twenties, John married Mercy Mary Acken from neighboring Somerset County. Of the fifteen children she would bear, four— William, Pearson, David, and Taylor—would follow adroitly in their father's footsteps in crime. Sometime around 1800, the Driscolls, along with John's parents and his four siblings, moved to Columbiana County, Ohio, on the Pennsylvania border. In their wandering westward, they would follow the National Road, the nation's first highway. A remarkable achievement for its time, the road was thirty feet wide and paved with crushed stone and topped with gravel. By 1818, the road had reached Wheeling at a staggering cost of $13,000 a mile.[6] Although still a work in progress when the Driscolls set out, the road would eventually take them all the way to its terminus in Illinois.

If the Driscolls were looking for a place with few laws and greater opportunity for outlaws, they had found it in Ohio. The first permanent settlement of New Lisbon had been established just four years earlier. The Driscolls built a log cabin west of town on a creek near the cabin of Sam and Thomas Davis, brothers who, over the next three decades, would become two of Driscoll's many partners in crime. Other neighbors and soon-to-be partners in crime were James Brody and his sons. James looked every bit the criminal he either was or was about to become. Diminutive in size, he had a "piratical look" with a low forehead, stiff black hair, and small blackish eyes set deep in a cretinous head. Over time, the Driscoll and Brody siblings would intermarry, creating a powerful and tightly-knit criminal syndicate.

By now in his mid-twenties, John Driscoll had grown to be a huge hulk of a man, six feet tall, weighing more than two hundred pounds, all muscle and sinew. Like many frontier Irishmen, he was a heavy drinker who became a blustering, swaggering bully when drunk. After a few belts of corn whiskey, he would invariably begin goading men around him into a fistfight, usually a large, muscular man like himself who presented a suitable challenge. Often these brawls, called "musters," took place at public venues such as the town square or the tavern, providing a kind of sporting spectacle for entertainment-starved pioneers. If his designated adversary proved unwilling to fight, Driscoll would simply sucker punch the reluctant soul.

On one occasion, after several libations at a tavern in New Lisbon, Driscoll began hurling insults at the patrons. Standing above the rest of the crowd was a large man named Isaac Pew. Approaching Pew, Driscoll let fly some insults and then coldcocked him. As Pew went down, Driscoll sprang upon him and bit off his ear. Such was life on the rough and tumble frontier that the proprietor of the tavern and associate judge of Wayne County Common Pleas Court, Christian Smith, looked on with indifference, making no attempt to arrest Driscoll.

The next time Pew saw Driscoll, he remarked to a friend, "He has my ear, now I'll have his nose." Pew approached Driscoll who, seeing the rage in Pew's eyes, began to retreat. As Pew pursued, Driscoll's brother William attempted to block his way but Pew rushed past him and lunged at John. Leveling John with a single blow, he then bit off part of his nose, leaving Driscoll ghoulishly disfigured for the rest of his life.

Around 1808, the Driscolls and Brodys moved to Wooster, the seat of Wayne County, Ohio. At the time the county had a population of three hundred, a single-room school made of logs, a gristmill, and not a single jail. Driscoll and his family settled in a cabin east of town on Apple Creek near an old mill. At first, Wooster residents regarded Driscoll as an upstanding member of the community. He voted in the town's first election and became one the first supervisors of Wooster when the town was organized in 1812. For some years, he made a living selling (or speculating) in farm real estate.[7]

Secretly, however, the Driscolls and Brodys were already plundering anything on four legs they could lay their hands on. During the War of 1812, two of John's sons were caught ripping off oxen from the US militia army that passed through Mansfield on its way to hunt Tecumseh. Three years later, Stephen Brody was convicted of his third offense of horse stealing—the penalty for which was a public cropping of one's ears—much as you would do to mark your prized heifer. Thereafter, he was known as "Cropped Ears."

As for John Driscoll, he was able to live nearly ten years in Wooster seemingly without personal suspicion or incident—apart, that is, from his drunken brawls. One night in 1820, Driscoll and a large party had gathered in the bar room of the Eagle Hotel owned by Horace Howard. After some heavy drinking, the guests became boisterous and Howard ejected them from the premises. As Driscoll was leaving the bar, he picked up a candlestick and carrying it outdoors with him, tossed it into Howard's garden. The next morning Howard had Driscoll arrested for theft of property. The jurors, however, ruled that Driscoll had not exhibited intent to steal and acquitted him. Though the act was more childish than malicious, it marked the first of his many arrests.

---

*John's brother Dennis seems to have gone his own way and eventually put down roots in Ohio where became a town trustee.

On another occasion, Driscoll was parading the streets of Wooster bellowing in his usual manner that he was mean fighter that no man could whip. Just then, Smith McIntire, who had just finished clearing off some land on his farm south of Wooster, rode into town to buy some tobacco and other goods. McIntire's quiet, courteous demeanor belied the fact that he could be a ferocious fighter when pressed. Hearing Driscoll boast, McIntire pointed toward him, saying, "I can whip anybody, but I don't know that man, and I am a stranger here, and more than that, I am a peaceful man," whereupon he quietly returned to his errands. But two members of the town, keen to see the bully Driscoll put in his place, had only to remark to Driscoll that (pointing to McIntire) there was a man that he had not yet whipped. Taking the bait, Driscoll rushed toward him and said, "Do you think you can handle me?" To which McIntire responded, "I do." Driscoll said, "Well, let us take a drink, and then to business." McIntire was a teetotaler, but to oblige Driscoll, he accompanied him to Nailor's Tavern where Driscoll threw back a few shots of whiskey. He then turned and faced McIntire. When the word "ready" was given, McIntire landed a single lighting blow that knocked Driscoll senseless. Eventually, a doctor had to be called and it was a few hours before Driscoll came to senses.

Determined to even the score, a short time afterward, Driscoll challenged McIntire to a second test, which he accepted. For his backers, McIntire had two of his friends, Driscoll, his son William, and his son-in-law Reason Brody. The contestants met and with the same result as the first. As Driscoll lay on the floor again unconscious, McIntire picked him up like a rag doll and, dragging him toward the fireplace, exclaimed, "I will make a burnt offering of him," until alarmed patrons interceded.[8]

Shortly after Driscoll's beating, sheriffs Michael Totten and Moses Loudon attempted to arrest Stephen Brody for stealing a heifer at a nearby mill. Brody resisted. In the ensuing struggle, Brody plunged a knife into Loudon's thigh the length of the blade. At his trial in Wooster, he was found guilty and sentenced to three years in prison. Given the close relationship between Driscoll and Brody, when more animals began to go missing in the county, residents immediately suspected John Driscoll. When a prominent general had a yoke of oxen stolen and sold in Cleveland, a young man named Ben Worthington was arrested and tried for stealing the animals. During the trial, Worthington testified as to the complicity of the Driscolls and Brodys in the theft as well as the existence of a gang of horse thieves whose leader was none other than John Driscoll.

If there was any doubt as to Worthington's claims, soon after his trial, Driscoll was arrested in Beaver County, Pennsylvania, for trying to sell horses he had stolen in Columbiana. In Ohio, as elsewhere on the frontier, horse stealing was a serious crime, punishable by fifty lashes in the first offense and imprisonment in the second. Driscoll was tried, found guilty, and sentenced to three years in the Columbus prison in 1829. At the time, prisoners were permitted to labor on the public works if secured with heavy weights and under guard. When working, Driscoll was always secured with a fifty-six-pound weight fastened to his leg with a chain. About eighteen months into his sentence, he decided he had had enough. One evening while pushing a wheelbarrow of dirt along the Ohio canal, he picked up the weighted ball and chain and started to run. Several guards immediately fired on him but missed and he escaped into the gathering darkness. At length he came to a farm residence where he found an axe in a woodpile and severed the ball from the chain. Having dispensed with this impediment to travel, he leisurely made his way back to his family in Wayne County where he filed the clasp of the chain from his leg. Despite a reward outstanding for his capture, whenever he was drunk, he would recount the details of his escape—the severing of the chain with the farmer's ax and the filing of the leg clasp—until neighbors could hear him roaring with laughter.

It wasn't long before authorities heard Driscoll was back in Wayne County and mounted an effort to recapture him. To elude his pursuers, he led a roving life for a time, stealing horses and concealing them in thickets, burning barns and houses of his enemies, finally quitting the country altogether for Ashland County. It was about this time that he changed his surname from "Driskel" to Driscoll.

Late 1830 found Driscoll holed up at a farm with his son Pearson and two of the Brody boys. Using the farm as headquarters, he picked up where he had left off—stealing horses. Horses stolen in Ohio were quickly passed along to the Lake Erie region, making it hard, if not impossible, to recover them. Prosecuting horse thieves was just as hard, for each time a suspected thief was apprehended, his cohorts would provide a ready alibi in court. By now, Driscoll and his accomplices had acquired the moniker "land pirates" for their brazen horse stealing, incendiarism, and burglary. After an intense period in which Driscoll stole a horse and another man's colt and robbed Hart's store near Haysville, residents became so frustrated they finally called in the Black Cane Company.

Headquartered in Richland County, Black Cane was a vigilante group created in 1820 in response to counterfeiting and horse stealing in the southern Ohio counties. Shortly after its establishment, Black Cane had discovered an extensive horse-stealing network that ran from the southern country up the Mohican Valley to Lake Erie. The company got its name from the black cane its members carried. The cane was made from the wood of the gnarly hawthorn tree, which was very hard and resistant to rot. After peeling off the bark, the cane was then burned and polished with oil to give it a glossy appearance. Its purpose seems to have been functional as well as aesthetic.[9]

Soon after being contacted, Cane leaders received a tip that the goods stolen from Hart's store were cached in a swamp ten miles south. The men hasted to the swamp but found nothing. A few days later, another tip surfaced that the merchandise had been removed from the swamp and was now in route to Lake Erie. On hearing this, Cane leader Judge Thomas Coulter and another member went in pursuit of a wagon they heard was headed north toward Monroeville. Halfway to Monroeville, they overtook the wagon and searched it but found nothing. Only later did they learn that the goods had been hidden under a false floor of the bed.

After his return to Richland, Judge Coulter began collecting on a number of judgments against defendants convicted in his court, many of which were against the Driscoll gang. Coulter had succeeded in collecting about $45 when it occurred to him that the Driscoll gang was aware he stored the fines in his desk drawer. One evening after Coulter had finished collecting fines, he decided to move all but $5 of the money (about $100) for safekeeping. His precautions came not a day too soon, for the next morning, Coulter found the desk lying in a farm field rifled of all its contents. At once Coulter suspected the Driscolls and ordered them to be placed under arrest.

Now whenever a member of the Driscoll gang was arrested in connection with such events, it was state prosecutor Jonathan Coulter (Thomas's brother) and Green Township constable William Irvin (both Black Cane members) who prosecuted them. With several of the gang now facing trial, Pearson Driscoll attempted to bribe Coulter and Irvin in return for their "cooperation" in court. When that failed, Pearson tried verbal intimidation—to no avail. Hoping to frighten them into cooperating, Pearson and Stephen Brody finally burned down their barns. The blaze at the Coulters was devastating, consuming several horses, equipment, large stocks of grain, hay, and nearly spreading to the house. While the barn fires raged, the Driscolls cut loose a large flatboat on the Blackfork River loaded with hundreds of barrels of whiskey, salt, and pork. They were hoping it would drift down to the Mohican River where they planned to take possession of it. But when a local citizen noticed it adrift downstream, it was safely recovered. Shortly after the inferno, Pearson was arrested and tried for arson and sentenced to three years in prison.

Three years later, on a bitter cold December evening, a Mohican Township resident, John Kidwell, spotted John Driscoll making his way stealthily through the woods on horseback in the direction of Pearson's house. By now, Pearson had served his prison time and had returned home. Assuming the old man was headed to visit his son, Kidwell set out on foot through the woods to communicate his discovery to the neighbors. A force of six Black Cane members was hastily assembled that included Jonathan and Thomas Coulter, William Irvin, David Ayres, and the Peterson brothers. Together, the six rode to Pearson's house, arriving late at night. As they reconnoitered the premises, Thomas spotted a brand new saddle hanging under the portico of Pearson's cabin, indicating John was inside. While two men remained outside, Thomas, Irvin, and Ayres opened the door and entered. The room was dark, so they quietly approached the fireplace and stirred the coals. As flames leaped up and illuminated the room, John Driscoll, who had been sound asleep, suddenly awoke. Before anyone had time to react, Driscoll sprang from his bed with a bowie knife, seized his rifle, and threatened to kill the intruders if they did not immediately leave the house. Gingerly, the vigilantes backed out and closed the door after them. As they retreated, Driscoll shouted that he would not be taken alive and would rather be shot down at his son's home than return to the penitentiary.

Coulter and his men were not about to wait out Driscoll in the frigid cold, telling him he would have five minutes to surrender or be killed. Several times Driscoll tried to rush through the door guns ablaze but each time Pearson and his wife restrained him. At one point, when Driscoll cracked open the door and thrust his arm through, Irvin dealt a sharp blow to his arm causing him to withdraw into the house momentarily stunned.

Now Driscoll had a picklock gun loaded with unusual percussion grains. These grains were about the size of a pinhead and the pick striking down on one exploded the powder. Of the five Black Cane men, four had flintlock muskets, the best firearm in use in those days. The other had a pistol. When the five minutes expired, Coulter gave the order to fire. At the same time, old man Driscoll raised his gun to fire at David Ayers who was standing within sight of the partly opened door. As John took aim, Pearson, not wishing to return so soon to prison, abruptly slipped his hand between the grain and the pick, preventing the discharge of the gun but wounding his own hand. At the same time, the five vigilantes all fired at Driscoll but in the extreme cold, their weapons failed to go off. The result was four faint, anticlimactic "snaps" followed by the flash of Ayer's pistol belatedly discharging in the dark.

For a brief moment, there was confused silence. Then the vigilantes rushed the house and began pushing out the chinking between the logs to secure portholes for the muzzles of their guns. With time running out, Pearce and his wife pleaded with Driscoll to surrender. As the muzzles began to poke through the walls, Driscoll finally announced his surrender. The vigilantes then rushed in and, securing Driscoll's arms with a rope, turned him over to the Peterson brothers. That same morning, the Petersons left with their charge for the Columbus prison, relieved they had finally caught one of the region's most notorious and elusive horse thieves. But when they stopped over night at the village of Sunbury, Driscoll escaped.[10] He fled to Steubenville, Indiana, with his family and the Brodys. They were not in Steubenville a year before angry residents drove them out.

By now, John Driscoll was getting tired. In his mid-fifties, he had spent most of his life running from one county to another and from one state to another. He needed to make a fresh start in a place where he could settle down and pursue a life of crime more or less unfettered, a place where there was plenty of opportunity to steal and the arm of law enforcement was short.

His son David had found just the place.

CHAPTER 2

# The Driscoll Gang

*Those land pirates who at that early period roved over these billowy prairies, as pirates roam the seas.*

—HENRY BOIES, *History of Dekalb County*

The Rock River Valley was an outlaw's paradise. Settlers living isolated and vulnerable in the prairie wilderness made easy prey and new ones were arriving every day. On flatboats drifting down the Rock and Illinois Rivers, farmers were shipping the fruits of their labors: ham, bacon, venison, poultry, hides, pelts, leather, and bushels of wheat, oats, and rye to market—all signs of a burgeoning wealth ripe for the harvesting. And the trackless forests and tallgrass prairie afforded natural cover for the outlaws' plunder as well as the outlaws themselves.

Best of all, law enforcement was in its infancy, undeveloped and unorganized. There were few sheriffs and even fewer jails. The court system was equally primitive. The entire state had but five circuit court judges who held trial on an itinerant basis in their districts. Since there were no formal courts, the largest room of a tavern or a spacious loft made do with an itinerant judge presiding. One settler described the informal nature of the frontier courtroom and the inexperience of its jurors at the time:

*The sheriff opens the court and calls the cases, the noise ceases. Upon a couple of planks are ranged twenty-four freemen, heads of families, housekeepers, forming the grand jury. What an assemblage! From the hunter in breeches and skin shirt, whose beard and razor have not met for a month—the squatter in hat and dressed in stuffs manufactured at home by his wife—the small dealer . . . sitting beside the blacksmith . . . The judge makes his charge with as much dignity as if he sat in Westminster, and the verdicts savor nothing of the whimsical appearance of the court and jury.*[1]

David Driscoll arrived in the Rock River Valley in 1834, settling in DeKalb County's South Grove, so called because it was just south of the Kishwaukie Forest. When his father arrived the following year with Mercy and their seven children, he bought out David's claim. David moved a few miles further south near the village of Lynnville along the banks of Killbuck Creek that he named after a stream in Ohio. Soon after, the rest of the Driscoll gang swept into the valley like a plague of locusts.

Fifty-five-year-old James Brody arrived the same year as John Driscoll with his sons John, Stephen, William, and Hugh. They settled six miles south of their boss in a grove of hickory and walnut timber in what came to be known as "Brody's Grove" in today's Dement Township in Ogle County. Other settlers had been loathed to take up land there as it was unproductive, thus providing a high degree of isolation for the Brodys' criminal activities. Samuel Aikens and his son Charles settled at Washington Grove in Ogle County a few miles west of the Brodys. His other sons, Thomas and Richard, settled amid the hardwoods at Lafayette Grove a half mile away. The Aikens may have originally intended to live normal lives in Ogle County. But after their extensive land speculations there turned sour, they allowed their houses and barns to become places of refuge and concealment for the Driscoll gang. In 1838, William and Pearson Driscoll arrived from Ohio, settling near David in a log cabin in South Grove.

From Ohio also came two counterfeiters, William K. Bridge and Norton Royce, who settled at Washington Grove and Lafayette Grove. Royce would produce such an abundance of counterfeit bills that he would become known as "director of the pirates' mint." To Inlet Grove in south Ogle County (it would become Lee County in 1839) came another group of counterfeiters: Adolphus Bliss and his wife Hannah, Corydon Dewey, and Charles West, known facetiously as "Bliss, Dewey, West, and Company." Dewey was Bliss's nearest neighbor on one side and West's on the other. That same year, Charles Oliver, a counterfeiter from Pennsylvania, settled in Rockford in Winnebago County just north of Ogle.[2]

Such is a brief outline of the persona dramatis of the Driscoll gang who came to roost and raise hell in Rock River country. Whether by accident or design, the dispersal of the gang over a wide geographic area would prove advantageous for their criminal activities, providing places of rest and refuge for outlaws and for concealment for their horses and other stolen goods. In the ensuing years, hundreds more outlaws would descend on the northern Illinois prairie like a plague of locusts, some linked to Driscoll, others operating more or less on their own and about which history tells us little.

Shortly after their arrival, the Driscoll gang went to work stealing horses, good horses, horses that were strong and fast. A coveted asset on the frontier, horses were easy to pinch from a hitching post or a stable. In some cases, neighbors, who were not themselves part of the gang, would inform a gang member of the location of a horse and of the neighbor's routines in return for a share in the profits.

Once stolen, horses were easy to hide and transport as well. At times, they were concealed amid the prairie tallgrass or in a dense copse of trees. Other times, the gang used barns with trap doors that allowed stolen horses to be kept underground during the day and moved to another "station" at night. The pirates stole corn from the farmers to feed them and at a suitable opportunity conducted them out of the county under the cover of darkness. Horses did not stay in one place for more than a day or two before being moved, making it difficult for farmers to trace them and even harder to catch the thief. Even if they could, it was usually impossible to prove ownership of the horse. Thus, once gone, a horse was usually gone forever.

To transport horses to market, Driscoll tapped into a network that was far more extensive than anything he had used in Ohio. It extended through the southern states to Arkansas and Texas, north to Wisconsin and the Great Lakes, west to Iowa Territory, and east as far as Lake Erie. Along the clandestine routes were stationed men and agents at convenient distances to receive and relay the animals, men to all appearances hard-working and upstanding members of their communities. A horse stolen at either end of the line or anywhere in the interior was passed from one agent to another so that none of the agents needed to be absent from his home or business for more than a few hours at a time. In other cases, horse thieves simply rode stolen horses from Wisconsin to Missouri and back again. Houses of the Driscolls, Brodys, and other gang members served as waystations along the way where horse runners received shelter and refreshment. Other times, runners would come up from the south with stolen horses and, unless in fear of immediate pursuit, would leave them with Dewey or West at Inlet Grove, or with Driscoll at Washington Grove, or Oliver at Rockford, who would then pass them along to the end of the line. Along this well-established line, horses passed continually like cargo. To avoid detection, they used secret signals, passwords, and handshakes that governed their transactions. One such handshake involved crossing the wrists at right angles and repeating the words "Robinson Crusoe." While visiting the Rock River Valley in 1841, William Cullen Bryant reported ten to twenty horses a night being brought to a station.[3]

John Driscoll planned, guided, and directed the horse-stealing operations in the Rock River Valley. A kind of paterfamilias of the prairie pirates, he concealed them when danger threatened, nursed them when sick, rested them when worn down by fatigue and forced marches, furnished hiding places for their stolen booty in caves and underground caches, and, of course, shared in the spoils.

If there was one thing Driscoll had learned in his early years of plundering the frontier—apart from horse stealing—it was not to make a spectacle of himself. In Illinois, the drunken brawls ceased. Instead of the menacing ogre, Driscoll projected an image of the kind-hearted, hardworking pioneer. Locals, unaware that he was an escaped convict, thought him an intelligent man, full of generosity toward his neighbors. In one instance, after he and his sons finished plowing their fields, they planted a field of corn for a woman whose husband had died in the middle of planting season. John Driscoll had definitely matured as a criminal.

Others in the gang inspired outright admiration in the community. Pennsylvania-born William Bridge possessed all the marks of an aristocrat: tall, handsome, educated, and charming. To his neighbors he seemed a model citizen, full of rectitude, charity, and kindness. Charles Oliver was a man much like Bridge, educated, witty, and urbane. At the Rockford House Inn, which he built in 1838 with a $4,000 advance from his father,

Oliver regaled locals with his store of witty anecdotes. Similarly, Dewey and West, who had started farms on government land, seemed to locals to be industrious settlers intent on making an honest living.

In this diabolical way, the Driscoll gang was able to operate for years while remaining unsuspected. Year after year horses disappeared, yet no one knew where or how. From time to time, a farmer would find a mangled corpse in some uninhabited woods or counterfeit money would flood the country with no clue as to its authors. To settlers, the epicenter of the criminal activity appeared to be Ogle County, though Lee, Winnebago, DeKalb, and other counties in northern Illinois were affected to varying degrees. Indeed, it was no exaggeration to say, as one historian did, that "[e]very grove from Inlet and Paw Paw to the Wabash might have been said to contain caches of stolen goods and horses and the cellar of many a tavern the bones of murdered men."[4]

By 1837, so many horses were disappearing that owners began taking measures to protect them—and themselves. Owners of fast or fine horses never left them unguarded for a single night unless the stable was doubly locked and barred and a watchdog left within the stable or at the stable door. Some farmers took to sleeping in their stable with their trusty rifles by their side. Those with several horses might hire an armed guard to stand watch at the stable during the night. For personal protection, settlers began carrying weapons and no man ever thought of going to his stable or his woodpile after nightfall without his gun.

On the frontier, horse stealing went hand in hand with another criminal activity: counterfeiting, a business as old as the American colonies themselves. The practice was first introduced by a British General, Sir Henry Clinton, in 1776 in an attempt to wreck the continental currency. Clinton's counterfeiters produced spurious paper so good he was able to flood the colonial economy with tens of thousands of dollars in worthless paper. Though his scheme ceased with the end of the war, the practice was quickly adopted by unscrupulous Americans. When Massachusetts began minting the colonies' first coins in the seventeenth century, counterfeiters quickly followed suit, producing bogus coins made of pewter. Early counterfeiting of bills entailed altering their denomination. By the early eighteenth century, skilled artisans began making plates with which to make bogus bills from scratch. To avert detection, some counterfeiters sent bills to Europe where they were copied (sometimes with spelling errors in non-English speaking countries) or used to strike plates. On the whole, the quality of these bills was surprisingly good and men from New England to North Carolina turned small fortunes in bogus currency.[5] Authorities were forever on the lookout for those passing phony bills though conviction was hard to obtain as the passer could simply plead ignorance. If convicted, however, the penalties were usually severe. Owen Sullivan, who for years headed a large counterfeit operation in New England, was finally caught and hanged in 1756.

As luck would have it for the Driscoll gang, the 1830s were a virtual heyday for counterfeiters. In 1837, President Andrew Jackson's refusal to renew the charter of the National Bank opened the way for states to create a free banking system. Essentially, anyone who could comply with a few simple regulations could create their own bank. "Wild Cat Banks," as they were called, had so few restrictions they often operated in wilderness shacks or the rear of a store. Each bank had its own currency design and degree of integrity. Counterfeiting was relatively easy given the number of banks issuing notes and the ignorance of the average person to detect forgeries. In the unregulated environment, bogus bills flooded the frontier currency system. Some counterfeiters printed bills in assembly line fashion, selling $100 notes for five or ten legitimate dollars. To some extent, businessmen could protect themselves against counterfeiters by subscribing to periodicals that contained detailed description of bogus bills. The average settler, however, had no such recourse and was forever at the mercy of some shady character passing the "long green." Eventually, the monetary situation became so dire that the government discontinued the sale of land in Illinois for anything but gold coins.

In Ogle County, much of the counterfeiting activity revolved around Adolphus Bliss's Log Tavern, which he built in 1838. Though the Tavern was a welcome sight to travelers, many a family and individual who had sojourned there might have reconsidered had they known the true character of the place. For it served equally as a mint, a rendezvous for counterfeiters, and a distribution point for spurious currency and coin. Bliss's wife, affectionately known as "Aunt Hannah," produced a steady supply of bogus bills fashioned from no less than five sets of dies sewn up in one of her feather beds. Whenever funds began to run low, all that was necessary to replenish the exchequer was to call on Aunt Hannah.

Robbery was another source of income for the prairie pirates. Because of the unreliable character of many banks, Illinois pioneers placed little faith in them, preferring to keep their money in their homes. This practice made them easy targets for armed robbers who became increasingly common—and violent—over time. Sometimes neighbors passed along information to the gang—called "getting up the sight"—as to the existence of a cache of money in a home and the owner's movements for a share in the profit, just as he would a horse. If the owner chanced to find the robbers in the house, he could be murdered, though these incidents were rare—at least in the beginning.

Stagecoaches were particularly vulnerable to highwaymen. So often were the stagecoaches attacked that passengers often prepared their wills and said their prayers before setting out upon a journey. The English insisted on carrying gold when traveling, a practice that made them particularly conspicuous targets. There were also government stagecoaches moving from LaSalle to St. Louis transporting gold revenue from land sales. Sometimes the bandits didn't bother to wait for the stagecoach to depart and would strike directly at the land office itself.

Families living in isolation on the prairie were particularly vulnerable to pirate predation. Out of the blue strange men would appear at homes with no indication as to what they were doing in the area. On one occasion, a woman with her cradled baby was visited by two men. After a brief conversation, the men snatched the baby from its cradle and walked off. The frantic woman gave chase. After the men had walked some distance, they set the baby on the ground and placed a butchering kettle over it.

A particularly unfortunate victim of the pirates was the frontier peddler whose itinerant, solitary nature made him easy prey. Peddlers made the rounds on a monthly basis passing from Chicago to Madison via Rockford and Belvidere. They traveled from farmhouse to farmhouse and from tavern to tavern peddling their modest wares. News of an approaching peddler was always greeted with excitement by women eager to obtain tin ware, calico, lace, ribbon, thread, needles, scissors—in short, all the little niceties of life they had left behind in the east as well as hard-to-find indispensable items. Men sought them out for tobacco and tools. Sometimes the peddler sold for coin; other times he bartered for furs and other valuable materials. He carried his wares unsecured on his wagon, his money too, unless he was staying at a tavern or roadside inn when he would entrust it to the proprietor for the night. Not surprisingly, peddlers routinely disappeared in Rock River country but for a long time no one knew why or how.

But settlers had their suspicions. As early as 1837, members of the Driscoll gang were turning up in court, David Driscoll for trespassing and William Bridge and several of his associates on unknown charges. Both were acquitted. As time went on, more and more of the gang were appearing in court on charges varying from trespassing and horse stealing to counterfeiting and robbery. Conviction, however, faced a mountain of hurdles. For one thing, specific proof against the pirates was often difficult to obtain. Witnesses were not paid by the state to appear in court and were often absent on the day of the trial. A defendant could also readily get a change of venue with the charge that the judge or jury was biased and therefore unable to get a fair trial. Wherever the trial took place, gang witnesses were always on hand to provide an alibi. If arrested, tried, and found guilty, pirates were always flush with money to post bail whatever the amount only to disappear into the vast frontier.

As if that were not enough to ensure a favorable outcome in court, several gang members secured elected office. Charles Oliver was the first to attempt to do so, running for justice of the peace in Rockford in 1837. The election was hotly contested and the polls were kept open until ten o'clock at night. Every man who could vote was sought out, taken to the polls, and made to vote for one or the other of the candidates. In the end, Oliver lost by only a few votes. A few years later, Dewey succeeded in becoming justice of the peace and West as constable. Whenever an arrest warrant was issued, Justice Dewey would inform his comrades of the fact and then place the warrant in the hands of Constable West for service. Knowing in what direction the outlaw had gone, West would start out in hot pursuit in a directly opposite direction. Small wonder then that he always returned his warrants marked "not found."[6]

With so much weighing in the pirates' favor, it wasn't surprising that the first four criminal trials in Ogle County had all resulted in acquittals. One of acquittals was against Sheriff Mudd—long suspected of being in league with the Driscolls—for a "palpable omission of duties." It would not be until 1839 that the county won its first conviction against a counterfeiter who received two years in prison.

Even when outlaws were caught and convicted, there were no jails or jails sufficiently secure to hold them. For several years after the first settlement of Winnebago County, the nearest secure lockup was eighty miles away at Galena and even that was a poor excuse for one. On one occasion, a man was locked up in the jail for some offense. The sheriff started home, but had scarcely left the shadow of the jail before his prisoner managed to get out. Upon the sheriff's arrival at Rockford, his late prisoner was among the first to greet his return! Until 1846, Ogle County had a makeshift log cabin jail in Oregon City that was relatively easy to break out of. Upon arrest, the suspect was brought to jail and taken upstairs where a trap door in the floor was raised. A short ladder ten or twelve feet in length was then lowered through it, and the prisoner backed down it into his cell. When the ladder was removed and the trap door lowered, the prisoner was considered secure in his cell. Yet, so faulty in construction was it that one prisoner using a jackknife was able to dig his way through the wall to freedom within three hours. To be sure, some counties had good jails but they refused to take prisoners from the newer counties unless the cost of keeping them was paid in advance. Few could afford to do so.

The hobbled wheels of justice meant that the ranks of the outlaws were never thinned out by imprisonment of any of their members. In lieu of incarceration, the guilty received fines or the whip, in some instances branding, only for them to return unchastised to their former life of crime. And with so many outlaws operating in the region, the administration of justice became an exercise in futility.

There had been one minor success against the Brodys. One of his neighbors, Ben Worden, had a fine pair of horses and to protect them against the pirates, Worden had adopted the practice of sleeping in the barn with them. When James Brody discovered this, he innocently asked him why. Worden replied that there were many pirates about and he feared they might be stolen. Brody, who liked Worden, said he need not fear for his horses would be safe for he, Brody, would personally see to it. Brody's assurances inadvertently raised suspicions in Worden's mind that he was one of the mysterious horse thieves.

If there was any doubt in his mind about Brody's culpability, it was put to rest by a discovery shortly after the incident. Searching the prairie one day for his cattle, Worden suddenly felt the ground sinking beneath his feet. On further inspection he found a large depression that had been carefully excavated and covered with planks, soil, and growing grass. In its center a stake had been driven, indicating a place where horses had been tethered and fed. Worden had previously noticed the Brodys periodically coming and going to the place, each time with a fine new horse. What could all this mean, he surmised, but systematic horse thieving.

Shortly after Worden's discovery, settlers drove the Brodys out of Ogle County. They resettled in Linn County, Iowa, where they continued to steal horses well into the 1850s. Among the effects they left behind were a large number of trunks, cases, and other personal effects, remnants of peddlers who at various times had come into the country and had mysteriously vanished from sight, particularly around Dement Township in Ogle County.

By the late 1830s, settlers in northern Illinois were living in a virtual state of siege. Every bump in the night was presumed to be the sound of a desperado lurking about. Fear and tension continued to mount until one day the pirates committed an act so audacious that it finally galvanized citizens into action.

For the first two years after the establishment of Ogle County, its seat of justice alternated between Oregon and Dixon. In 1839, the county finally began work on its first courthouse—an imposing two-story brick structure—at a cost of $1,822. By March 1840, construction had neared completion sufficiently to use it for the sitting of the spring term of the circuit court due to begin on Monday, March 22. In the jail adjacent to the courthouse were six members of the Driscoll gang awaiting trial. With their spanking new courthouse, citizens were heartened that, at long last, the wheels of justice were beginning to roll.

All day on Sunday, the town was full of men known to belong to the gang watching the movements of the court officers—the sheriff, the clerk, the judge, lawyers—all preparing for trial in the morning. On Sunday evening, court clerk Benjamin Phelps, who had been keeping the court's books and papers at his residence, loaded the papers onto a wheelbarrow and started to haul them to the courthouse for the trials. Along the way, he ran into E. R. Dodge, a lawyer from nearby Ottawa, who, because the hotel was full, was on his way to Phelps's residence to see if he could put him up for the night. Phelps happily agreed and turned back with Dodge, taking the records with him.

That night, as a storm raged, the Driscoll gang set fire to the courthouse in the dual hope of destroying the indictments against their confederates and facilitating their escape. When citizens reached the burning building, they found the prisoners already up, dressed, and waiting for their rescuers. But they were nowhere to be found. Though the jail stood but a few yards from the burning courthouse, it had escaped the flames. Not so lucky was Hugh Ray. Ray, who lived two miles from Oregon, was working on construction of the courthouse and was sleeping in the building at the time. By the time he awoke, flames had engulfed the entire building and he barely escaped with his life. Although none of the prisoners had escaped, it would be seven years before citizens could afford to build a new courthouse.

Audacious though it was, the fire had failed to free the prisoners and the sitting of the court went forward in a nearby building, Judge Thomas Ford presiding. During the trial, the jury found the evidence complete and conclusive against all six prisoners. Yet, once again, the confederates had secured a place for one of their own on the jury who refused to consent to a verdict of guilty. At this, the exasperated eleven jurors adopted a novel method of securing a conviction. Seizing the recalcitrant twelfth, they threatened to lynch him in the jury room unless he concurred in the guilty verdict. The holdout quickly shed his opposition, the verdict of guilty was pronounced, and the six criminals each received a year in prison. But before they had served a single day of their sentence, they managed to break out of Oregon jail and disappeared.

By 1841, citizens of Rock River country had become fed up with law enforcement's inability to rein in the Driscoll gang. For five exasperating years, they had endured robberies, burglaries, arson, horse stealing, and destruction of property. The country was awash in counterfeit money. People were reduced to living in terror of men who feared nothing and who seemed to actually enjoy the dangers of their trade. With the burning of the courthouse, the attempted packing of the jury, and the escape of the convicts, the gang had made a total mockery of the justice system. Worst of all, communities remained vulnerable to further predation. With its nefarious tentacles reaching in nearly every corner of society, the Driscoll gang appeared bent on taking control of the entire region.

The law wasn't working. It was time to work outside it.

## CHAPTER 3

# The Regulators

*Lynch law is not unknown in more civilized regions, such as Indiana and Ohio. Now lynch law, however, shocking it may seem to Europeans and New Englanders, is far removed from arbitrary violence . . . Many crimes would go unpunished if some more speedy and efficient method of dealing with them were not adopted.*

—JAMES BRYCE, *The American Commonwealth*, 1888

A few weeks after the burning of the Oregon courthouse, frustrated residents of White Rock and Paine's Point conferred with Judge Thomas Ford to find a way to rid themselves of the Driscoll gang. Ford had been serving as an itinerant judge on the Military Tract and Rock River Valley circuit since 1830. Many a time he had presided over the trial of a gang member only to see him walk free through jury tampering or bribery. Not only did this trouble him as a judge but also as a part-time resident of Ogle County. He sympathized deeply with the predicament of its citizens, many of whom were close friends and neighbors.

In fact, during the trial of one outlaw, Ford had come under fire from the press for an unusual comment he made from the bench. A lawyer defending his client on criminal charges had argued that "it was better that ninety-nine guilty men escape than an innocent man be convicted," to which Ford caustically replied, "That is the maximum of the law alright, but the trouble here is that the ninety-nine guilty have already escaped!"

Ford, too, realized that law enforcement was useless in the face of a powerful gang like the Driscolls. So the judge offered an extraordinary bit of advice: form a company of armed men, round up the outlaws, and "punish them with a blacksnake." Ford was a fervent believer in the power of the whip to deter men from crime. He had seen men sentenced to ten years in the penitentiary with apparent indifference but never saw a man who did not wince when faced with a whip.[1] For the first chastisement, Ford recommended thirty-six lashes with the whip, sixty for the second, and that suspected gang members be ordered to leave the country within ten days. In other words, Ford was advising them to form a vigilante group.[2]

It wasn't the first time citizens had taken the law into their own hands. As settlers began pouring into the Rock River Valley in the mid-1830s, "local protection organizations" sprang up to deal with problems arising from the area's rapid growth such as claim jumping, land speculating, and the appearance of drifters and scofflaws. In the absence of legal authority, scores of these organizations—usually called "Settlers' Association," "Claims Association," or "Claims Club"—followed. Sometimes the associations numbered no more than five or six settlers, depending on the size of the community. Oregon, the seat of Ogle County, started a Claims Protection Society in 1835 to settle issues of overlapping land claims. Members often drafted their own laws in keeping with state and federal laws—or their imperfect understanding of them. The club had elected officers who recorded all property transfers and boundaries. If the problem concerned troublemakers, they were whipped and sent packing.

Yet, such groups were more like today's neighborhood watches and no match for heavily armed and well-organized bands of hardened criminals like the Driscoll gang. To drive them out of the country called for the more muscular approach of earlier regulators that had been so successful.

Following their meeting with Ford, fifteen Ogle County residents, all of whom had been victims of the Driscoll gang at one time or another (recall Locke's admonition here) held a meeting in a log schoolhouse at White Rock. In addition to Yankee settlers, there were Canadians, Scotsmen, even Native Americans, all united in their desire to rid the country of the Driscoll menace. After a long discussion, they came to the inescapable conclusion that law enforcement was neither capable of checking the outlaws nor could it protect people and property. Accordingly, they formed "The Ogle County Regulators" (aka "The Ogle County Lynching Club"), whose mission was to rid northern Illinois of the pirate scourge once and for all.[3] Widely viewed with favor, lynching on the Illinois frontier, otherwise known as "Jerking to Jesus," meant any form of corporal punishment from tar and feathering to whipping, scalping, and other forms of physical punishment. (Only after the mid-nineteenth century did it become synonymous with hanging.) Although a harmless whipping was thus the Regulators' intention from the start, they were about to take the meaning of the term to a whole new level.

To impose a modicum of order on the impromptu group, Ogle County Regulators adopted by-laws and rules. Members were made to solemnly pledge to die in the cause if necessary. John Long, a mill owner and early resident of the county, was voted captain. The rank and file consisted of Ogle County's most respected citizens, like lawyer E.S. Wellington, and twenty-year-old farmer Ralph Chaney, and his brother Phineas. Within days, more men joined and the organization soon had "divisions" in Boone, DeKalb, Lee, McHenry, and Winnebago Counties. At Inlet Grove, another vigilante group was formed, the "Association for the Furtherance of the Cause of Justice." So many men came out in support of Ogle's Regulators that, according to one observer, "had a red flag been hoisted during the night over every house sympathizing with the Regulators, it would have seemed the whole country had the smallpox."[4]

Once organized and armed, the Regulators set out to order the Driscoll gang to leave the state or be stripped naked and whipped. "You are given twenty or thirty days to leave the country, and if found here after that time you will be lynched," was the brief and threatening message that condemned the suspected party, without a trial, to banishment, at whatever sacrifice of his property, and at whatever sudden breaking of the ties that bound him to his home.

The first bandit visited was John Earle who had enlisted a twenty-year-old accomplice to steal his neighbor's horse. When Earle refused to leave, the Regulators dragged him from his house, removed his coat and vest, and pinioned his arms. With a rawhide whip, six Regulators administered five lashes apiece, blood following every stroke. A deacon of the church, clearly driven by some divine inspiration, was said to have inflicted the most vigorous strokes. Earle quietly withstood the ordeal without flinching. When it was over, he remarked, "Now as your rage is satisfied, and to prove that I am an honest man, I will join your company." Not only had the beating deterred him from further criminal behavior, Earle had become one of the Regulators and according to Ralph Chaney, "a good worker."

Next stop was the home of a man named Daggett in Franklin. Daggett, who had been a Baptist preacher back east, was charged with being an accessory to the theft of four horses from the Rockford area. Taking him into custody, the Regulators tried him by their adopted rules. Daggett was found guilty and sentenced to five hundred lashes on his bare back. As the vigilantes were stripping him to administer the punishment, his teenage daughter rushed frantically into the midst of the men, begging for mercy for her father. Her agonized appeals together with the solemn promise of Daggett that he would leave the country secured an immediate remission of the sentence.

Satisfied with their first day's progress, the Regulators dispersed to their homes. About two o'clock that night, however, several Regulators rode to Phineas Chaney's to tell him they had found the owner of the horses Daggett had stolen. Feeling they had let Daggett off too lightly, they now wanted to go back and give him the whipping he deserved. Ralph Chaney opposed the scheme, arguing that they had already tried Daggett and agreed to spare him punishment in return for his departure. The other Regulators, however, were itching for a whipping. Exacting a promise from Chaney that he would not oppose them, they proceeded to Daggett's house, dragged him from his bed, and led him to an oak tree two miles from his cabin. Tying him to the tree, they administered ninety-six lashes, a chastisement later denounced by the more conservative Regulators. A doctor was brought along who occasionally examined Daggett to prevent fatal injury. As he was being whipped, Daggett confessed that he had indeed helped to steal the horses but insisted that he did not know where they were as they had already passed outside the area. After the whipping, he was untied and allowed to leave. The next morning Daggett moved to Indiana where his family followed soon after. He was never again seen in Rock River country.

When he heard of the treatment of Daggett, William Bridge and several of his cohorts obtained a warrant for the arrest of those who had whipped him. As the sheriff was absent, the warrant was given to Coroner James Clark, who, apparently, approving of the Regulators' actions, did not serve it.

As they were returning from Daggett's, the Regulators came upon one Lyman Powell on the road between the Driscoll's and Killbuck Creek. Powell was known as something of a harmless village idiot whose only crime seems to have been in working as a handyman for the Driscoll gang. The Regulators interrogated him closely to obtain evidence of his culpability or that of the Driscolls in a crime but got nothing from the frightened Powell. Assuming the horse he was riding had been stolen, they seized it, lashed him with hickory sticks, and left him standing, bereft and confused, by the road. Their punishment would have seemed just but for the fact that the unfortunate Powell had purchased the horse in good faith from a nearby stable.

Shortly after, one Daniel Ross was taken by the Regulators and made to hold onto a limb of a tree just high enough to allow his toes to touch the ground. Whenever Ross attempted to let himself down, the Regulators applied a blacksnake to his backside, thus forcing him to assume his former uncomfortable position.

At long last, the Regulators had begun to exact their righteous retribution. Yet, the men they had singled out thus far were not the Driscolls who would not go so easily into the good night. Indeed, when John Driscoll heard about Daggett's treatment, he was livid. He called an urgent meeting of eighty outlaws in the barns of Aikens and Bridge—first in one barn and then adjourning to the other—to discuss an appropriate response. The plan: to murder every man, woman, and child in the hamlet of White Rock.[5]

When the plan leaked out, terror swept over White Rock. Citizens immediately armed themselves with rifles, shot guns, pistols, pitchforks—anything and everything that could serve as a weapon of defense. Every boy who was old enough and big enough to handle a weapon was enlisted. Tearing down a cross fence, they drove nails into the side facing outward and laid it across as a barricade on the lane leading to White Rock. One hundred residents then assembled behind the barricade, bracing for the threatened attack. As the Driscoll gang marched on the hamlet, a cooler-headed confederate met them en route and persuaded them to adopt less extreme measures.

As residents of White Rock were nervously bracing for their arrival, the outlaws had turned and headed for the farm of John Long, the captain of the Regulators. They then burned down his new gristmill and broke the legs of his only horse, leaving it to die in agony. After Long received a threatening letter from the Driscolls, he abruptly resigned from the Regulators.

For a brief moment, it seemed the tactic had worked. But the Regulators were not about to be intimidated. They quickly replaced the faint-hearted Long with the formidable John Campbell. A Canadian, Campbell was one of the first settlers in White Rock, having come to Illinois in 1838 with his wife and young son from Toronto. No sooner had Campbell assumed his position that he received a letter from William Driscoll threatening not only his life and the life of his family, but also the life of every one who dared to oppose the Driscoll gang. William then brazenly challenged him to come to his home in South Grove on June 22 for a show down.

Unlike Long, the threat only piqued Campbell's ire all the more. He immediately assembled the Regulators from Ogle and neighboring counties—an impressive 196 men in all. Mounted and armed with muskets and wearing armbands, they rode to Driscoll's house like a great army, two abreast with a bugle sounding and the American flag unfurled. As they neared Driscoll's cabin, they halted just outside of gunshot to plan their attack. Osborn Chaney volunteered to sneak up to the house to assess the situation inside. As he crept up to the house, the front door flew open and nearly a score of desperados, all armed with pistols and muskets, dashed out and made for the woods. Old man Driscoll mounted his horse and raced off. One man remained behind who had a message from John Driscoll for the Regulators: Driscoll had gone to Sycamore to muster three hundred of his men and would return to the prairie to fight them in two hours. Keen for a showdown at last, the Regulators dismounted and sat on the ground, checking and loading their weapons.

Meanwhile, Judge Ford was holding court in Sycamore when news reached him that a large army of men was marching through the western portion of the county threatening acts of violence. Fearing things had gotten out of hand, the judge dispatched DeKalb probate judge Frederick Lovell, district attorney Seth Farwell, the county sheriff, and two other men to inquire as to their intentions. No sooner had Ford's men started on the Oregon State Road in search of the Regulators when they came upon old man Driscoll, who must have thought the timing a stroke of good fortune.

At three o'clock in the afternoon, Driscoll returned to the Regulators but instead of his confederates, he had brought Judge Ford's emissaries. Sheriff Walrod inquired as to the nature of the strange gathering. Displaying their constitution, Campbell explained that they were the Regulators, recently constituted, whose mission was to scour the countryside, investigate persons suspected of crimes, and warn them to desist. If they were believed guilty they would be ordered to leave the country or be lynched if they refused. Campbell stressed that they did not desire to interfere with the courts but only to assist them in the enforcement of justice in cases in which they were "unable to reach a verdict." He then proceeded to enumerate all the crimes the Driscolls had committed. How, for example, William Driscoll and another man had robbed Waterman's store in Boone County and stashed the goods in Hickory Grove, and how Driscoll had later gone in the dead of night and stolen the goods from his own confederate, thereby "making himself the meanest thief on the face of God's earth." After citing several other Driscoll transgressions, Campbell fired an angry glare at Driscoll and ordered him to leave the state in twenty days. While Campbell was reciting his long litany of crimes, John Driscoll sat on his horse seething with rage. (Ralph Chaney, who could hear the old man's teeth grinding, believed it was then that Campbell had received his death sentence from Driscoll.)

All in all it had been a cordial meeting between the Regulators and Ford's emissaries. Satisfied with what they heard from Campbell, the men from DeKalb said that any time they needed help, to call on the town of Sycamore, and they would be happy to supply at least one hundred capable men to assist them. Upon their return, the men gave a favorable report to Judge Ford, who expressed no opposition to their activities and may well even have approved in light of his earlier advice.

Turning to Driscoll, Campbell again ordered him to leave the state, saying, "If after that time you are found east of the Mississippi River, we will brand your cheeks with 'RS,' and crop your ears, so that none shall fail to know your character as a Rogue and a Scoundrel wherever you may be seen." Told he could name the day of his departure, Driscoll indicated he would leave in twenty days. Satisfied with his response, the Regulators dispersed to their homes.

Driscoll, however, had no intention of leaving. Instead, he called an urgent meeting at Bridge's farm to respond to the Regulators' ultimatum. Bridge was already chafing from the notice he had received to leave by June 17. He had gone to Dixon and complained about the order, pleading for assistance to defend himself and his dwelling against the lawless violence of the Regulators. To his chagrin, the people of Dixon instead joined in passing a resolution fully approving of the Regulators' actions and gave him four hours to leave town.

As the beleaguered outlaws discussed their options, William Driscoll, who had been in Iowa the previous winter, proposed a plan that had worked there. John Long, he reasoned, had been frightened into resigning merely by burning his mill. Murder his successor and no other person will dare to risk his life to be captain and the organization will collapse. Everyone thought the plan sound, so sound, they also agreed to kill Phineas Chaney whom they may have anticipated would be Campbell's successor. David and Taylor Driscoll were tasked with murdering Campbell (the designated killer of Chaney is unknown) and made to swear not to depart "until he was a corpse." The dates for the murders were set at Friday, June 25, for Chaney and the following Sunday for Campbell.[6]

On Friday, Chaney's would-be killers rode to his house late at night. But when they approached the house, they were greeted by Chaney's two ferocious watchdogs which promptly treed the men in the corncrib. Hearing the fracas created by the dogs, Chaney rose from his bed and started out to see what was wrong. Remembering the gang had recently made threats against his life, he thought it more prudent to return to bed. Meanwhile, the two men remained stuck in the crib until daylight when they managed to quiet the dogs and slip away.

At school the next morning, William Bridge's little daughter Hettie inadvertently reported the incident. She said she always slept in a trundle bed, which was drawn out from beneath the bed occupied by her father and mother. In the morning just before dawn, she said she had overheard her father tell her mother, "Chaney was killed last night by some men that had been sent to do that work." This statement of a child, too young and innocent to manufacture such a tale, left no reason for the settlers to doubt later that Bridge had known all about the scheme.

On Sunday morning, old man Driscoll was seen wandering suspiciously around Campbell's premises. Instead of going home, he spent the night at a neighbor's house. Later that day, as was his custom, John Campbell went to church at a schoolhouse one mile away, returning in the afternoon. After supper, Campbell lay down to take a nap. About sundown, he started across the lane in front of his house toward the barn to finish some chores. In the lane was a hedge of hazel brush thick enough to hide his murderers. Waiting nearby with horses for the getaway were John, William, and Pearson Driscoll. As Campbell stepped through the gate from the yard into the lane, David and Taylor emerged from behind the bushes and remarked, "We want to go to the burnt mill but have lost our way." Before Campbell could answer, Taylor Driscoll raised his gun and shot Campbell point blank in the chest. Campbell staggered back several paces through the gate and fell dead.

When Mrs. Campbell heard the gunshot she came rushing out of the house to find her husband's body lying lifeless on the ground. As the men ran for their horses, she cried out, "Driscolls, you have murdered John Campbell!" Hearing this, the two halted. Taylor Driscoll turned and slowly raised his rifle, pointing it ominously toward her. He then lowered it without firing and the two resumed their retreat.

Meanwhile, Campbell's son, thirteen-year-old Martin, had seized his father's double-barreled shotgun. Running around the back of the house, he aimed and fired at the fleeing Driscolls. Although the gun was double-charged with buck shot, having been loaded for some time and exposed to the damp, it failed to go off.

First on the murder scene were Ralph and Phineas Chaney who had heard the shot from their house three-quarters of a mile away. They found

Mrs. Campbell in the front yard sobbing over her husband's body. When they heard that the Driscolls had killed Campbell, they rode off to inform Ogle County Sheriff William Ward . . . and the Regulators.

When Ward and his men arrived at the Campbell's, they found tracks of five horses in the dirt, one of which had a broken shoe. Taking a few men, Ward set out to follow the tracks while several stayed behind to dig Campbell's grave. The broken shoe tracks led the posse directly to David Driscoll's house in Lynnwood. Sheriff Ward entered the house while others went to the stable where they found a horse that had just been ridden and was still covered with dried sweat. An examination of the horse's feet revealed part of a shoe that corresponded exactly with the tracks discovered at Campbell's. In the house were John Driscoll and several women of the household, including Mercy. Ward then began to question him.

"Who rode that animal in the stable this morning?" Ward asked.

"I rode it," replied Driscoll, "from South Grove."

"Who rode it to South Grove last night?"

"I rode it there yesterday afternoon."

"Who rode it from near Campbell's place yesterday evening?"

To this last question, the old man had no answer and from that time forward maintained a stubborn silence. One of the female members of the Driscoll household, a daughter-in-law, entered the room and remarked that the old man "was a bad and dangerous character and that if he had received his just deserts, he would have been shot long ago."

"Driscoll," the Sheriff announced, "that broken horse shoe and the tracks it left have placed you in a quandary from which you will find it difficult to extricate yourself. I hereby place you under arrest, in the name of the people of the State of Illinois, on suspicion of being accessory to the murder of John Campbell." At this Driscoll finally spoke, saying "I always calculate to hold myself in subjection to the laws of my country."[7]

According to Phineas Chaney, when the Sheriff announced he was under arrest, one of Driscoll's daughters who had been looking on suddenly turned and faced her father and their eyes met and "there was that kind of a look I can hardly describe passed between them, and as she held his eye she nodded her head to him. Nothing said, but such a look I never saw in the world."

Oddly incongruous with the tense exchange that had just taken place, Driscoll's wife then served him breakfast. The Sheriff told the old man to eat and get ready to accompany him to jail. Mercy placed a dish of pie before him, but he ate sparingly. When he finished, Ward told him to bid his wife and the rest of the family goodbye, as he might never see them again. Calmly, Driscoll turned to his wife and said with grim finality, "Take care of yourself, and do the best you can." Ward then placed him on a wagon between two guards who left for the Oregon jail.

Meanwhile, dozens of Regulators were fanning out over the countryside in search of David and Taylor Driscoll, Bridge, and Richard and Thomas Aiken. William and Pearce were arrested at their homes in South Grove. William insisted he was innocent, arguing on the day of Campbell's murder he had been in Sycamore. While there, Mr. Hamlin, the postmaster, had called him into his office and read to him startling news that the postmaster at Oregon City had written on his package of letters for Chicago so that in passing the news might be broadcast to all the post offices along the route. William claimed to have been surprised and saddened by the news of Campbell's death. It boded no good to him, he said. Confident of his innocence, he offered no resistance and quietly went with the Regulators, saying if tried he was quite certain he would be acquitted. Before leaving, the Regulators set fire to William's house, forcing his wife and children to take shelter in an outhouse. There they lived for some time as neighbors feared any generosity shown them would invite revenge.

The Regulators then took the two brothers to White Rock so that Mrs. Campbell might identify the killer. Toward evening they arrived at Campbell's house. John's body was now lying inside. William and Pearce were brought in and without any hesitation Mrs. Campbell said that neither of them was present at the murder. Martin, who had also seen the assassins, was equally confident that neither of them was the guilty pair.

With no jail to incarcerate them, the vigilantes placed the two Driscolls under guard in the upper room of the Campbell house for the night—a morbid act under the circumstances—and agreed to meet the following morning. The sentry was not particularly vigilant, and as the night wore on, the sleepless captives talked of attempting an escape. "They are determined to kill us tomorrow," Pearce said. "I can see it in their looks and manner." "No," said William, "we can prove our innocence so strongly that they cannot fail to discharge us." After a long whispered discussion of their chances, the advice of the elder brother prevailed and they decided to stay put.

Meanwhile, word of Campbell's murder had spread like a prairie fire to Sycamore, Oregon, and Rockford. By dawn on Monday, a phalanx of angry Regulators and sympathizers from near and far had gathered at Campbell's. Rockford was practically deserted, most of its male residents having joined the manhunt. Phineas Chaney, who had hitherto taken issue with some of the draconian measures of the Regulators, was now clamoring the loudest to avenge Campbell's death.

Other companies of Regulators from the remoter settlements were also pouring in. There was a company from Payne's Point, led by E.S. Wellington, one from the Pennsylvania settlement led by Dr. Hubbard, one from Oregon led by a Methodist clergyman named Crist, and a company from Daysville. The Regulators wanted blood and it was beginning to look as though any Driscoll blood would suffice. To ensure this time justice would be served, they would try the prisoners themselves in a kangaroo court.

But to do this they needed custody of John Driscoll.

About nine o'clock on Tuesday morning, a party went to the Oregon jail and demanded Sheriff Ward turn over John Driscoll. When Ward refused to comply, the Regulators battered down the door with heavy timbers. Judge Ford, who happened to be in Oregon at the time, warned the Regulators not to take the law into their own hands. But the momentum was all on the Regulators' side now and they were not about to let the Driscolls slip through their fingers. Seizing Driscoll from his cell, they tied a rope around his neck and put him in a wagon. They then descended to Rock River to cross on Ozier's Ferry to Daysville, about twelve miles south on the other side. Ward gave chase immediately to recover his prisoner. When he reached the Regulators, he grabbed Driscoll from the wagon and started back, declaring indignantly that Driscoll was his prisoner and he intended to keep him. The abruptness with which this was done left the Regulators momentarily stunned. For several seconds, no one spoke or moved. All of a sudden, John Phelps sprang from the wagon and exclaimed, "If we are going to be men, let us act like men, and not like a lot of boys!" The Regulators then started for Driscoll. As they wrested Driscoll from the Sheriff, Phelps looked reassuringly at Ward and said, "You have done your duty." They put Driscoll back in the wagon and continued to the ferry.

As they were descending the embankment, sixteen-year old Michael Seyster happened to be riding into town on an errand. Needing a fresh horse to draw the wagon, the Regulators seized the boy's horse, leaving the bewildered teenager to follow along in the wagon to recover it. When the Regulators reached the other side of the river, a man from Washington Grove told them that the Rockford Regulators had already taken William and Pearson to the mill.

The trial was to take place at Stephenson's Mill in Washington Grove ten miles to the south. On the way to the trial site, Chaney temporarily halted outside Daysville. There, he and Obed Lindsay took the old man aside to interrogate him. Hearing that the infamous Driscoll was in Daysville, a crowd of over a hundred men gathered. Driscoll admitted that he had been a bad man and that he had done many unlawful and vicious things but that he had never committed murder. He confessed to having stolen—or participated in the stealing of—as many as fifty horses. Chaney asked if the number might rather reach five hundred, to which he replied, "Maybe it might. I have lost count. I have paid out hundreds of dollars to young men for stealing horses from men against whom I have had a grudge and from which I never received a cent of profit. I paid these hundreds of dollars in small sums of from ten to twenty dollars each. I did not expect any profit from such expenditures. All I wanted was sweet revenge." Then, referring to the time his son went to prison for arson in Ohio, he added, "I also did a great wrong towards my son, Pearson, whom I was the means of sending to the Ohio penitentiary. I had a grudge against a man that lived seven miles away and determined to burn his barn. Pearce lived half way between my place and the man against whom I held this grudge. I went to Pearce's stable in the dark hour of night, took out his horse, rode to the barn, set it on fire, and returned the horse to the stable. The roads were muddy and the horse was easily tracked. The tracks led to Pearce's stable and he was arrested, tried, convicted, and sentenced to the penitentiary for three years, and served out his time."[8]

When Chaney had finished interrogating Driscoll, they started for Washington Grove. All the men who had gathered to see Driscoll followed along. Driscoll sat dazed and sullen in the wagon, fearing that the trial was to be a mere farce and that his fate was already sealed.

At ten o'clock, they arrived at Washington Grove. The Rockford Division still had not shown up causing a delay in the proceedings. By now, word of the impromptu trial had spread far and wide and several hundred men had turned out to see the Driscolls get their comeuppance at long last. Some of the men were from Winnebago, some from DeKalb, some from Lee, but the majority was from Ogle County, the epicenter of Driscoll's criminal operation. Also present were William Driscoll's friends. At the time of his arrest, he dispatched a messenger to those in Sycamore who knew of his innocence to solicit their attendance at the trial and testify on his behalf. Five of them, including Ben Worden, arrived to find over a hundred Regulators raging around John Driscoll like angry hornets.

Now a few paces from the mill on Grove Creek, Stephenson had also built a distillery. During the delay, a barrel of whisky was rolled out, its head removed, and a dipper attached to its rim. As they waited, the agitated men began to slake their thirst.

In due course, William and Pearson were brought up. Upon seeing the angry mob now imbibing heavily, William sensed he was doomed. Friends who knew him to be innocent tried to reassure him of an acquittal. "No," he said glumly, "they will kill me, but they will kill an innocent man."

The rope was removed from John Driscoll's neck and replaced with a one-inch leather halter taken from a horse's head. He and his sons were then led to an old black oak tree. Lawyer E.S. Leland (who later became an Illinois circuit court judge) volunteered to serve as judge. Jason Marsh, a lawyer who had come to Rockford only two years earlier from New York, volunteered to serve as defense attorney; Charles Latimer, a British lawyer, agreed to serve as prosecutor. Determined to simulate courtroom proceedings as much as possible, Leland ordered the 120 Regulators to form a circle around the tree to serve as a rather large jury. Among them were James Gale, an early settler and first mayor of Ogle County, George Philips, who later served as mayor, and Peter Smith, who would later become a bank president. Leland then ordered that anyone who objected to the nature of the proceedings to withdraw. Under this ruling, the number of jurors was reduced to one hundred and eleven men. A few chairs were placed in the circle for the "court officials" and witnesses were sworn in by one of the Regulators.

Taking a seat on the ground at the foot of the tree, Leland ordered John Driscoll brought into the circle and arraigned before him. Although now sixty years of age and grey-haired, he was still as burly and powerful as in his youth.

"What are the charges against this man?" Leland asked. Even though the question was standard courtroom protocol, it left the Regulators somewhat confused. In their all-consuming desire for revenge, none of the Regulators had bothered to ask what crime he was being charged with. Finally, someone spoke up, charging him with minor offenses. After several others spoke up, the main charge was that he was one of the "horse thieving fraternity" and that they would be afraid for their lives if he were to be released.

During questioning, Driscoll admitted to having stolen a yoke of cattle and fifty horses in Ohio. After he was caught stealing the fifty-first, he served five years in the Columbus penitentiary (conveniently omitting to mention his escape). "When I came out," he said, "I resolved to lead an honest life. I moved away to this county, and I have since kept my pledge." On the night Campbell was shot, John Driscoll said he went to Ben Worden's house and asked permission to stay all night with him. He told Worden that something might happen that night and he wanted to be with an honest man, so he could prove himself innocent. The prosecution then submitted the broken horseshoe track and other evidence to the jury, which Driscoll could not explain away. Beside this, there were other crimes that had been traced to the hands of the Driscolls and upon which he was also questioned.

When questioning was completed, Leland addressed the jury, "What shall be done with this man?" Someone stood up and shouted, "We hang him!" The judge put it to vote and the sentence was carried with a shout of unanimity.

The old man was then taken out of the ring and William was brought in. Accusations against him were called for. At first, none of the Regulators could charge him with a specific crime. Hamlin, the postmaster, who had come expressly to exonerate William, now tried to get a hearing. He asked to say a word or two in William's defense, but each time he tried, he was met with a storm of hisses and shouts of "No, not a word!" Two other men made some defense of William, but as they raised their voice in excitement, they were seized and placed under guard. Several Regulators attempted to remove Hamlin until Leland protested that he had a right to be heard and that he be allowed to make his statement.

When Hamlin finished, Leland turned to William and asked, "Did you ever instruct your brother David to go to the Captain's at twilight, pretend to be lost and then shoot him down as they once did in Iowa, saying, 'damned them (the Regulators), they will all run then, as they did there?'" William denied he had done so. Henry Hill, a respected Ogle County resident, was then sworn in and examined. Hill testified that he had heard William Driscoll give the accused the instructions just quoted and named the time and the occasion. Suddenly, William's memory was refreshed and he answered, "I remember it now. I did use the language, but only in jest," causing Leland to admonish, "Driscoll, you will find that jesting away good men's lives is a serious matter and that it will not be tolerated in this community."

Others witnesses were called who corroborated William's instructions to David at the meeting at Bridge's. This was considered sufficient to establish his guilt as an accessory to Campbell's murder. William said he had lived honestly and had done no injustice to anyone, unless it was in a "certain trade" on one occasion, which he regretted. Nothing he could say, however, was of any avail. The crowd cried, "Hang him! Hang him!" and he was removed trembling from the ring.

Lastly, Pearson was brought in but no evidence or charges could be brought against him and he was released.

Examination of the accused was now terminated. Both John and William, the Regulators concluded, had been given a fair and just opportunity to demonstrate their innocence as accessories to Campbell's murder. After consulting with John Driscoll, Jason Marsh announced that his client had no further confession or statement to make.

As the Regulators began to prepare for the sentencing, Marsh proposed to Charles Latimer, as an additional formality, to defend the prisoners and present their case in summary remarks before the court. Marsh then made a plea for clemency for the Driscolls. "And I must say," Ralph Chaney said, "he did himself credit, and full justice to the prisoners in his speech." Latimer followed on behalf of the people, delivering an impassioned argument that nothing but blood would palliate the crimes that had been committed and that "as long as the gang of outlaws was permitted to remain on earth no community would be safe from their depredations and crimes. If not the authors of the untold robberies and murders that had been committed in the country, they were at least accomplices and had all shared in the plunder." In summation, Latimer said the people were justified in taking the course they had, that their safety demanded it, and that the murder of Campbell must be avenged. If the actual murderers could not be found, then those who planned the sinister deed must suffer in their stead.

When Latimer finished, the son-in-law of Campbell moved that a sentence of death be passed upon the two prisoners. After further deliberation, Leland said that while David and Taylor were the murderers, William and John were, by their presence at Bridge's, accessories to the crime. He then put the question to the men in the circle within which the prisoners had been tried.

"What say you, gentlemen, guilty or not guilty?"

"Guilty," came the unanimous reply from the jury. Raising their right hand, they then voted for a sentence of hanging. A death-like silence fell over the crowd. The prisoners, although calm and motionless, turned deathly pale. Leland then moved that Pearson Driscoll be released, to which the jury assented.

The trial had consumed the greater portion of the day.

When the sentence was pronounced, John Driscoll grumbled he would rather be "shot like a man than hung like a dog." The defense submitted a motion for a change of sentence, which was granted with a few dissenting voices. The old man was the first to speak. Turning to a bystander, he said, "If you are going to shoot me down, for God's sake take this noose from my neck, for it is choking me." Campbell's son-in-law untied it.

William called his brother Pearson and said, "They are going to kill me, and I want you to take that money of mine that is hid and give my children a liberal education and spend it for their support until they become men and women and grown. There is a plenty of it." Pearson expressed his willingness to do so but added, "I don't know where your money is; you have never told me." William began to speak but stopped short, exclaiming, "Oh, my God! I can't do it!"

One hour was given to them for prayer and two ministers present prayed with the condemned men. One of the preachers, the captain of the Oregon City Regulators named Crist, prepared himself by drinking a dipper full of whiskey from the now half-depleted whisky barrel. Kneeling down next to William, he began to pray long and loud. As William begged for forgiveness, at one point he broke down, confessing to having committed six murders with his own hand.

All this time, old man Driscoll stood erect and emotionless, refusing to join in prayer with the others. He was determined to die in the same fearless and defiant way he had lived. As the praying continued, the allotted hour stretched into two—and the crowd continued to imbibe from the whiskey barrel.

Several Regulators, who were not drinking, were now having second thoughts about what they were about to do. Postmaster Hamlin began frantically circulating among the crowd attempting to secure a postponement of the execution or a commutation of the sentence to banishment beyond the Mississippi within twenty-four hours. Leland favored the idea. Though unwilling to argue on their behalf himself, he urged Hamlin to keep up his efforts in favor of clemency. Even John Phelps, who had so defiantly wrested old man Driscoll from the Sheriff, favored it. Some called for a full remission of the sentence; others favored remanding them to the custody of Sheriff Ward, thereby evading the grave responsibility they had taken upon themselves. In the midst of all the clamoring, Latimer again made an impassioned address for the people, urging the immediate execution of the Driscolls. This had the effect of stifling the pleas of those seeking clemency and dispelled from the minds of the prisoners all hopes of a stay of execution.

Nothing more remained to be said. The time had now expired. Leland instructed the executioners to form a single line, divided into two, as equal as the number would permit, fifty-five in one section and fifty-six in the other. One division was detailed to execute the old man, and the other William. In the firing line were some of the leading men of the area: doctors, lawyers, postmasters, county officials, farmers, merchants. Each of them was given a rifle, though not all of the guns were loaded so that none of the men could know who was actually responsible for their deaths.[9]

John would be executed first. Now young Michael Seyster, who had followed the Regulators to recover his horse and had observed the proceedings with consternation, could not bear to be witness to the execution and withdrew with several men to a ravine out of sight. Some of the Regulators were now weeping, realizing they had gone too far. The old man was blindfolded and his arms bound behind his back. He was led ten paces to the left side of the line and instructed to kneel on the grass. Several Regulators suddenly decided not to take part in the execution and quietly slipped to the rear of the firing squad and pitched their rifles against a tree. Seeing this, Marsh shouted that all must join in and ordered the faint-hearted to pick up their guns and fall into line. When all were ready, Leland counted to three and gave the signal to fire. In a single volley, an ear-shattering report of rifles split the air and, as William and Pearson looked on, John Driscoll, the outlaw who had eluded authorities from Ohio to Illinois for more than thirty years, fell forward on his face without a sound.

At the sight of his father's execution, William dissolved into hysteria. Choking down sobs, he begged for mercy. In response to his desperate pleas, the crowd cried, "Shoot him! "Shoot him!" It was said that as terror overcame him in his final hour, William's hair had turned almost white. He was blindfolded and made to kneel on the grass. Leland counted to three and, as the guns fired in unison, William crumpled to the ground forty feet to the left of his father. As the victims lay prone, their backs revealed multiple holes where the bullets had gone through. John's vest contained more than forty bullet holes.

Some of the Regulators now felt that they had made a mistake in killing John first. If they had shot William first, they argued, the old man would have known they were serious and might have made a full confession as to his crimes and accomplices. But it was too late.

As the bodies of the two Driscolls lay on the ground, Leland told Pearson he could take charge of them and that help would be provided to bring them home and prepare them for burial. Pearson indignantly said he would have nothing to do with the bodies. His brother should not have been executed, he said, as he had been raised in a life of crime. As for his father's punishment, he had nothing to say.

Spades and shovels were then produced and a single shallow grave was dug on the spot where they had been killed. While carrying the elder Driscoll to the grave, Ralph Chaney noticed that his skull had also been shattered. Drawing their caps over their faces, the men rolled the blood-soaked bodies, unwashed and un-coffined, into the hole and covered it over. Six weeks later, friends removed the bodies and brought them back to South Grove where they were washed, placed in a casket, and given a decent burial.

Before the Regulators dispersed to their homes, they destroyed what remained of the houses and barns of both John and David to make sure the sons at large would have nothing to return to. For several weeks after, Mrs. Driscoll was forced to live in a corncrib amidst the charred ruins. The remainder of the family scattered to different parts of the country—some to California, some to Minnesota, and some to unknown localities. Even though he was acquitted, Pearson was warned to leave the country, which he promised to do. A few weeks later, he moved to Cook County and abandoned his life of crime.

Shortly after the executions, the Regulators began scouring the countryside for David, Taylor, William Bridge, and the Aiken boys. (The *Rockford Star* had posted a $500 reward for their capture.) The Regulators first went to Bridge's house but were unaware he was hiding in an excavation underneath it. When the Regulators left, Bridge fled to Henry on the Illinois River, taking refuge at Grant Redden's, the leader of a Mormon gang. The vigilantes were able to track him down in Hancock County concealed in the garret of Redden's house. The Regulators arrested him and took him before justice of the peace William J. Mix for questioning in connection with Campbell's murder but discharged him for lack of evidence.

It seemed the Regulators had finally prevailed. What happened next, however, would put an end to "regulating" in Rock River country.

## CHAPTER 4

# The Trial

*[T]here is even now something of an ill omen amongst us. I mean the increasing disregard for law that pervades this country—the growing disposition to substitute the wild and furious passions in lieu of the sober judgement of courts, and the worse than savage mobs for the executive ministers of justice.*

—ABRAHAM LINCOLN, *The Perpetuation of Our Political Institutions*, 1837

Judge Thomas Ford's devotion to the law bordered on the religious. In a way, he owed his life to it. As a child in Uniontown, Pennsylvania, he had lost his father in a coal mining accident. His second father was thought to have been murdered by a highwayman.[1] Left destitute, his twice-widowed mother took her large brood of children to Spanish Missouri in the hope of obtaining free land. When she realized she had been lured on a false promise, she packed up and moved to Monroe County, Illinois, in 1805. At the time, few people were living on the frontier and life was pitiless. Schools were primitive and Thomas, though small and frail, often had to abandon his studies to labor as a farm hand with his siblings. He often studied at home and though he was an able student, he showed little ambition. Thanks to the encouragement and financial support of his elder half-brother, Forquer, he eventually entered Kentucky's Transylvania University studying law as Forquer had. But after a year, his brother's business failed and Thomas was forced to withdraw. He returned to Illinois some four hundred miles on foot. On his way back, he ran out of money and was forced to teach school for three months. As it was a new settlement, Ford helped to build a schoolhouse, an achievement that he later referred to as one of the proudest of his life. When he returned home, to make ends meet he worked as a farm hand, pursuing law studies in his spare time. When he finally completed his studies, Forquer had regained his financial footing and made him partner in his law firm.[2]

In 1829, Ford set out on his own, setting up a law practice in Galena where the discovery of lead had sparked an economic boom. His business, however, attracted few clients. Once again, Forquer came to his aid, securing him an appointment as state attorney in the Military Tract Zone. There, he prosecuted one prairie pirate after another only to see the

Thomas Ford as Circuit Court Judge
*Source: Courtesy of the Abraham Lincoln Presidential Library and Museum*

cases dismissed. He nonetheless served ably until 1835 when he became circuit court judge in the same district. Over time, Ford developed a reputation as a straight-talking judge with a strong sense of moral probity and an abiding concern for social order. Five years later, he was appointed state Supreme Court judge in the Northern Judicial Circuit around the Rock River Valley.

Now Judge Ford had a big problem.

In advising Ogle County residents to form a group to drive out the Driscoll gang, he was in some measure responsible for having stirred up the Regulators. That the Regulators went far beyond what Ford had in mind when he counseled them and that he had tried to stop them when they seized John Driscoll from the Sheriff mattered little. What mattered was that a sitting judge had countenanced extrajudicial action, action, moreover, that led to the summary killing of two men who, whatever their other misdeeds, had been innocent of murder. At worst, John and William were merely accessories to murder and as such would have been sentenced to no more than three to five years in prison by a formal court, a far cry from the harsh death sentence they had received at the hands of the Regulators.

Ford had already come under criticism for admonishing from the bench a member of the Driscoll gang, Norton Royce, during a particularly exasperating trial. Royce had been one of the prisoners in the Oregon jail when it was wantonly burned down, forcing the embattled judge to hold court in a makeshift room. Royce had been on trial with two other men for counterfeiting and had many sympathizers on the jury who were attempting to influence the outcome. Even more frustrating, the defense attorney had made so many peremptory juror challenges that Ford was obliged to summon no less than forty-nine talesmen. Despite the tiresome maneuvering of the defense, the jury nonetheless found Royce guilty though he received the minimum sentence—one year in prison. The next day, the defense attempted to quash the judgment and move for a new trial, but Ford had overruled him. Fearing retaliation by the gang for his action, Ford had admonished Royce:

> *I am going away on business, and will be obliged to leave my family behind me. If the desperadoes dare to injure them while I am gone,*

*I will come back, call my neighbors together, and follow them until
I have overtaken them, when the first tree shall be their gallows; and
if the injury is done while I am on the bench trying a case, I will leave
the bench and follow them up until they are exterminated!*[3]

It was an extraordinary—even impeachable—remark for a sitting judge. Yet, such was his awareness of the daring and invincibility of the prairie pirates that he felt obliged to issue an outright threat. Several newspapers quickly condemned him for his comment, one calling it "a strange and startling declaration." The Peoria *Register* also rebuked him, intimating he bore some responsibility for the mob violence. "When the chosen minister of justice tramples the law under his feet," wrote the editor, "we ought not to be surprised at the extremes of those who are too ready, with such high examples, to spurn its salutary restraint."[4]

Still, most newspapers had applauded the work of the Regulators. Referring to those who had presided at the Driscolls' trial, the Ottawa *Free Trader* had enthused, "A more respectable assemblage of individuals could hardly be convened in the northern part of Illinois."[5] More to the point, the Galena *Gazette* had noted, "The violation of the law should always be condemned. But, if forced to choose between professed villains and professed honest men, we shall not hesitate to be found at the side of the latter."[6] The overwhelming consensus was that the Regulators had acted in the interest of social order and were thus justified in their actions.

The Democratic Rockford *Star*, however, took strong exception. After learning that the Regulators planned to issue monthly reports of their vigilante activities in the Rockford newspapers, its editor, Philander Knappen, wrote a long editorial excoriating the Regulators:

*Now, be it known to all the world that we have solemnly resolved that the
proceedings of the Ogle County, or any county volunteer lynch company
cannot be justified or encouraged in our columns. The view we take of the
subject does not permit us to approve the measures and conduct of the said
company. If two or three hundred citizens are to assume the administration of lynch law in the face and eyes of the laws of the land, we shall soon
have a fearful state of things, and where, we ask, will it end if mob law
is to supersede the civil law? If it is tolerated, no man's life or property is*

*safe; his neighbor, who may be more popular than himself, will possess an easy, ready way to be revenged by misrepresentation and false accusation; in short, of what avail are our legislative bodies and their enactments? We live in a land of laws, and to them it becomes us to resort and submit for the punishment and redress as faithful keepers of the laws, and thus extend to each other the protection and advantages of the law . . . we wash our hands clear from the blood of Lynch law.*[7]

In the same issue of *The Star*, two letters to the editor had appeared. One signed *Vox Populi* (written by a Whig named Jacob Miller) lambasted the actions of the Regulators, disparaging them as "banditti." In a long and impassioned argument Miller asked,

*Shall all Civil Law be sacrificed and trampled in the dust at the shrine of Mobycracy? Shall the life and property of no one receive any protection from the civil law, but both be subject to the nod of an inconsiderate and uncontrollable mob? Shall these things he so? Or will the people rise en masse, and assert the laws of the land, and enforce the same against the murderers and lynchers? The latter course is certainly pointed out by justice, and I trust in God that justice will be meted out to all who have had a hand in this bloody business.*[8]

The second letter, signed simply "B," was written by Charles Latimer, who had been the prosecutor at the Driscolls' trials. Latimer staunchly defended the Regulators' actions.

Even though *The Star* had given both sides their due, Miller's editorial infuriated the Regulators. A few nights later, several of them broke into the newspaper's office and completely ransacked it. Financially ruined, Knappen was forced to sell his paper.

Underlying the entire discussion was whether to hold the Regulators accountable for the killing of the Driscolls. To try them for murder, it was thought, would be wildly unpopular. It might also embolden the outlaws. Everyone knew William and John Driscoll had been committing crimes in the region with impunity for years. Something had to be done and, as far as most citizens were concerned, they had gotten their just deserts.

On a personal level, Ford could scarcely try men who were his friends and neighbors and among the most respected citizens in northern part of the state. John Phelps was Ogle County's oldest and wealthiest settler and founder of Oregon. He had built the second house in Oregon after Jonathan Jenkins. For a time in 1835, Ford had even boarded with Phelps until setting up his own cabin on Phelps's land.[9] And when Phelps's brother Ben was commissioned Ogle County court clerk in 1837, it was Ford who had generously posted his bond.

On the other hand, to do nothing amounted to tacit approval of their actions. As a judge, Ford needed to put them on trial if only to clear his own involvement in the matter. As a prominent Democrat he also harbored aspirations for elected office and was well aware, come election time, his Whig opponents would exploit his involvement in the extrajudicial killings. His solution to his dilemma resulted in one of the most bizarre trials in the annals of American justice.

At the commencement of the fall term of the Ninth Ogle County Circuit Court in 1841, Ford empaneled a grand jury to hear evidence against Jonathan Jenkins and 111 others for the murder of William and John Driscoll. Jenkins, the first person named in each of the indictments, had nothing to do with the execution of the Driscolls. However, the Lafayette Grove resident was considered friendly with the Driscolls, and it was feared that he might furnish some damaging testimony against the Regulators. So, too, might the nine Regulators who had opted out of the jury. To prevent them from testifying, they were also placed on the indictment list. Of the twelve grand jurors, ten were selected because it was feared their testimony might also be harmful to the defense; the remaining two were known Regulators. As if that were not enough, the grand jury foreman, S.M. Hitt, was a brother of one of the Regulators.[10]

When the case was presented for consideration with a list of the names of those charged, the name at the top of the list was called first. If it happened to be the name of a juryman, the juror was temporarily excused. When he had left the room, the charges against him were then examined and disposed of after which the person was recalled to the jury.

The next name was called and the same procedure was observed until the entire list was completed.

On Friday, September 24, the grand jury handed down indictments charging 112 men with the murders of John and William Driscoll (the 109 men who had been in the firing squad plus Jenkins and the two trial lawyers). Since two of the men on the grand jury were Regulators, they had in effect presented indictments against themselves. The trial took place the same day. Since there was no courthouse, the trial was held in a building owed by Ralph Chaney. The case was entitled "The People v. Jonathan W. Jenkins, Seth H. King, George D. Johnson, Commodore P. Bridge, Moses Nettleton, James Clark, Lyman Morgan, William . . ." and so on, naming all 112 accused. Among those indicted were the four Chaney brothers, Richard, Phineas, Ralph, and Osborn, and John Phelps and his brother Benjamin, all of whom had been in the firing squad. Seth B. Farwell appeared for the people and John D. Caton for the defense before a twelve-member jury.[11]

As Caton had spoken to only a few of the accused before the trial, he now convened a meeting with them outside the courthouse on "a little isolated peak of the prairie." As the accused gathered around Caton, he called out their names one by one. To his surprise, four of the 112 were absent. So, too, was the sheriff in whose custody they were supposed to be. Unfazed, Caton instructed four of the men that when the clerk called their names in court to answer as "proxies" for the absentee defendants. Caton's clients then followed him into the tiny courtroom. With so many accused in such a tiny room the men crowded right up to the table where the lawyers sat.[12]

As the clerk began to call the name of each Regulator, Caton listened anxiously. When the first three absentees were called, the proxies promptly answered—with no challenge. But when the fourth name was called, someone near the door shouted out, "That ain't him." For a moment, a puzzled silence fell over the courtroom. Judge Ford calmly asked for the name to be called again. Again the name was called and the proxy answered. This time he was not challenged and the clerk continued the absurdly lengthy roll call.

When arraigned for trial, the defendants all pleaded "not guilty," and the trial proceeded. By law, each of the defendants had a right to the peremptory challenge of twenty men. This would have necessitated the availability of 2,040 potential replacement jurors, a number of men greater than there were in the entire county. Yet, such, presumably, had been Ford's prior arrangement that the defense made few or no juror challenges.

So far so good. The first hiccup occurred when out of the blue, a Peoria attorney named Lincoln Knowlton, a well-known sympathizer of the Driscolls, asked to assist the people in the prosecution of the case. Blindsided by the request, the prosecutor quickly denied it on the grounds that he was not "of the sober and discreet type the case required." The implication was that Knowlton was a drunk. Had Ford allowed the motion, Knowlton would likely have moved for a new venue or the ten indicted jurors to testify against the Regulators. Later, Ford bluntly defended his action, calling Knowlton "a drunken lawyer . . . for the horse thieves."[13]

After brief addresses by Farwell for the people and Caton for the defense, Farwell then called several witnesses. Caton described what happened next:

> *The truth was that no one was present at the trial and execution but the defendants, and no one could be found who had heard any one of them say a word about it. All the witnesses had heard rumors, with which the whole atmosphere was filled and had been ever since the event happened, but of course, these widely differed from each other, and some of them were wildly extravagant, but this was not legal testimony. I did not object to them, because I wished to demonstrate by their contradictory character how unreliable mere rumors are. I called no witnesses, no argument was made to the jury on either side, and I asked the court to instruct the jury that mere rumors were not evidence, which, of course, he did, and explained the law in his own way as to what evidence was necessary to authorize a conviction.*[14]

Just where the dozens of men were who had observed the Driscoll execution is unclear, though most likely no honest citizen in the country was willing to testify on behalf of the banditti. Since no evidence could be presented, the cases went forthwith to the jury for a decision. Without leaving their seats, the jury returned a verdict of "not guilty" in the murder of John Driscoll. The same jurors then sat on the trial for William's murder. Since the second indictment tried the case on the same facts as the one they had just heard and on which they had rendered a verdict of not guilty, the outcome of the second trial was assured and the Regulators were acquitted of all wrongdoing.

On the following day, State Attorney Seth Farwell dismissed the indictments as to Jonathan W. Jenkins and the nine others who had not been acquitted. Thus ended a criminal case that was remarkable not only for the number of accused but for the extraordinary nature of the judicial proceedings: a grand jury composed of some of the accused, the rapid arraignment, the vast number of juror challenges allowed by the law and the significant use of none, as well as the speed with which a verdict was rendered. The trial's outcome was reported in the newspapers without comment, though the *Ottawa Free Trader* did honor the Regulators with a new title—"The Rock River Rangers."[15]

It had been a virtuoso judicial performance on Ford's part. What was most remarkable was that the entire trial had met the tacit approval of the public. None of the newspapers, which had previously been so critical of the Regulators, raised a single objection. According to Caton, some of those who were sympathetic to the prosecution begrudgingly quit the county shortly after the trial. He was succeeded on the bench by Caton, who called the Regulator trial "the most important case, nominally at least, in which I was ever engaged." It certainly was the most unusual. That Ford wished to forget the entire embarrassing episode was clear. For in his *History of Illinois*, he made no mention of the affair, even though his book purported to be about "interesting events" in the state's early history.

Less than a year later, Ford was put forth as a candidate in the gubernatorial election on the Democratic ticket when the party's candidate, Colonel Adam Duncan, died unexpectedly. His Whig opponent and incumbent, Joseph Duncan, tried to portray Ford as an advocate of Lynch Law in Ogle County, a charge, of course, that Ford denied.[16] Duncan's strategy failed to gain any traction and on August 1, 1842, Ford became governor of Illinois.* Even though Ford was now in the statehouse in Springfield, the prairie pirates would dog his career.

---

*Ford did lose Ogle County, which had been a Whig district since its inception.

## CHAPTER 5

# Pirates Redux

*It is important to recognize that there has never been a "golden age" of law and justice in our history.*

—SAMUEL WALKER, HISTORIAN

It had been a tumultuous six months in the Rock River Valley: the brazen burning of the Oregon courthouse, the righteous rampage of the Regulators, the wanton murder of Campbell, and the dramatic execution of the Driscolls. With Ford's theatrical trial of the Regulators, the entire pirate scourge seemed to have come to a quiet denouement.

Nonetheless, for a year after the Driscoll killings, people remained uneasy. Oregon's residents never went to sleep until its citizen sentries had gone on duty. Even then, they felt unsafe, for no one knew the moment when the night watch would be overpowered and a general slaughter of its citizens—as the Driscoll gang had threatened—would begin. Nothing untoward happened, however, and little by little tranquility returned to the valley. Settlers concluded that with the loss of their boss the worst of the outlaws had moved off while others had abandoned their life of crime altogether.

But they were sorely mistaken. Taylor and David Driscoll were still at large; Bliss, Dewey, West, the Aikens, and many other outlaws had no intention of leaving a place they called home—or of abandoning their chosen trade. They were laying low, quietly moving stolen horses up and down the frontier, patiently waiting for the time when settlers let down their guard.

That time came on the night of September 18, 1843, when William McKinney's store in Rockford was broken into and robbed of a trunk containing $1,000 in silver pieces. Bradford McKinney, William's brother, had been sleeping in the store when he was awakened by an intruder.

"Who's there?" Bradford called out in the dark.

"Bradford, your brother, wants the trunk," came the reply.

"But who are you?" Bradford demanded.

"Your brother wants the trunk."

"Stop! The trunk cannot go. Who sent you for it?"

"Look here," said the robber. He then took Bradford's hand and ran his bowie knife lightly across his fingers. "Do you feel that? It is very sharp and I won't hesitate to use it. Keep still and you shan't be hurt, but the trunk must go!"

Needing no further persuasion, McKinney handed over the trunk. The next morning, he found it discarded a short distance from the house, emptied of its contents. In their haste, the robbers had left eight pieces of silver in the trunk. McKinney found several more pieces near the house and in the prairie grass the following spring. He offered a $200 reward for the apprehension of the careless thief but he had absconded without a trace.[1]

Scarcely had the disturbance created by the McKinney robbery died down when the gang perpetrated an even bolder one. The Dixon Land Office had recently received a large amount of gold from the sale of government land. Periodically, a stagecoach belonging to Frink, Walker, and Company in Rockford would transport the gold to deposit in a Chicago bank. Upon learning of the existence of the gold, one of the pirates went to the Dixon office to inquire when they planned to make the twenty-four hour trip. Suspecting a ruse, the employee gave October 2 as the departure date—only it was for a passenger stagecoach leaving a week later than the one carrying the gold.

On the appointed day, the stagecoach departed for Chicago with several passengers on board. While the coach was in full motion, several men on horseback rode up behind it and removed the baggage from the rear of the coach. So deft had the robbers been that it was not until the following morning that the passengers discovered all their baggage missing. In a news article the following week, the *Rockford Forum* aptly noted the key to the pirates' success: "What renders these transactions still more exciting is the fact that they are committed by those who are perfect scholars in the business of the movements of the town."[2] Scholars indeed. For whenever large sums of money were reported to be in a home or business, word seemed to reach the pirates in a flash, though the sums to be had were often wildly exaggerated.

Such was the case of William Mulford of Ogle County who was rumored to have received a transfer of $15,000 from New York. When it reached the long ears of the gang in Washington Grove, they hastily devised a plan to secure it. On October 28, a stranger appeared at the Mulford house. Using the alias "Haines," he professed to be in search of employment. Mulford offered to hire him for six months but Haines said he could work but three; they discussed wages but could not reach agreement on that either. After further discussion, during which time Haines carefully surveyed the premises, he took leave, promising to call again in a few days.

True to his word, late one night ten days later Haines and two other masked men armed with pistols, knives, and clubs, broke into Mulford's house. One of the men ordered Mulford to sit down. He then took a candle from the table, cut it into three pieces, lighted them, and placed one in each of the two windows for two men outside keeping a lookout. With the third piece, he began his search of the house, telling the Mulfords not to stir from their bed or they would be shot. When the thieves demanded the keys to the bureau drawers, Mulford said they were in the stable behind the horses. This was merely a ploy to give him an opportunity to get to his rifle in another part of the room. As soon as the men went to the barn, Mulford attempted to go for his gun but one of the robbers stationed at the door rushed in and, holding a pistol to Mulford's head, ordered him to sit down.

Finding no keys in the barn, the robbers returned to the house enraged, swearing they would "chain the old devil" and set the house ablaze unless he revealed the location of the keys. Mulford, however, remained mum. But when Mrs. Mulford began to hear chains clanking, she realized they were serious and finally produced the keys from behind a cupboard. Unlocking the bureau drawer, the men found $400 in a crisp brown envelope as if it had just been taken from the bank—a far cry from what they had believed was in the house. Furious, the robbers demanded to know where Mulford had stashed the rest of the $15,000. Mulford repeatedly insisted that $400 was all he had, but each denial served only to convince Haines he was lying. Haines then began to ransack the house while his partner watched over Mrs. Mulford with a rifle. After emptying the cupboards and turning over the furniture, he went to the cellar where he found several large cakes of tallow. Bringing them up, he proceeded to cut up the cakes with a single slash of his bowie knife in the hope they contained the money. Finding nothing, he went to a bureau in the bedroom and began to empty each drawer of neatly folded linen, shaking them out and throwing them on the floor as he went along. After all the trouble it had taken her to clean and fold them, Mrs. Mulford bristled as she watched her fresh linens one by one being soiled. Finally, she could bear it no longer and blurted out, "Mr. Haines, you conduct yourself very differently from what you did the other day when you wished to obtain employment!" Incensed by the old woman's cheek, Haines rushed over and held a bowie knife to her face. "Bitch," he said, "you lie down and cover up your head. If you utter another word while we are in the house, I will make a stain on the floor that will last long after you are gone!"[3]

Haines then sat down in front of the old man and coolly counted the $400 on his knee. Just then, he suddenly realized he had been exposed, for Mrs. Mulford had addressed him by name. Turning anxiously to his comrades he said, "By God, I must be missing. I'm known and this is no place for me. A minute more boys and I'm off!" He hastily finished searching the rest of the house before departing. As he was leaving, Haines suddenly stopped. Turning to Mulford he asked, "Old man, do you intend to follow us?"

"I don't know," said Mulford implacably.

"Do you intend to follow us, I say?"

"I can't tell. I haven't thought about it."

"You must tell. What do you say old man?"

"I don't know that it will do any good."

"You'd better not," Haines warned. "Take my advice and keep still. There are a good many of us, and you could not catch us if you tried." As he started for the door, Haines took down a fowling piece from the lintel, but the old man begged him not to take his gun. Haines promised he would leave it where he could find it when they were gone. "We shall leave a man with a loaded rifle to guard your door," Haines said, "and if anyone ventures out before sunrise, a bullet will end their prying. Good-bye, old man, we are off and follow if you dare!"

With this parting salutation, the robbers fled. For a time, the Mulfords sat quietly in the darkness straining their ears for any sound of the robbers. Hearing nothing, they ventured out to find all were gone. At the spot designated by Haines, Mulford found his gun. The next morning, neighbors scoured the country for miles around but found not a trace of the desperadoes.

Within days of the Mulford incident, the banditti went on a robbery spree, relieving a peddler of all his goods in Troy Grove south of Rockford and robbing the Haskel house at Inlet Grove. Mr. and Mrs. Haskel were awake in bed at the time and never heard the intruder creeping along the floor.

Soon after, a major breakthrough came in the fight against the pirates. Charles West, the partner of Bliss and Dewey, had been arrested in Lee County for the robbery of a peddler whose goods were found in his possession. While West waited for the next term of the court to begin, he was placed in Dixon jail. It did not take long for West to realize he had no stomach for incarceration and he proposed to turn state's evidence and disclose all he knew concerning the prairie pirates.[4] It was the first such instance of a pirate willing to do so and it would lead to a mass roundup of the Driscoll gang. Among West's many revelations was that a noto-rious Indiana horse thief and Mormon, William "Judge" Fox, and John Baker had committed the robbery at Troy Grove. The two had tempo-rarily stashed most of the stolen goods in a house in Inlet Grove owned by a man named Sawyer before transferring them to Iowa. When authorities went to Sawyer's house, they found a portion of the peddler's goods there. Sawyer was tried and sentenced to two years in prison.

Another of West's disclosures was that Bliss was innocent of the Haskel robbery while Dewey had merely been an accessory, having "got up the sight." (The two were already serving a three-year sentence for the crime). The actual culprits were William Fox and Robert Birch. Like Fox, the twenty-seven-year-old Birch had been stealing horses and robbing houses since his adolescence. Birch had first come to Illinois's Clark County with his father, "Old Coon," and brother Tim. Birch roamed the Mississippi and Missouri Valleys using the aliases Brown, Bleeker, Harris—and Haines. Both had been on the run since breaking out of jail earlier in the year after being convicted with Tom Aiken for horse stealing in Warren County.

By far the greatest of West's revelations concerned the McKinney and Mulford robberies. A man named Irving A. Stearns had confided the details of these robberies to him while negotiating over a horse he wished to buy from West with some of the Mulford money. During the negotiations, Stearns revealed that Charles Oliver had hatched the plan for the raid on the Mulford house. Oliver and William McDowell (of Winnebago County) cased the premises while Birch and Bridge broke into the house. McDowell and Birch had collaborated in the McKinney robbery as well. Although Stearns had not been involved in either robbery, he had received a share of the Mulford money.

Based on West's testimony, a night session of the grand jury was hurriedly convened and indictments were handed down against Oliver, McDowell, and Bridge for the Mulford robbery and against Bridge and Aiken for other robberies disclosed by West.

At that time, the sheriff of Winnebago County was out of town. There was no deputy, and next in authority to the sheriff, the coroner, was the father-in-law of McDowell, which rendered him uniquely unqualified to be entrusted with the arrest of McDowell and Oliver. Under the law, two justices of the peace could appoint an officer to act in cases of emergency where there was no sheriff or in his absence. Acting under this law, Chauncy Burton and Willard Wheeler, the Winnebago justices of the peace, and Goodyear A. Sanford, the former sheriff of Rockford, were called out of bed and deputized to make the arrest. By this time, it was late and the arrests were deferred until the morning when Sanford took them into custody without incident. Soon after, authorities arrested Bridge at his home in Ogle County and placed him in the Rockford jail. No bail was set and the men were kept in custody until their trial.

Now ever since the Mulford robbery, Rockford prosecutor Jason Marsh had been working to ferret out the robbers. That summer, he received a letter from the warden of the penitentiary at Jackson, Michigan, to the effect that a prisoner in his charge, Isaac Stearns, knew about the robbery and was willing to testify. As it turned out, shortly after divulging the details of the robberies to West, Stearns had ridden to Michigan where he was caught and convicted for horse stealing. With West's testimony in hand, Marsh hastened to the Michigan penitentiary to interrogate Stearns. Feigning ignorance of the details of the robbery, Marsh asked what Stearns had to say on the subject and it mirrored precisely the sworn testimony of West. When court convened, Marsh sent for Stearns to testify as a key witness in Oliver's trial.[5]

Charles Oliver's trial began on August 26, 1845, before a ten-member jury on charges of conspiracy. The courthouse was filled to capacity by Winnebago County residents anxious to see justice delivered to a man they had so long trusted. Thomas C. Browne was the presiding judge and James L. Loop, the district attorney. Assisting Loop in the prosecution was nearly the entire legal profession of Rockford—Jason Marsh, James M. Wright, Anson S. and Cyrus F. Miller, and Thomas D. Robertson.

From the moment of his arrest, Oliver had assumed an air of utter insouciance toward the charges against him. Since he had merely planned the robbery and had not executed it, there was no one who could testify against him. The only witness to fear was Stearns whom he imagined to be safely locked away in a Michigan penitentiary. Acquittal, thus, seemed a foregone conclusion.

Upon arriving in Rockford, Stearns was sequestered until called to appear in court. When the time came to testify, he was ushered into the courtroom concealed by a circle of ushers. Soon after, Oliver entered, chatting and laughing with his attendants as if he were simply a casual spectator instead of a prisoner on trial for a felony. When the trial began and the names of witnesses for the prosecution were called, the name "Irving A. Stearns" was announced. The words fell on Oliver's ears like with a thud. His face turned deathly pale and he now sat trembling by his counsel's side.

Stearns's testimony was direct and unequivocal and a rigid cross-examination failed to weaken it to any degree. Then West took the witness stand, testifying that although Oliver had only planned the robbery, he had received a share of the stolen money. As in the testimony of Stearns, a sharp cross-examination failed to bring out any contradiction in the details of his account. On Saturday afternoon, the case went to the jury for a decision. The jury was out an hour and a half when it returned with a guilty verdict and a sentence of eight years confinement in the state penitentiary in Alton. Thus ended the most dramatic criminal trial in Winnebago County.

After serving five years, Oliver was pardoned and released. He went clean and rejoined his wife and family in New York. A few years later, he visited Rockford and mingled freely with the people among whom he had once been so popular and who had convicted him. To some he explained why the gang had not robbed them as well. To Goodyear Sanford, who had once been county treasurer, he said, "The boys often wanted to go for you, but I wouldn't let them, because you was such a clever fellow!"

William McDowell's trial began on November 26 and the case went to the jury five days later. After an all-night session, the jury brought in a verdict of guilty with a sentence of seven years in prison. The court ordered that the first month of the imprisonment be in solitary confinement. After serving five years, McDowell was pardoned. He stayed in Alton working as a carpenter and never returned to his former life of crime.

William Bridge requested a change of venue to Ogle County where he was convicted and sentenced to the penitentiary for eight years. His land in Winnebago County was sold and from the proceeds the Mulfords were reimbursed for their loss. After his release, Bridge drifted off to Iowa. There he fell into his old vices and was finally killed resisting arrest by a local sheriff.

Adolphus Bliss would die in prison while serving a three-year term for the Haskel robbery of which he was innocent. After serving his prison term, Dewey returned to his home and settled down to work his old farm. Sawyer also served out his time and likewise returned home to farm.

None of the Aikens boys—Charles, Richard, and Thomas—was ever apprehended for their many crimes, though their fate was comparatively worse. Charles died at his home at Washington Grove in 1841 from the effects of a terrible whipping administered by the people of Fort Madison, Iowa, for an unknown criminal offense, probably horse stealing. After the whipping, Iowans had tied him to a log of wood and threw it into the Mississippi River. How he escaped from drowning was a mystery. By the time he reached home, he was more dead than alive. For a few days, he suffered in agony and then expired. Those who prepared him for burial described his body as cut into gashes from his shoulders to his heels. Richard died the same year from sickness contracted from exposure while hiding day and night from the Iowa Regulators and law officers. After his escape from Warren County jail, Thomas Aikens quit the Rock River Valley for good. Rumor had it that he relocated far up the Missouri River where he settled down to farm and, to all appearances, lived an honest life.

Old man Sam Aikens, who had never been involved in criminal pursuits, died at Washington Grove in 1847 a broken man, disgraced by the disreputable lives into which his three eldest sons were drawn.

After remaining away for four years, probably in Iowa Territory, Taylor Driscoll returned to Ogle County in 1845. He was at once arrested and indicted for the murder of John Campbell. For nearly two years, he languished in different jails. When his case finally went to trial, his lawyer requested a change of venue on the grounds that the Driscolls were so reviled in Ogle County they could not get a fair trial. The trial was moved to McHenry County where it resulted in a hung jury. In the second trial, the court allowed the defendant's counsel wide latitude in cross-examining witnesses for the prosecution, especially Mrs. Campbell. Under cross-examination, she had sworn that on a recent occasion she had seen Pearson Driscoll at a certain time and place. She was as positive of it, she said, as she was that she had seen Taylor Driscoll shoot her husband. When the defense proved beyond a question that it was not Pearson but another brother whom she had seen, Pearson having been forty miles away at the time, her credibility was suddenly called into question. Finding her mistaken in identifying a person whom she had seen only a few months before, the jury was easily persuaded that she might have been equally mistaken in the identity of Taylor, whom she had not seen for six years. He was subsequently acquitted.

David Driscoll fled across the Mississippi into the Iowa Territory where he joined a large band of horse thieves in Jackson County. He was later shot by a sheriff while resisting arrest.[6]

With the rout of the core of the Driscoll gang, many pirates abandoned their life of crime while others slipped off into the Iowa frontier.* Peace finally returned to Ogle and neighboring counties. Those who had moved off would reappear in Illinois, in due course, more hardened and daring than ever.

*A strange sequel to the Driscoll affair occurred many years later. Local residents long believed that several caches—one amounting to $30,000—from the gang's robberies and stagecoach holdups remained buried near their hiding places on a farm south of DeKalb. It happened that the DeKalb farm once owned by William Driscoll later became the property of a man named Byers. One day in autumn, while Byers was threshing wheat, three men came on horseback and entered the grove west of the house. After surveying the premises, they located a spot and began digging. Byers ordered them to stop and get off his land. Producing a revolver, one of the men told him to mind his own business and return to his work. After their departure, Byers went to the spot and found a shallow hole in the ground. Beside it was a small, empty box and at the bottom of the hole the mark from which the box had been dug.

CHAPTER 6

# Unholy Alliance

*Having passed my whole life on the frontier . . . I have frequently seen that a first few settlers would fix the character of a settlement for good or for bad, for many years after its commencement. If bad men began the settlement, bad men would be attracted to them, upon the well-known principle that "birds of a feather will flock together."*

—GOVERNOR THOMAS FORD

In his observation of frontier settlement, Governor Ford was referring to the locus of his latest pirate woes: Hancock County. Located on a horseshoe bend of the Mississippi, Hancock was founded in 1829 when it had reached a population of 350, deemed sufficient to establish it as a separate administrative entity from Adams County. As part of the Military Bounty Tract, Hancock had been on Ford's itinerary from its inception during the four years he had served as state attorney. With few exceptions, Hancock's delinquents had been for Ford "hard cases" much like those in Ogle County.[1] Indeed, many of its horse thieves, counterfeiters, and robbers had been part of, or in league with, the Driscoll gang before its demise.

Of equal consequence in Ford's view were the "birds of a feather" that were flocking in massive numbers to Hancock: the Latter Day Saints. The charismatic Mormon Prophet, Joseph Smith, had come to Illinois as a fugitive from Missouri during the harsh winter of 1838–1839. When he and his three thousand followers crossed the Mississippi at Quincy, ragged and hungry, Adams County residents were sympathetic and aided them. Despite the warm welcome, Adams had too many Gentiles to Smith's liking, so he pressed on to Hancock

County, which was mostly wilderness. There, along the river, Smith bought some disease-infested swampland near the hamlet of Commerce. The following year, he drained the swamp and began construction of the new city of Nauvoo ("beautiful place" in Hebrew). He then summoned the faithful from all parts of the world and thousands poured in. For the next four years, the population of Nauvoo would double each year and continue to grow after that, making City Beautiful one of the most important—and nettlesome—cities in the state.*

Hancock residents were initially well disposed toward Mormons, viewing them as a quiet and industrious people who had been unjustly persecuted in Missouri. Not long after their arrival, however, Gentiles began to notice their property—clothing, agricultural implements, food, what one settler called "petty depredations"—mysteriously disappearing. They immediately suspected the Mormons, believing the Prophet himself was sanctioning theft of Gentile property.

While the accusation against Smith was untrue, Mormons were stealing from Mormons and non-Mormons alike. Some of the thieves were Danites, or "Sons of Dan," a shadowy Mormon militia that grew out of conflict with non-Mormons in Missouri.[2] The term Danites derived from Genesis 49:17— "Dan shall be a serpent by the way, an adder in the path that biteth the horse's heels so that his rider shall fall backward." Initially formed to protect the Mormon Church in Missouri, over time the Danites became increasingly violent, burning homes and robbing anyone perceived as an enemy of the church. Danites also believed stealing from Gentiles was sanctioned by God. Although Smith later repudiated them, some Danites were serving in the city's police, the Nauvoo Legion. There were also Mormons who tithed stolen goods to the church, which knowingly accepted them. Others were criminals lurking in Nauvoo; still others were escaped convicts from the east who had converted to Mormonism and pretended to believe in the teachings to obtain the special legal protection the religious enclave afforded.

---

*Even though Smith had encouraged everyone to settle in around Nauvoo, the poor quality of the land led many to settle across the river in the village of Montrose in Lee County.

According to George Q. Cannon, a Mormon historian,

*There were a number of bad men in those days, who, professing to be Latter Day Saints, were guilty of many evil practices. Not content with doing wrong themselves, they tried to lead others to engage with them by telling them that Joseph [Smith] knew all about their acts, and that he had given them authority to steal. They endeavored to screen themselves by using the names of Joseph and Hyrum and other leading men. They said it was not wrong to steal anything from a Gentile; the prophet Isaiah had said that Zion should suck the milk of the Gentiles; and Micah had said that the gain of the Gentiles was to be consecrated to the Lord and their substance to the Lord of the whole earth. When, therefore, they stole property from men who did not belong to the church, they said they were "consecrating" or that they were "milking the Gentiles," and justified themselves for doing so, and called it perfectly right.[3]*

The Prophet seemed genuinely disturbed by the criminal element in the community. He likely saw the potential for theft to destabilize the fledgling community of Zion, especially since crimes were being perpetrated against Mormons as well. In October 1840, he appointed six elders to weed out the town's corrupt elements and bring them to justice. The stealing only worsened, however, as did relations between Gentiles and Mormons. The following year, in a speech to his followers on the state of the church, the Prophet specifically addressed the problem of crime among the Saints:

*I wish you all to know that because you were justified in taking property from your enemies, while engaged in war in Missouri, which was needed to support you, there is now a different condition of things. We are no longer at war and we must stop stealing. When the right time comes, we will go in force and take the whole state of Missouri. It belongs to us as our inheritance but I want no more petty stealing. A man that will steal petty articles from his enemies will, when occasion offers, steal from his brethren too. Now I command you, that you who have stolen must steal no more. I ask all the brethren to renew their covenants, and start anew to renew their religion. If you will do this then I will forgive you your past sins.*[4]

Yet, despite his lip service to crime, Smith did little to eradicate it. Indeed, after he received approval for a change in Nauvoo's legal status, the city actually became a safe haven for criminals, Mormon and non-Mormon alike.

As the city grew in population, Whigs and Democrats began to see Mormons as a powerful voting bloc, even though Smith had indicated he would not support either party. So when, in December 1840, Mormons presented a request to the state legislature for a city charter that allowed them to govern themselves, it passed both houses without so much as a single vote taken. Among other powers, the charter gave the Mormons the power to enact laws and establish their own independent militia and courts. All powers were vested in Smith who served as mayor, lawmaker, commander of the militia, and judge of the municipal court. In effect, Nauvoo had become a state within a state. Governor Ford condemned the charter as being undemocratic, noting that "the great law of separation of powers was wholly disregarded."[5] By far, the power that would have the greatest implication for the two hundred criminals living in Nauvoo was the writ of habeas corpus. The writ gave Mormon courts jurisdiction in all cases of arrest of Nauvoo residents.[6]

Less than a year after the passage of the bill, Mormon's independence was tested when the governor of Missouri issued a warrant for the arrest of Smith and several Mormon leaders on charges related to the conflict with Missourians known as the 1838 Mormon War. With no explanation, the arresting agent returned the warrant without executing it. The warrant was reissued, and this time Smith was arrested. Appearing before Judge Stephen A. Douglas, Smith argued that since the warrant was returned the first time it was no longer valid. Douglas dismissed the case.[7]

Meanwhile, Nauvoo courts were liberally applying habeas corpus to protect city residents from arrest. Just why Smith tolerated the practice in view of his incontrovertible power (he was ex-officio judge of the mayor's court and chief justice of the municipal court) and public statements condemning crime in the community is unclear. At times, he himself even exonerated criminals such as escaped convict Jeremiah Smith. Smith had been indicted in Washington, DC, for embezzling the government. After fleeing to Nauvoo, he was promptly arrested by the deputy district marshal, but a municipal court presided over by Smith ordered his release.

One explanation for the unwillingness to prosecute Mormon criminals was the deep-seated Mormon hostility toward Gentiles after years of Gentile persecution. In New York, Mormons had endured the hatred of Christian churches, making continued residence there hazardous. In Ohio, the Prophet was tarred and feathered. In Missouri, non-Mormons who stole from them routinely went unpunished. So too did the Missouri militia that massacred seventeen men and boys at Hawn's Mill in 1838. Nor were Mormons ever reimbursed by the government for the loss of their land and property when they were expelled from Missouri. Smith complained bitterly that the law was "always administered against us and never in our favor." It mattered little that much of the Gentile hostility stemmed from Smith's depreciation of other religions as "abominations" or that he had threatened to exterminate those who attacked them. In the minds of Smith and other Mormons, what mattered was that they had been harried from state to state and made to endure injustice and physical and mental abuse at the hands of non-Mormons.

Gentile's relations with Mormons took a turn for the worse when a resident of Missouri found a cache of goods stolen from a store in Tully about thirty miles south of Nauvoo. When several Tully residents came to retrieve the goods, they happened upon several Mormons in the river bottom claiming to be looking for horses stolen from them. Assuming they were complicit in the theft of their goods, Tully residents took them captive and imprisoned them in a log cabin. Over the next two days, they beat them severely, the Mormons eventually confessing to the theft. Whether they were actually guilty is unclear, though the confession confirmed Gentile's suspicions that the church was encouraging the Saints to steal. In a November 1841 newspaper article, church leader Hyrum Smith, Joseph's brother and confidante, vigorously denied the charges, as did Council of Twelve president Brigham Young. The Prophet issued an

The Mormon Prophet Joseph Smith
*Source: Courtesy of the Abraham Lincoln*
*Presidential Library and Museum*

even stronger disavowal a few days later. Nevertheless, within days of the confession, elders convened a "General Court-Martial" of the accused and sanctioned two of its apostles.

As crime increased in and around Nauvoo, by 1842, the initial warmth Illinoisans had accorded Mormons began to cool. Residents of Hancock and surrounding counties were now convinced that Mormons condoned the theft and robbery of Gentiles and that the Nauvoo courts regularly set criminals free.

On July 20, 1842, former Missouri governor Lilburn Boggs issued a warrant for Joseph Smith's arrest on new charges of conspiring to murder him. Boggs had been reading in his study when he was seriously wounded by a shotgun blast. Three weeks later, Missouri sheriffs arrested Smith in Lee County, Illinois. Once again, a Nauvoo municipal court ordered his release on a writ of habeas corpus. As frustrated sheriffs rode to Springfield to protest the action, Mormons passed a new ordinance authorizing the court to free anyone arrested on malicious intent or religious persecution. After Illinois governor Carlin backed the sheriffs, Smith went into hiding. Carlin promptly issued a $200 bounty for his capture.

When Smith resurfaced four months later, Thomas Ford had become Governor and assured Smith the charges would not hold up in federal court.† They didn't. Following Ford's advice, Smith stayed out of politics and focused on the construction of his impressive city. While laying low might have been good advice for the Prophet, it did little to resolve the problem of crime—or the deteriorating relations between Mormons and Gentiles.

By the summer of 1843, Illinois citizens wanted Smith and his Mormons out of Illinois. In addition to fears of the growing political and economic power of the Saints, there were angry complaints that they were harboring thieves, harassing Gentiles when they entered Nauvoo to recover their property, and abusing the power of habeas corpus to escape justice. So much counterfeit money was issuing from the city that a half-dollar counterfeit coin in circulation was dubbed "the Nauvoo Bogus" because its provenance was the city of the Saints. There were also fears that the Mormon vote would decide the legislative elections in 1844. Rumors were also circulating that Nauvoo's militia was now equipped with thirty cannons and six thousand small arms. (The actual amount was considerably less.) Compounding these problems was Nauvoo's size. By 1843, it had become the second largest city in Illinois after Chicago, with a population of nearly fifteen thousand—and growing. By virtue of its size alone it was attracting its normal, big-city quota of "counterfeiters, blacklegs, bootleggers, slave traders, gamblers, and every other disreputable type of person," as one historian observed.[8]

As tensions escalated, Gentiles began attacking Mormons traveling alone or living on isolated farms. When new fears arose that Missouri

---

†Surprisingly, as candidate, Ford had pledged to abolish the Nauvoo charter but carried Hancock County by an overwhelming majority.

would attempt to arrest the Prophet, the city council passed an ordinance mandating life imprisonment for anyone attempting to arrest him on the old Missouri treason charge. It also forbade the governor from pardoning anyone convicted by the Nauvoo court. In December, the council passed yet another ordinance preventing any officer from arresting a Nauvoo resident without having the writ countersigned by the mayor. According to Governor Ford, many people had begun to believe the Mormons were about to set up a separate government for themselves in defiance of the laws of the state.[9] Indeed, they had already done so.

Ironically, Smith's embattled theocracy began to unravel from within in 1844. Several members of Smith's inner circle had become disaffected with the Prophet, mostly over his practice of polygamy. After starting their own press, the *Nauvoo Expositor*, Mormon dissidents published an article—in what was to be the one and only issue—claiming that the Prophet was a polygamist who wished to become a theocratic king and calling for the repeal of the city charter. Fearing continued criticism would incite Gentile violence against him, Smith had the press destroyed and its founders ejected from the church. The dissidents fled to Carthage, the seat of Hancock County, where they attempted to file charges against Smith and his men but a Nauvoo court dismissed them. On June 17, Carthage citizens, concerned the violence would spread, asked Governor Ford to call out the state militia and restore order in Hancock County.

There was good reason for fear. County residents had adopted a resolution vowing to exterminate all the Mormons not only in Illinois but in Iowa and Missouri as well. The day after the destruction of the press, a public assembly adopted the following resolution:

> *Resolved . . . that we hold ourselves at all times in readiness to cooperate with our fellow citizens in this state, Missouri, and Iowa, to exterminate—UTTERLY EXTERMINATE—the wicked and abominable Mormon leaders, the authors of our troubles.*
> *Resolved . . . that the time, in our opinion, has arrived when the adherents of Smith as a body, shall be driven from the surrounding settlements into Nauvoo; that the Prophet and his miscreant adherents*

*should then be demanded at their hands, and if not surrendered, A WAR OF EXTERMINATION SHOULD BE WAGED, to the entire destruction if necessary for our protection, of his adherents.*[10]

With civil war looming, Ford demurred, opting instead to ride to Carthage to assess the situation for himself. When he arrived, he found an angry, 1,700-strong county militia poised to attack Nauvoo. His first act was to place the militia under the command of regular officers. He then proposed to Smith that he be tried in Carthage by non-Mormons and that Ford would personally guarantee his safety.[11] When he received Ford's offer, Smith was holed up in the largely Mormon town of Montrose, in Lee County, Iowa, intending to flee west. At the last minute, however, friends and relatives persuaded him to return on the grounds that fleeing was inconsistent with his exalted role as Prophet. Reluctantly, at midnight on June 25, Smith turned himself in with his brother Hyrum and several others. The next day, the Mormons were charged with rioting and destroying the press and released on bail.

Within days, Joseph and Hyrum were rearrested on trumped-up charges of treason. They were placed in the Carthage jail in the very midst of their enemies. This time, in view of the nature of the charge, the judge refused bail. Ford refused to override the judge, even though he had lured Smith back with assurances of his protection. Leaving two companies to guard the Carthage jail, Ford disbanded the militia. He then went to Nauvoo where he told Mormons they had been aggressors in the conflict and urged them to keep the peace. When the militia from Warsaw heard of Ford's order to disband, they protested against "being made tools and puppets of Tommy Ford" and headed to Carthage to "talk things over" with their counterparts, the Carthage Greys.[12] On June 27, 1844, the remnants of the two militias rushed the jail and murdered the Prophet and his brother. Whether the guards had been in on the attack is unknown.‡

---

‡Six months later, the Illinois state legislature moved to limit Nauvoo's power by revoking the city's charter on the grounds that it had been "much abused" by Mormons.

For non-Mormons, the Prophet's blood was insufficient; they would eventually settle for nothing less than the total expulsion of Mormons from Illinois. As anti-Mormon sentiment simmered in Hancock and the surrounding counties, several attacks by Mormon cutthroats operating out of Nauvoo would only add fuel to the fire. On April 25, 1845, John Miller, a fifty-eight-year-old minister, who had emigrated from Ohio with his family, offered to pay $1,000 in cash for a farm near Whiteside County, Illinois. Within days, two strangers appeared at Miller's isolated one-room cabin near the hamlet of West Point, Iowa, carrying a whip and saying they had just moved to the area and were searching for their lost ox. When Miller indicated he had not seen it, the men retreated to the house of old "Mill" Walker nearby. Authorities had long suspected Walker of harboring thieves and fugitives but could never establish any connection between him and robberies occurring in the area.[13]§

The next morning they returned to Miller's. Attempting to learn of the location of the money, one of the men asked Miller to cash a bank note so they could pay for their lodging. Suspecting the note might be counterfeit, Miller declined. The following night, Mrs. Miller heard the latch being lifted and looked up to see the blackened faces of three intruders, armed with pistols, bowie knives, and cudgels. One was holding up a lantern. A fourth member of the gang was outside standing watch. In addition to Mrs. Miller were her husband and their two daughters and their husbands, Henry Leisi and Jacob Risser. Before she could wake her husband, two of the men pounced on Miller and Leisi and began bludgeoning them. While the two men attempted to fight off their aggressors, Jacob Risser laid still on the floor in one corner of the cabin, trembling with fright.[14]

The robbers had expected the peaceable Mennonites to be an easy mark, so they were unprepared for the fierce resistance put up by Leisi and Miller, who had been a soldier in Germany. At one point, Miller was able to break free and began beating one of the robbers with his unloaded shotgun. Just as Miller was about to push him out the door, his attacker turned and thrust his bowie knife into Miller's side, piercing his heart. As

§According to Reid, after Walker's death in Quincy many years later, $100,000 in silver coins was found concealed beneath his cellar floor in rusty sardine and oyster tins.

Leisi rushed to his aid, he was stabbed several times in the back and head. Briefly he struggled with his attacker when a shot rang out and Leisi crumpled to the floor. The robbery now having gone sour, the assailants fled with nothing. Miller attempted to give chase but fell dead on the ground outside.[15]

It wasn't until after midnight that neighbors who had heard the shots arrived at the scene and the bell of the Catholic Church was sounded. One of the first to arrive was Colonel Reid who found Miller in the front yard "lying dead, stabbed through the heart by a big bowie-knife, and his bloodless face upturned, looked from his open, glassy eyes with an excited stare upon them, like that of a soldier dying in the midst of a charge. A little deep, worn path, leading from the house to the smoke house, was filled with his heart's blood, which had flowed into it from the place where he had fallen."[16] The bowie knife was the kind used to sharpen mill saws. Inside was Leisi who was critically wounded and moaning in agony. Word was sent to Lee County sheriff James L. Estes in West Point, who arrived just before dawn with Drs. Holmes and Sala. The women were in the bedroom trembling and choking down tears as they described to Estes the details of the horrific event. Holmes attempted to administer aid to Leisi who had multiple skull fractures and was bleeding profusely from a severe knife wound to the chest.

Local residents immediately pointed the figure at Mormons—and their instincts were correct. For when Estes, a Kentucky backwoodsman, surveyed the premises, he found four sets of footprints that he tracked to the Mississippi—in the direction of Nauvoo. He immediately organized county residents into companies that fanned out in search of the killers. But it wouldn't be Estes's men who would succeed in tracking down the killers but a quirky amateur detective named Edward Bonney.[17]

Edward Bonney was born and raised in Essex County, New York, in 1807. Though related to the famous political leader Daniel Webster on his mother's side, he apparently did not acquire much by way of education or skills in his youth. In 1837, seeking greater opportunity on the frontier, he left New York with his wife Maria and the first of several daughters. In Indiana, Bonney purchased a hundred acres of land on which he built a grist and a saw mill. He hoped the mills would attract the building of a canal or railroad that would serve as the basis of the new city of Bonneyville. By 1841, neither happened and the town failed to take off. After liquidating his interests, he ran a hotel and tavern in Indiana for a while.

By his own account, Bonney had aimlessly "fiddle-footed his way" to Nauvoo where he found work in a general store in 1844. There, he befriended Joseph Smith, becoming his aide-de-camp and one of three non-Mormon members of the Council of Fifty, an elite organization dedicated to the coming theocracy on Earth. For Bonney, who professed no interest in matters of religion, it was likely more of a career move. After Smith was murdered, Bonney claimed to have found a calling fighting criminal elements within Nauvoo. His efforts were mostly in vain however, for he wrote,

> *In case of an arrest at Nauvoo, the accused were immediately released by the city authorities, and the cry of "Persecution against the Saints" raised, effectively drowning the pleas for justice, of the injured, and the officer forced to return and tell the tale of defeat. This done, the fugitive found a safe shelter under the wide-spread wings of the Mormon leaders and laughed at pursuit.*[18]

Disenchanted with the crime in Nauvoo, in 1845, he moved to Montrose in the Iowa Territory where he bought some land and opened a livery stable. The business offered a reliable means to support his large family but was personally unsatisfactory. So when he heard about the savage attacks on Miller and Leisi, he volunteered his services to help find the culprits.

In becoming a "self-appointed agent of justice," Bonney was a wannabe, someone who longed to be where the action was and the action, as he saw it, was in fighting crime.** By posing as one of the bandits, he was able to infiltrate the ranks of the banditti and bring some of its worst malefactors to justice. In so doing, he became a one-man vigilance committee and bounty hunter who operated on the margins of the law.

Affecting the role of the dashing detective, Bonney donned a black top hat and long coat under which he hid a pair of rifle pistols, a revolving

---

**The line between the law-abiding and the law-breaking can often be curiously thin as Bonney himself had been notorious passer of "the long green" while in Nauvoo.

six-shooter, and a bowie knife. He also sported an ingenious sword cane tipped with a steel spike that screwed into an iron socket. When removed from the socket, the seemingly foppish cane instantly became a deadly sword. At the head of the cane was a twelve-inch dagger, which was detached by means of a spring. In his stable, he set up an office.

At the Miller house, Bonney got a description of a fur-brimmed cloth cap found there. He immediately recalled having seen a young man by the name of Hodges in Nauvoo three weeks earlier wearing a similar cap. After passing along the information to Sheriff Estes in West Point, Bonney rode to Nauvoo to trace the suspect.

The young man seen wearing a cap was William Hodges, one of eleven children born to Curtis and Lucy Hodges, who had converted the entire family to Mormonism in Kirtland, Ohio, in the early 1830s.[19] In 1836, the family followed the Mormons to Clay County, Missouri, where Curtis and one of his sons bought land with the intent of settling down. Two years later, however, when Gentiles turned against the Mormons, a mob attacked Curtis, seriously wounding him in the side. Angered by their hostile treatment in Missouri, they followed Smith to Nauvoo. Some think it may have been then that the Hodges brothers turned to the bad.††

Once in Illinois, Amos, Ervine, William, and Stephen formed an alliance with Gentile horse thieves and counterfeiters reinforced by an oath of allegiance and mutual protection. William and Stephen had already been convicted in Iowa for horse stealing and were suspected of robbery there as well. Amos, who was president of the Thirteenth Quorum of Seventy, a kind of Mormon priesthood, was wanted in Iowa on robbery charges.[20] William was also a church elder, having preached only a few days before the assault on the Millers.

After speaking with a few merchants in Nauvoo, Bonney learned that William and Stephen Hodges were staying at the house of Amos and his wife Lydia in a rundown part of town. Of the three, only Amos was

---

††In 1843, Curtis was driven out of the church after abandoning his family in Nauvoo and leaving for Indiana where he remarried. He subsequently moved to Tennessee where he fleeced Mormons living there by posing as an indigent travelling church elder. Hyrum Smith pardoned him a year later.

married and none had any employment whatever. Bonney learned that on the afternoon of the murder, William, Stephen, and another Mormon, Thomas Brown, were seen rowing in a skiff up the Mississippi toward the mouth of Devil's Creek in Lee County, Iowa. (The twenty-one-year-old Brown was a known horse thief and counterfeiter and had already done time in Brown County for robbery.) Early the next morning, William Hodges, who had previously worn a cap similar to the one found at the Miller's, was seen going from the river toward his home bareheaded. That same day, his brother Stephen was spotted in a grocery store with a bloodstain on his shirt. When questioned about it, he said nothing but returned to his house and put on a clean shirt. The evidence, though circumstantial, was sufficiently suspicious for Bonney to pass the information to Stephen Markham, captain of the Nauvoo Legion, to help arrest the attackers.

After the murder, the Hodges had gone straight to Brigham Young, Smith's successor, asking what they should do. Young's approach to stealing in Nauvoo was laissez-faire at best, but this, after all, was murder. Believing they were guilty, Young told them to surrender to the authorities. (Young would later deny the Hodges were—or had ever been—Mormon.)[21] After threatening to kill Young for his perfidy, the Hodges turned for help to the Prophet's brother, William, who warned them to get out of Nauvoo. Instead of heeding his advice, William and Stephen took refuge in Amos's house. Tom Brown and a fourth accomplice, Artemus Johnson, both Mormons, had already fled to Missouri.

At 2:00 a.m. on June 13, Markham moved on Amos's house with a posse of twenty armed men. Several of the men surrounded the house while Markham and Bonney went to the door. Peering through the front window, Bonney saw three men armed with pistols and one sliding a bowie knife into his shirt.

"Who's there?" a nervous voice inside called out. When Markham identified himself, the outlaws refused to open the door, threatening kill anyone who attempted to enter. When the Hodges heard that Markham had come to arrest them, they agreed to surrender on the condition that he do so in morning. After a brief consultation, Bonney and Markham concurred and ordered the men in the posse to guard the house all night lest they attempt

Brigham Young
*Source: Courtesy of the Abraham Lincoln
Presidential Library and Museum*

an escape. When daylight came, Markham knocked on the door and the men surrendered without a fight, confident they would be acquitted in a Mormon court. They were detained in the Mansion House, a stately hotel for visitors to Nauvoo. While the Hodges were in detention, William Smith unsuccessfully tried to convince the Nauvoo police to set them free.

A preliminary hearing was scheduled for June 15 in Nauvoo before Aaron Johnson, a Mormon justice of the peace. A Mormon lawyer, Almond Babbitt, represented the Hodges. On the morning of the hearing, with a large group of irate Iowans looking on, several members of the gang filed in to provide alibis for the Hodges on the night of the murder. Fearing the Hodges would be released if the hearing went forward, the prosecution requested a continuance, which was granted until the following morning. Bonney immediately took the prosecution witnesses to Lee County where a grand jury was in session to obtain an indictment against the Hodges, Brown, and Johnson.

After the witnesses gave testimony, an indictment was issued and Bonney rushed back to Nauvoo for the hearing. Tension in the courtroom was high, with angry Iowans on one side and supporters of the Hodges on the other. When Bonney produced the indictment, effectively placing the prisoners beyond the reach of Mormon machinations, cheers went up from one side of the courtroom while angry curses issued from the other. "All now seemed quiet," Bonney wrote, "and yet the slightest cause would have resulted in the complete destruction of Nauvoo and the expulsion of the Mormons."[22]

To secure the prisoners and defuse the tension in Nauvoo, Sheriff Estes requested custody of William and Stephen. Babbitt acquiesced only after Iowans threatened to destroy Nauvoo if the two prisoners were not remanded immediately. Estes placed them in the Fort Madison jail and released Amos for lack of evidence.

Though barely alive from the attack, Leisi believed he could recognize his attackers on sight. Gathering several men unknown to Leisi, Estes brought them to his house and lined them up alongside the Hodges brother. After surveying them, Leisi singled out Stephen Hodges, saying, "That is the man who stabbed me with the bowie knife." Then, pointing to William he said, "That is the man who shot me." Later, the ball extracted from Leisi's body matched a pistol found in their possession. Leisi would die shortly after identifying his killers.

On May 15, a West Point grand jury indicted William and Stephen Hodges, Tom Brown, and Artemus Johnson for Miller's murder. At the arraignment the following week, Sheriff Estes told the Hodges they could stay in the Carthage jail or be moved to Iowa. Choosing Iowa over the jail where Joseph and Hyrum Smith had just been murdered, they were placed in the Des Moines County jail.

Meanwhile, Bonney, who had been offered a $500 bounty for the capture of those still at large, took off in search of Brown. On May 28, he took a steamer to Quincy where he met with Adams County sheriff James Pitman. Pitman said that he was well acquainted with Brown and his confederates as Brown resided in the county. He suggested Bonney meet with one of Brown's relatives, a Mormon named Bingham, who had done time for larceny, and another gang member named Agard. At once, Bonney rode north. On the way to Bingham's, he met a man on horseback who turned out to be Agard. Bonney innocently said he was looking for Bingham as he wished to buy some land in the area. Agard immediately became suspicious, saying he had a map at home and would meet Bonney the next day at a grocery store where he would be happy to show him a layout of all the tracts of available land in the area. The next morning at the appointed hour, Bonney went to the grocery but Agard was nowhere to be seen.

The next day, Bonney rode back to Bingham's house. Pretending to be a horse thief from the eastern part of the state, he said he had a horse for sale. Interested in the offer, Bingham said business was slow as "the boys up north had their hands full," alluding to the Miller and Leisi murders. The Hodges, Bingham conceded, were guilty but they would never catch Brown. "He's too smart for that," he added. In that case, Bonney said, he could use a clever man like him for he planned to steal a chest of money at a Dutchman's house in Shawneetown. Convinced by now that Bonney was indeed one of the bandits, Bingham gave him some contacts in St. Louis who might know of Brown's whereabouts. The next day, Bonney arrived in St. Louis to find that he had just missed Brown and that an unsuccessful attempt had been made to arrest him. With no idea as to the direction of his flight and the trial of the Hodges about to begin, Bonney curtailed the manhunt and returned to Burlington.

On June 12, Mormon defense lawyers filed an affidavit for continuance so that John and Aaron Long, William Fox, and fifteen others could testify that the accused were with them in Nauvoo at the time. The motion was denied. The trial began on June 20 at the Old Zion Methodist Church, Judge Charles Mason presiding. Sheriff Estes gave testimony about what he had observed at the scene of the crime, including the fur-brimmed hat, and how he had followed the tracks to the Mississippi River. Testimony was then given by Leisi and Mrs. Risser and Mrs. Miller, as well as neighbors who had stated having seen the Hodges near Miller's house on the day of the murder.

For its part, the defense argued that the hat found at the scene could not have been that of William for he had burned it in February. Artemus Johnson's wife, Almira, testified the Hodges brothers were in Nauvoo with her and Artemus at the time of the crime. But when it came time for their sister-in-law Lydia to testify, she flatly refused. "For God's sake do not call me to prove it," she protested to Jonathan Hall, their lawyer. "They were gone all night, came home in the morning, said they had been unsuccessful and probably got themselves into trouble."[23] Lydia had also knitted the hat for William, evidence that did not come up at the trial. In the end, the presence of so many defense witnesses proved a liability, for a cross-examination of them revealed so many contractions as to the facts of the case that the jury concluded they were all lying. On June 22, the jury delivered a guilty verdict. Judge Mason sentenced them to be hanged "at some convenient place" in Des Moines County.

William Fox had been unable to testify during the trial because he was with Amos Hodges and Robert Birch (aka Haines) robbing a Mormon merchant named Rufus Beach. Just prior to the robbery, Amos had consulted with Brigham Young about the propriety of robbing a fellow Mormon. Because Fox and Birch were not Mormons, Young disapproved of the idea, secretly tipping off Beach just in case.[24] As Young had suspected, in late June, Fox and Birch went ahead with their plan. Breaking in to Beach's, they began to remove a leather trunk containing $4,000 when they were greeted with a hail of gunfire. Amos was arrested but Fox and Birch managed to escape to Grant Redden's cabin on Devil's Creek in Iowa.‡‡

As these events were transpiring, Ervine Hodges was busy trying to help his brothers. He first tried to induce Brigham Young to break them free but Young wanted nothing to do with the Hodges. Ervine then threatened Young he would go public with all he knew amount Mormon involvement in crime. Young refused to be intimidated. Ervine was later

---

‡‡Fifty-five-year-old Grant Redden was baptized Mormon in 1841. He had taken in William Bridge when the latter was on the run from the Ogle County Regulators, evidence of his links with the Driscoll gang. Redden had likely first worked with John Driscoll when the two were living in northern Ohio. Grant and his sons William and Return Jackson also worked with the Hodges, Birch, and the Long brothers.

seen in the streets of Nauvoo angrily complaining to a police officer and William Smith.

The following night, June 23, as Ervine was walking home through a cornfield after visiting his brothers in Burlington, he was murdered with his own knife. Allen Stout, who was standing guard in front of Brigham Young's house, reported hearing the "sounds of dull blows followed by what sounded like the screeching of an ox." Ervine was stabbed four times in the left side and struck several times in the head. Though mortally wounded, he managed to stumble into Young's yard groaning, "I am a butchered man." When asked just before he died who had attacked him, he replied, "men whom he took to be friends." By now several men had gathered around the dying Hodges, one of whom asked again who had stabbed him. His last words were he "could not tell."[25] Though the killers were never apprehended, several newspapers believed Brigham Young had ordered his killing for threatening to expose criminal activities in Nauvoo. While such a revelation would indeed been an embarrassment to Young, neither he nor the church was directly involved in criminal activities. Given Ervine's threat to expose gang identities, the more likely scenario was that a gang member had silenced him, most likely Return Jackson Redden. "Jack," as he was known, was a Mormon and, along with Birch and two others, had sold some land to help raise $1,000 to pay for the Hodges' lawyers.[26]

Upon hearing of Ervine's death, Young said that it was "far better for Alvine Hodge [sic] to die, than to live any longer in sin, for that he might now possibly be redeemed in the eternal world. That his murderers had done even a deed of charity for that such a man deserved to die."[27]

Two days after Ervine's murder, William Smith posted bail for Amos who attempted to flee Nauvoo by dressing in women's clothes. He did not get far before being murdered, most likely by Fox and Birch in retaliation for having disclosed the Beach robbery to Young. Surprisingly, Mormon authorities in Nauvoo made no attempt to pursue Fox and Birch for the robbery and the two would live to strike—and more viciously—and another day.

While the Hodges were in jail awaiting trial, Judge Charles Mason offered to commute their sentence to a limited prison term if they would reveal the names of their associates. Initially, William agreed to do so but at the last minute declined. Most likely, when he heard of Ervine's murder, William realized the same fate would befall him if he turned state's evidence.

On July 15, the day of the execution, their father was permitted to come to see them from the Alton penitentiary where he was doing time for larceny. Nearly ten thousand people turned out to witness the hangings. The steamer *Mermaid* offered passenger service from Bloomington to Burlington to witness the event, complete with plenty of food and drink. Several other steamers provided similar service. What should have been a solemn affair had turned festive as people picnicked and politicians gave stump speeches. Around noon, with their hands in manacles, the brothers, clad in long white robes, were escorted from the jail and seated on their coffins in a wagon. Because it was feared Mormons might attempt a last minute rescue, a large armed militia surrounded the prisoner wagon. As the procession made its way to the execution site, a band in the rear wagon played a solemn funeral dirge. When they arrived at the scaffold, a priest from Mount Pleasant sang a hymn,

While the lamp holds out to burn,
The vilest sinner may return.[28]

While their sisters looked on anxiously, the condemned men then ascended the platform. Stephen spoke first. In a loud ringing voice, he proclaimed his innocence, claiming they were being punished because they were Mormon. As the crowd listened attentively, Stephen, among other things said, "[H]ow can that jury who brought in a verdict of guilty sleep calmly on their pillows at night?"[29] William then spoke in a somewhat trembling voice, also proclaiming his innocence. Their manacles were removed, ropes placed around their necks, and black caps drawn over their heads. Just before the execution, the "New Purchase" ferry came in loaded with passengers from Nauvoo who barely had time to get to the scene of the execution before it took place. Des Moines sheriff John H. McKenny cut the ropes retaining the drops on which they stood and their bodies shot downward. As the bodies twitched spasmodically, their sisters wailed in grief. One of the witnesses standing near the gallows, described the grim scene:

*He [Stephen] stood near the north end of the trap and when the south end fell, made an inclined plane down which his feet began to slide, until the tightening rope checked the motion. The consequence was his neck was not broken, and he died of strangulation. He struggled in his agony, drawing up his limbs, relaxing them and again drawing them up, his muscles twitching and his body in contortions. It was a sickening sight and I never want to see the like again. The crowd gazed on the gruesome spectacle with horrified interest, varying of course with temperament and age. One woman fainted. It was said she was their sister.*[30]§§

Their bodies were buried in the Mormon Nauvoo cemetery but, after a vote of church elders who believed they were guilty, they were later removed. Of the entire affair Brigham Young later said, "I am glad there is three of them gone. Amos is the only good one in the entire family."[31]

If the status of Mormons in Hancock County was bad, it was about to get even worse for those living in Iowa. On October 16, a public meeting at the Courthouse in Fort Madison was held to nominate candidates for legislative elections scheduled for November 1. That the meeting had been inspired by the recent spate of Mormon-led murders and robberies was apparent from the resolutions adopted, first of which was that Mormons depart "as early as practical."[32] In addition, two explicitly anti-Mormon candidates were chosen to run, Colonel William Patterson and General Jessie B. Browne, two of the county's oldest settlers. To ensure victory, one was a Whig and the other a Democrat; both were running on an anti-Mormon ticket. The resolutions were subsequently publicized along with a list of a dozen Mormon criminals taken from District Court records, part of which read,

*A system of petty Mormon thieving is extensively carried on in this county, that our citizens can scarcely any longer exercise a peaceful forbearance. Every old settler has lost something. No one feels secure. Each man before retires to rest, bolts and barricades his house, and hospitality reluctantly opens the door after nightfall, fearing it might*

---

§§Soon after the execution, two of their sisters eloped with a Dr. Lyon, a married man, then living at Fort Madison, and moved to Texas.

*let in the cut-throat and thief, instead of the stranger seeking a shelter.*
*All good men reprobate violence, and therefore the "Latter Day Saints"*
*have been solicited to depart from among us . . . It is hoped that the*
*vote given for it will be so decided as will leave no doubt of the wishes*
*of the people in regard to the Mormons leaving the county, and when*
*you cast your suffrages for the Anti-Mormon candidates remember*
*that you are thus exercising your moral power to induce the deluded*
*people called the "Latter Day Saints" to depart in peace. Remember*
*that your [sic] are doing an act which will save you county from future*
*scenes of violence, and the tax-paying community from burdensome*
*levies upon them.*[33]

The announcement also estimated the cost to taxpayers of Mormon crimes in the county totaled between $5,000 and $6,000.

On election day, the anti-Mormons prevailed, prompting many Mormons to subsequently leave the county. When the family of one of the worst criminals, a horse thief named Ben Brooks and his two sons, refused to leave, a small group of vigilantes, armed with long cowhides, took them out of bed one night. Rowing to an island between Montrose and Nauvoo, they whipped them severely and, putting them in their own skiffs without oars, shoved them off in the river with orders never to return.

Meanwhile that fall in Nauvoo, Brigham Young announced Mormons would abandon the city in the spring. Over the winter, he set out with an advance party of 1,600 of his followers in search of a new home. By May, twelve thousand Mormons, nearly 90 percent of Mormons living in Hancock County, had crossed the Mississippi for an unknown destination. The city that had once been the largest in the state was nearly empty. Among the last to depart was Bill Hickman, a former Danite and personal bodyguard to Joseph Smith and Brigham Young. Hickman used a homemade cannon to guard the city until the last of the residents could be evacuated. Joining the exodus west were Thomas Brown and Artemus Johnson, both of whom had been reinstated by the church. Two years later, Brown was murdered in Winter Quarters, Nebraska. Artemus Johnson would die in Utah years later.

Several others, like Fox and Haines, were still at large.

# CHAPTER 7

# The Brown Gang

*This section of the country is infested by horse thieves and petty robbers of almost every description.*

—The *Galena Democrat,* FEBRUARY 1840

If nothing else, the extraordinary number of witnesses willing to perjure themselves on behalf of the Hodges—William Fox, Robert Birch, and Aaron and John Long—to name some of the worst cutthroats—was testimony that the gang was indeed as thick as thieves. Their close ties grew out of years of criminal conspiracy in Iowa Territory under the direction of a shrewd boss named William W. Brown.

Brown had come to Bellevue, Iowa, in the spring of 1837 probably from Elkhart County, Indiana, by way of Michigan.[1] When he and his attractive wife Betsy and daughter Roxana rolled into town with a team of steeds pulling wagons laden with fine furniture, residents immediately took notice. Educated and refined, the Browns quickly became welcomed additions to the frontier community. Little did people know that Brown had welched on a $300 debt to his brother-in-law back in Indiana and was now about to fleece the settlers in the Iowa borderlands.

Nestled in the bluffs along the Mississippi, Bellevue was a prairie pirate's idyll: newly established and surrounded by wilderness. In October of the year Brown arrived, the US government began surveying the town to make lots available for official purchase. Three months later, Bellevue became the seat of Jackson County in the newly established Territory of Iowa. Much like the Driscolls in the Rock River Valley, Brown had gotten in on the ground floor.

William A. Warren Late in Life
*Source: Courtesy State Historical Society
of Iowa, Des Moines*

Wishing to appear on the right side of the law, Brown made a bid for the county's first sheriff by forging his name on a petition to the governor as well as on letters of endorsement to the legislature. A House clerk reviewing the letters, William A. Warren, whose name had also been submitted for the position, was surprised to see letters from people who suspected Brown to be an outlaw. On further inspection, Warren was shocked to see his own name signed on one of the letters.[2] The forgery exposed, the job went to Warren.

A former Kentucky backwoodsman, twenty-eight-year old Warren was a frontier lawman right out of central casting: handsome, affable, and cool in a crisis. Warren had come to Bellevue in 1836 from Dubuque where he had helped found Jackson County and the Iowa Territory. He had served in the war against Black Hawk, and even though he had seen no action, he earned the rank of captain, a title he retained even after he became sheriff. He was rarely without his clay pipe that had a stem so short the bowl almost touched his lips.[3] One wonders if the good captain would have taken the job had he known that it would pit him against some of the most vicious outlaws in the Mississippi Valley. Though he and Brown were on opposite sides of the law, they shared a mutual respect for one another right up to their final dramatic clash known as "the Bellevue War."

The events that led to the war (it was actually a titanic gun battle) were much like those that led to the execution of the Driscolls: a vexing epidemic of robberies, horse stealing, and counterfeiting that persisted for years after Brown's arrival. Even though time and again the crimes were traced to Brown's men—if not directly to Brown himself—punishing them proved to be as elusive as it had been in Illinois.

About a year after Brown's arrival, an incident occurred that illustrated just how clever he was. One day, one of his men, Arnold Godfrey, was seen driving into town with a team of magnificent horses. Suspecting they had been stolen, Sheriff Warren immediately placed him under arrest. Under questioning, Godfrey repeatedly denied the charge, insisting he had purchased the horses in good faith in Missouri. The two repaired to Brown's Hotel where, in Brown's presence, Godfrey repeated his story. Rather than side with Godfrey, Brown accused him of lying. To test his guilt, Brown advised Warren to print handbills describing the horses and if in thirty days they were not claimed, they should be returned to Godfrey. Brown even generously volunteered to distribute the handbills while Godfrey awaited the results at the hotel.

Five days later, a man named Jenkins came to see Sheriff Warren. Producing one of the handbills, he claimed the horses were stolen from his home in the Rock River Valley and that he could identify them by their distinguishing marks. The bay, he said, had a scar on the inside of the right leg just below the flank, and the sorrel mare a slit in the left ear.

The next morning, Warren escorted Jenkins to Brown's Hotel where they found the marks on the horses just as Jenkins had described. Brown, however, refused to accept Jenkins's claim. At this, Jenkins became furious. Drawing his revolver, he said, "Show me the man who brought the horses and I will rid the country of him and put him where he can steal no more!" Warren insisted he let the law handle the matter. Brown, however, proceeded to take him to Godfrey who was outside town piling wood for Brown. When Jenkins had advanced within thirty paces, he drew his revolver. Frightened, Godfrey took off across the frozen river to an island. Jenkins followed in hot pursuit firing in rapid succession. At the third shot, Godfrey cried out and fell on the ice, but instantly recovered and ran on. Having emptied his pistol, Jenkins returned to claim his horses. After paying Brown for keeping them, Jenkins said that if Brown ever needed any assistance, he had only to send for him and he would come with fifty men to help rid the town of such worthless miscreants. He then rode off toward Illinois with his horses in tow while several Bellevue citizens crossed to the island to find Godfrey. He was nowhere to be found, however, leaving folks to conclude he had crawled away into the high grass and died. To Brown's many supporters, his role in the affair was further proof that he was not the villain some had presumed but a man of integrity and good will.

Not long after the incident, a stranger arrived in Bellevue asking to see Sheriff Warren. Wisconsin judge Ebenezer Brigham said he was in search of a span of horses stolen from him which were advertised in the Bellevue handbill. As Brigham proceeded to give the exact same distinguishing marks that Jenkins had, the truth suddenly dawned on Warren: *Jenkins had been Brown's accomplice in the scheme all along.* The clever charade—the handbills, the shooting and flight of Godfrey—had all been a farce to make it appear that Jenkins was the true owner of the horses. Warren and just about everyone else in town had been completely bamboozled.[4]

A local legislator, Colonel Thomas Cox, had once served with Brigham in the Illinois legislature. When he heard the story of his colleague's loss, he declared open war on Brown. He had a warrant issued for Brown's arrest but Warren refused to serve it, fearing it would spark a civil war between the growing number of townsmen for and against Brown.

As Warren demurred, Brown continued to plunder the countryside. In the fall of 1838, Tom Davis, a farmer who lived near the forks of the Maquoketa River, was about to take a fine yoke of oxen to Dubuque that he hoped to sell for the handsome sum of $125. On the night before he went to market, the oxen suddenly vanished. Fortunately, a heavy rain had fallen and tracks in the mud revealed the trail of the cattle in the direction of Bellevue, mysteriously disappearing just outside town. Continuing on to Bellevue, Davis informed Warren who immediately mounted a search party.

As soon as Brown was informed about the theft, he joined in the search with his usual alacrity. A visit to the slaughterhouse turned up nothing, nor did a reconnaissance of other suspected areas. Returning to town, Warren met with an informant inside the Brown gang, Lyman Wells, who told him that the missing cattle were in a ravine along South Mill Creek and that one of Davis's neighbors, Samuel Groff, had stolen the cattle with one of Brown's men. Sure enough, Warren found the cattle in the ravine and drove them back into town. Upon seeing the cattle, Brown feigned jubilation over their recovery, offering Davis $125 for them, which he accepted.

Despite the informant's reliability, Davis refused to accept Groff's guilt for he considered him a good neighbor and a pious member of the Methodist Church. The next morning, Davis called on Groff to tell him where he had found the stolen animals. Upon hearing the cattle had been recovered, Groff suddenly began acting strangely, indignantly denying any knowledge of the theft, which Davis interpreted as a clear sign of his guilt. Although lacking witnesses or proof, he filed charges against Groff, which only increased the animosity between them.

The matter might have gone forever unresolved until a bitter lawsuit between them arose in April 1839 in a new dispute over land Davis owned. During the trial, Brown, who was Groff's attorney, had confided to his client that he was unlikely to win and that the best thing he could do would be simply to kill Davis. Brown had even given him the rife, telling Groff facetiously to "go shoot squirrels on the island with it." Twenty minutes later, Groff was seen in a saloon loading the rifle, muttering it would be "the death of Davis."

When warned of Groff's intentions, Davis scoffed, dismissing Groff as a coward who would never dare to shoot him "unless it was in the back." A few days later, while Davis was walking down Front Street, Groff rested his gun on a picket fence and fired on him. In a tragic irony, the ball struck Davis in the back and passed through his chest near his heart. As Davis crumpled to the ground, Groff walked casually past him with his rifle at his side. Davis died thirty minutes later. A bystander who had witnessed the shooting, Shadrach Burleson, chased down Groff and demanded he turn over his rifle. Calmly, Groff turned and handed over the weapon as if nothing were amiss. When Sheriff Warren appeared on the scene, he asked Burleson to take the prisoner down to the blacksmith shop and have him heavily ironed. With no county jail, he was placed in a room under heavy guard, his ankles shackled with ten-pound weights made of wagon wheel iron.

To ensure conviction, Groff was indicted and tried on the very day of the murder. Under Iowa law, a prisoner could not stand trial at the same term of court as the indictment. With no jail and the next court session not for another six months, the judge and prosecutor agreed to call a special term to try Groff. Empaneling a jury proved difficult, as the murder had been the subject of a good deal of confabulation in the community and most citizens already had firm opinions as to Groff's guilt or innocence. Finally, after considerable wrangling, a twelve-man jury was assembled, though it still contained several men who were known to have said the Groff was guilty. Groff's conviction thus appeared a foregone conclusion.

Indeed, the testimony against Groff was so overwhelming that the defense chose to plead insanity. Defense witnesses testified how Davis's unfair accusations had pushed his client, a sensitive man, over the edge mentally. By evening, the case went to the jury. After an hour, the court received word of a verdict and hurriedly reconvened. Everyone expected a verdict of guilty so when Foreman Thomas Marshall arose and announced, "We, the jury, find the defendant 'not guilty'," a shudder of disbelief swept through the court. Outraged, the state's attorney denounced the jury for perjury and quickly moved that the court set aside the verdict. The motion was denied and Groff walked free.[5] That night, angry citizens, exasperated with the inability of the justice system to rein in Brown and his men, hanged the jury in effigy.[*]

Crime in Jackson took a turn for the worse that winter when Brown purchased a seven-room hotel in Bellevue for $2,000, renaming it "Brown's Hotel." The hotel quickly became a convenient stopping place

---

*Groff was later killed by Indians in Minnesota Territory.

for travelers who, as Sheriff Warren later mused, "ate at his far-famed table, drank his good liquor, listened to his enlivening talk, and came away feeling that the generous landlord was a most valuable addition to the community." Near the hotel, Brown opened a meat market and general store, often selling his goods on credit to struggling pioneers, generosity that endeared him to many. He subsequently won a government contract to supply summer steamships with wood he harvested from a river island using local labor. Like a benevolent mobster, he lent money to all and sundry and borrowed just as much. To many, Brown still appeared as enterprising and big-hearted, the kind of man that was bringing much-needed prosperity to the fledgling frontier town.

Others, however, had taken note of the seedy individuals lounging about his hotel with no visible means of support. Among the twenty or so regulars were William Fox, Aaron and John Long, Richard Baxter, Robert Birch, James Thompson, and Samuel Chichester. Some had been tutored in the art of frontier crime by Brown himself.

It wasn't long before residents began to notice more of the "long green" turning up in town. In addition, horses were seen being brought into town by strangers from Missouri who exchanged them for horses brought by other strangers from Wisconsin and Illinois. And each time a suspected horse thief or counterfeiter was identified, he turned out to be a guest at Brown's Hotel, or one of his employees. The silver-tongued Brown was always quick to cover for them with a handy alibi and seldom was anyone caught or punished. Such was the high regard Brown commanded among townsfolk that few believed the good hotelier was responsible for all the horse stealing, counterfeiting, or any other crime.

By January of 1839, Cedar, Jones, and Linn Counties were also reeling from the crime wave. (Later that year, John Brody and his four sons settled in Linn County after being driven from Illinois.) The three counties invited Jackson to unite with them in forming an organization to crack down on outlaws in eastern Iowa. In response, Sheriff Warren, Thomas Cox, and James Kemper (J.K.) Moss, a prominent merchant, formed a committee to represent the town.

On their way to Linn County, they stopped at the house of Joshua Bear, who angrily displayed eight $10 counterfeit bills that he had just received from a man named One-Thumbed Thompson in payment for a fine horse. Bear assured them that he was just as eager as they to stamp out counterfeiting and agreed to accompany them.

Just before sunset, the party reached the Wapsipinicon River where they found an unoccupied cabin at a place called "Nigger's Point," so called because it had been built by a black man who had mysteriously disappeared. Putting the horses in a makeshift shed covered with hay, they made camp for the night. As Warren and Bear were descending to the river for water, they came upon the carcass of a horse partly consumed by wolves. Soon after nightfall, Bear slipped out to spend the night near the dead horse shooting wolves. He managed to shoot one before the rest scampered off over a hill. Taking cover, he waited for them to return. Over the course of the night, he succeeded in killing and skinning ten wolves, declaring that in all his hunting, he had never before seen so many animals. Bear quickly lost all enthusiasm for the association, declaring he intended to remain there harvesting wolves.

Leaving Bear behind, the three men continued several miles up the Wapsipinicon where they picked up two more settlers before proceeding to Linn Grove. In Linn, dozens of irate delegates had gathered. The first and only recorded statement was that of Cox, who made an impassioned speech advocating the use of violence. Moral suasion, he declared, was wasted on the bandits; "hemp," he declaimed, was the best cure for such evil. At the conclusion, they agreed to form a vigilante organization christened the "Citizens' Association."[6]

The next day, the Bellevue party returned to where they had left Bear, who had in the meantime sold his wolf skins to a passerby for three pieces of gold. He accompanied the party back to Bellevue, intending to make some purchases with his sudden windfall. As he was about to pay for the goods, he discovered the pieces of gold were not gold at all but coated brass. After inquiring in town, Bear learned that the wolf hides had been purchased by Brown. When confronted, Brown insisted the man from whom he had purchased the skins was "above suspicion" and would at once give him good money when informed that the coins were bogus. Once again, the trail of the swindle led to Brown and, once again, he had insulated himself from direct involvement in the crime.

As tensions built between Bellevue residents over Brown, a man named Pearce came to town, claiming to be from the east. Pearce proceeded to buy several lots from Bellevue residents who were friends of Brown. He paid cash, mostly bogus bills drawn on the Bank of Chautauqua, New York. When Pearce learned of all the horse stealing and counterfeiting plaguing Bellevue, he indignantly declared he would not bring his family to such a place and offered to sell his properties at a loss. Brown found ready purchasers, which allowed Pearce to depart happily with a sack of good money.

Meanwhile, Sheriff Hallock had arrived from Galena, having traced the trail of Pearce's counterfeit bills to Bellevue. By now, Pearce was long since gone and Hallock returned to Galena empty-handed. Sheriff Warren, however, was able to track Pearce by drawing on his backwoods skills. Leaving Bellevue at nine o'clock on a bitter cold night, he followed Pearce's tracks in the snow to a farmhouse where the counterfeiter had taken dinner and had given the owner a ten-dollar bill—which subsequently proved to be counterfeit and for which the farmer had given change. Warren pressed on to Sabula only to find that Pearce had left at sundown for Savanna. At dawn, Warren crossed the river to Illinois where he finally found Pearce at a hotel eating breakfast. When Pearce finished his meal, Warren placed his hand on his shoulder and informed him that he was under arrest. Pearce indignantly asked what authority an Iowa sheriff had in Illinois. Holding a revolver to Pearce's breast, Warren replied that the weapon was all the authority he needed. A body search of Pearce turned up $8,000 in bogus bills tucked in the collar of his overcoat, about half that amount in good notes, a bowie knife, and a revolver, all of which Warren confiscated.

With Pearce was a young, slightly built man who furtively asked if he could give bail for his companion for his appearance at a Galena court. Warrren rebuffed him and started across the river to Bellevue with his prisoner, the young man hiring a buggy and following. At Sabula, the young man asked the Sheriff's permission to ride along, which he granted. At dusk, they reached the house of Anson Newberry where Warren halted with his prisoner for the night. After supper, Warren and Newberry chatted until late. With few beds in the house, to keep an eye on the two, Warren arranged for Newberry to occupy a bunk on the floor with Pearce, while he would share the bed with Pearce's friend. Both Pearce and his strange friend objected strongly to the arrangement but under the circumstances could do nothing. The next morning, as they approached Bellevue, the young man asked to confide a secret to the Sheriff, revealing that she, as it turned out, was the wife of a prominent Bellevue contractor. She asked him not to make known her identity until she and her husband left Bellevue some years afterward. Warren surmised the woman had come to Savanna to secure a part of the booty, which Pearce never had an opportunity to turn over.

By the time Warren reached Bellevue with his prisoner, the parties from whom he had purchased lots with counterfeit money were clamoring for his lynching—and for Brown's as well. For Pearce's safety, Warren decided to take him to Galena where he was arraigned before a judge. Pearce's attorney demanded the good money belonging to his client be remitted—in part so he could be paid for his services. He then waived examination and got his client released on $1,000 bail. Once free, Pearce absconded. The bond was never paid. After receiving threats to take him to court, Brown returned most of the money to the victims. Although later taken to court, to the mounting frustration of Bellevue's residents, he was acquitted.

In May, four horses stolen near Freeport were tracked to Bellevue. Warren and the owner of two of the horses got word that the thieves were heading for the woods at the forks of the Wapsipinicon and Buffalo Creek. Leaving Bellevue about 10 a.m., they reached Canton in the evening. There, they learned that that very morning the thieves had disposed of one of the horses to a Mr. Rankin, who paid $100 in cash and a note for $100 more. As the thieves had left Canton in a westerly direction, Warren and Rankin followed the trail, leaving the owner of the horses at Canton until their return.

On reaching a place called the Scottish Settlement, Rankin learned his note had already been sold to another man at half its face value. The pursuers continued westward when they came upon a half-breed named "Indian Jim" camping with several other Indians. Indian Jim told the Sheriff that the thieves numbered four or five and were holed up in a cabin about four miles away on the other side of the river. As the river was not fordable, Warren and his men made camp for the night. In the morning, Jim ferried them across in his canoe and allowed them use of his ponies on the opposite shore.

The men proceeded through a small ravine down toward a stream. When they reached the stream, they spotted smoke curling up from a small cabin almost completely hidden from view by dense undergrowth and timber. Rankin identified the horses hitched out front as his. Concerned they might be outnumbered, Warren instructed Rankin to remain in the brush with the ponies while he assessed the strength of the party in the cabin. Posing as a hunter, he entered the cabin to find a man preparing breakfast. When Warren inquired about the five plates on the table, the man said that his friends were on a hunt and expected back at any moment. In one corner of the room, Warren noticed a small forge and a pair of bellows—counterfeiting tools. When he inquired about the horses, the cook said they belonged to travelers who had stopped a few days to look at the country nearby. Pointing to the double-barreled shotgun Warren was examining, he remarked that was theirs, too. At this, Warren identified himself, announced the horses and the gun were stolen and started out of the cabin with the shotgun over his shoulder. When he got back to Rankin, he advised on an immediate retreat but Rankin refused to go until he had recouped his money. Fearing the men would soon return, they hastened to the river for reinforcements. There they saw Indian Jim ferrying three white men to the other side. On reaching the bank, Rankin spotted another of his horses, leading Warren to conclude the three on the ferry were the very men expected for breakfast at the cabin. He called to Indian Jim to come over for them, which he did, bringing the owner of the cabin, One-Thumbed Thompson. As soon as he saw Warren, Thompson feigned surprise saying, "What in the devil brought you into the wilds of the forks of the Wapisi?" When Warren recounted the tale of the stolen equines, Thompson disavowed any knowledge of the theft, claiming the men had assured him they were in honest possession of them. To demonstrate his innocence, he offered to help Rankin recover his money as well as his horses. After being gone about an hour on the other side of the river, Thompson returned with Rankin's money, including the $50 they had received in the sale of the note, which he handed over with the horses on the condition that Warren would not arrest them.

Warren's hapless deputy, James T. Hanby, however, who had been "spoiling for a fight," would not be so easily placated. When he learned about the counterfeiting tools in Thompson's cabin, he lit out with five members of the Citizens' Association to bring the culprits to justice. Before departing, Hanby melodramatically declared to Bellevue's citizens that "ere five suns should have rolled over their heads, he would return with the occupants of the cabin . . . or had fallen in the discharge of his duty."[7] While riding out, a heavy rain began to fall. With no sun to guide them through the wilderness, they soon lost the trail and were forced to take cover in a tent with a couple of claim hunters. Tethering their horses near the river bottom a few hundred yards from camp, they spent the night drinking and conversing with the hunters until late. On awakening late with a hangover, Hanby discovered the claim hunters had vanished with their horses, one of which belonged to Hanby. After searching in vain for the hunters—who were the very counterfeiters Hanby was in pursuit of—they found a trail that led them to Indian Jim's camp. Jim thought it would be useless to cross the river as the counterfeiters had already abandoned the cabin after Warren's visit. Hanby, however, had come a long way to demonstrate his bravado and insisted on seeing for himself. Crossing the river after dinner, he came upon the cabin with smoke arising from its tiny chimney. Cautiously, he and the others surrounded the house. Upon reaching the door, Hanby burst in with pistol cocked exclaiming, "Surrender or die!" The terrified occupants immediately surrendered and begged for mercy. As he handcuffed his prisoners, Hanby demanded they turn over the bellows and forge but the bewildered men declared they knew nothing about them.

On reaching the ferry with his prisoners, Hanby ran into a friend of his named Russell. When informed of the arrest of "three counterfeiters," Russell informed Hanby that two of the men were in fact his neighbors and the third a friend from the east. Realizing that Indian Jim had been right, the mortified Hanby released the men and sheepishly offered his apologies. The posse then returned to Bellevue, on foot and on horseback, worn out and nearly starving, a good deal humiliated by their experience. So went the Citizens' Association's first assault on crime in eastern Iowa.

The relentless crime, notwithstanding, many citizens continued to regard Brown as an upstanding member of the community who was innocent of any wrongdoing. Indeed, so popular was he, that Bellevue's residents chose him overwhelmingly as the Democratic nominee for a seat in the state legislature. Until then, everyone had assumed the nod would go to fifty-three-year-old Colonel Thomas Cox, the incumbent and uncontested leader of the party in Jackson County. A huge, aggressive, hard-drinking man with a florid complexion, Cox had served as a member of the Illinois militia and legislature and expected to face no challengers from within the party. Angered by what he perceived as betrayal by Brown and convinced he was the ringleader of the horse thief fraternity, Cox raised a drunken mob to drive him out of Bellevue. Upon arrival at the hotel, Cox demanded Brown pack up and leave town. Brown politely refused, saying he would appear before any official tribunal they would name and abide by its decision. On Cox's command, the mob rushed the hotel, killing seven of Brown's guests. The remaining six were whipped and ordered to leave the country. One of those whipped was William Fox who vowed that henceforth he would never do another day's work but rob, steal, and murder for a living, a promise he would keep. Brown was unharmed.

Cox subsequently ran for the legislature as an independent and won. But his assault on the hotel had done little to deter Brown and his men. On the night of September 14, 1839, the Collins family was awakened by the furious barking of their dog. When Dennis Collins opened the door to investigate, William Fox and Arnold Godfrey burst in brandishing pistols. Fox ordered Collins to strike a light. When he refused, Godfrey knocked him to the floor. They then made the same demand of Mrs. Collins who was still in bed. When she too refused, Fox dragged her onto the floor and beat her until she finally revealed where a candle could be found. Lighting the room, the robbers found a strong box and emptied all its valuables and $40 in cash.

The next day, Collins went to Bellevue to report the incident to Warren and to find a doctor for his seriously injured wife. While walking down the street, he happened to see Godfrey and Fox and reported it to Deputy Hanby who arrested them immediately. Brown posted half of their $500 bail.

At the trial, the prosecution made a seemingly airtight case for conviction. The prosecution showed how the week prior to the robbery, One-Thumbed Thompson had been in Collins's house and seen a strong box with cash, news which he promptly passed to Fox. Deputy Hanby testified seeing the two bandits on the evening of the robbery headed in the direction of the Collins residence. Andrew Farley, the Collins's nearest neighbor, said that at midnight just before the robbery, Fox and Godfrey had called at his house to inquire about the road to the Collins house. Last to testify were Dennis Collins and his wife who unequivocally identified Fox and Godfrey as their assailants.

Yet, when the defense rose, Brown trotted out ten of his boarders who testified that on the night of the robbery, the men were at his hotel playing cards and could therefore not have been at the scene of the crime. With so many witnesses providing an alibi, the charges against Fox and Godfrey were dismissed. As a stunned prosecutor and his witnesses exited the courtroom, Brown's men laughed in derision before repairing to the hotel for a night of drunken celebration at having suborned the justice system yet again.

And so, the plundering continued. In the autumn of 1839, a Galena rancher, Buncombe Gillette, sold a yoke of fine oxen to James Thompson, Brown's second-in-command. Being of some means, Gillette set the money aside for several weeks. Upon hearing of counterfeit money being used to purchase cattle, he examined the money only to find that he had been swindled. He traced his cattle to Tête des Morts in the possession of one David Zigler, who had purchased them in good faith from Thompson. By a writ of replevin, Gillette recovered his cattle and resold them legitimately to Zeigler who, in turn, filed counterfeiting charges against Thompson to recoup his money. During the trial, Thompson denied the charge, declaring he had never been a mile north or east of Galena, nor had he ever before seen Gillette. He then asked for more time to procure witnesses, a motion promptly granted by the prosecution so that Gillette's hired hands might also be summoned to identify the prisoner. The case was postponed for five days and Thompson was released on bail—once again posted by Brown.

On the day the trial resumed, Gillette appeared with two of his hired men and his attorney from Galena. Under oath, Gillette's men identified Thompson as the man who had purchased the cattle. The defense, however, had once again come in force, bringing William Fox, Aaron Long, Arnold Godfrey, and another of Brown's men as witnesses. The outlaws testified that on the day of the purchase the four had been with Thompson nearly a hundred miles away in Davenport attending the horse races, thus making it was impossible for him to have been anywhere near Galena on the day of the crime. Since Thompson had produced the greater number of witnesses, he was acquitted.

After the trial, Thompson and several of his confederates rode to Dubuque where they succeeded in unloading a large quantity of bogus bills, or "shoving the queer," as Sheriff Warren wryly put it. The method employed was to make small purchases at various stores and receive good money in change. Although they succeeded in getting away from the city without detection, Sheriff Cummins was able to follow the money trail to Bellevue. From the description Cummins gave, however, Warren concluded that the parties he was in search of were actually Aaron Long and Bartlett Denison, who were staying at Brown's Hotel. The two sheriffs proceeded to the hotel, seconded by thirty-year-old James Mitchell and Henderson Palmer, two of Brown's most strident enemies. When Brown's men saw the sheriffs approaching, they gathered their weapons and ran upstairs, shouting down for them to keep their distance. Calling Palmer and Mitchell to his side, Cummins started up the stairs. Long and Denison fired and a ball passed through the collar of Mitchell's coat. As the men continued their charge up the stairs, the outlaws immediately dropped their weapons, disavowing any deadly intent in the discharge of their guns. Cummins arrested Denison, Long, and Brown on charges of resisting an officer and an assault with intent to kill. Thompson was also arrested on the counterfeiting charge and taken to Dubuque with the other prisoners. At their trial, no solid evidence could be offered against Thompson and he was released. The other three were to appear at the next term of the district court, but through an error in the indictment, the charges were dismissed. Once again, Brown and his men had managed to slip through the net of justice.

Three weeks later, an old French trapper, Battice Rolette, who worked the islands, came to town and sold his furs to J.K. Moss for $200. That evening, the old man celebrated his good fortune over several shots of rye whiskey at Brown's saloon where he carelessly exhibited his money. Knowing bandits were also in the saloon, Rolette's friends advised him to remain in Bellevue for the night and depart in the morning when it was safer. Too drunk to heed the warning, Rolette got into his canoe late in the evening and started for home. James Thompson and Chichester followed. As soon as the old man reached his cabin and had retired for the night, they burst into his cabin and demanded his money. The drunken Roulette began yelling uncontrollably until he was knocked down and gagged. Thompson then took his money and stuffed it into his belt.

By happenstance, encamped on the island about a hundred yards below Rolette's cabin were Deputy Hanby and two men from the Citizens' Association, John T. Sublette, one of the original settlers of Bellevue, and Andrew Rodafer. Hearing the old man's cries, they rushed to the cabin and took Thompson and Chichester completely by surprise. After finding the money in Thompson's belt, Hanby arrested them. The outlaws waived examination and posted bail for appearance at the next term of court.

While all this was this was transpiring, Bellevue's citizens were meeting at Moss's store to devise a way of checking the increasing bandit activity in the country. Naively, they decided to invite Brown to a meeting and lay the whole matter before him and ask his cooperation in getting rid of the outlaws. On the appointed evening, Brown appeared with none other than James Thompson who, in addition to being Brown's deputy, had now become a partner in Brown's grocery store. Upon seeing Thompson, Mitchell jumped to his feet, saying to Brown, "You are here by invitation and while you may harbor and protect counterfeiters and robbers, you have no authority or permission to bring them to this meeting. Mr. Thompson can retire!"[8]

Thompson, who had vowed to get even with Mitchell for the role he played in his arrest earlier in the year, drew his revolver. Hearing the commotion, several of Brown's men outside rushed into the room brandishing their weapons. Only Brown's quick intercession prevented bloodshed. As Brown's men exited the room, Thompson bellowed, "Mitchell, you are a marked man, and if ever I catch you alone, the language you used tonight shall be atoned for!"

With the outlaws gone, the meeting proceeded. Moss diplomatically told Brown that the citizens were confident he could do much toward ridding the town of the desperadoes by disavowing their actions and ceasing to allow them to make his hotel their headquarters. If he did so, citizens would be forever grateful and extend their full cooperation in any project he might wish to undertake. After listening attentively to the proposition, Brown replied in his usual evasive manner:

> *Gentlemen, I would to God I could comply with your request, and that I might stand in your estimation tonight as I did when first I came among you. Your confidence and kindness in making this proposition is fully appreciated and, were it in my power, I would gladly accept it. But it is impossible. It would be no use for me to try to conceal from you the relation in which I stand to these men, and if, by counsel, I can prevail upon them to leave and seek honorable occupation elsewhere, I will do so.*[9]

The following morning, however, citizens were pleased to see nearly all of Brown's boarders had shouldered an ax and were starting across the river to the island to cut wood for him. So grateful were Bellevue's citizens that they resumed their former friendship with Brown and began calling at his house as they did when they first arrived. To visitors, Betsy Brown appeared to have been very much disturbed at her husband's recent fall from grace and the class of men he had about him. She appreciated the renewed warmth of her old acquaintances and expressed the hope that she and her husband might again reach their former respectable station in society.

Not long after the woodchoppers had gone to work, however, some of the farmers near Sand Prairie noticed their hogs missing. Suspecting they were being used to supply the woodcutters with meat, they crossed over to the island to investigate but got only stonewalling from the woodcutters. Several farmers then went to Brown to complain that his men were plundering their hog pens and asked his assistance in stopping it. Brown replied that he had engaged them cut wood by the cord and, apart from this, he had no control over them. Nonetheless, he offered to assist in searching their shanties for the meat. With Sheriff Warren leading the party, the farmers proceeded to the island and, after a thorough search, turned up nothing. As they were about to depart, they stopped to examine a haystack which had been disturbed in one spot. Following a sort of rabbit hole in the stack, they came upon a large bin containing two barrels of fresh pork and one of beef. Since the hay was on "Negro Brown's" premises, they seized his wife who protested that she was merely a cook for the woodmen. Though she knew nothing about the source of the meat, she said Driscoll brought it daily to the cabin. Just which of the Driscoll boys was moonlighting on the island was unclear, though it was likely David.

When Warren returned to town, he met with his informant Lyman Wells who said that Warren had not investigated far enough: the haystack contained another compartment in which Fox and Brown had concealed a bounty of goods stolen from merchants in Galena. Now that the haystack had been discovered, Brown planned to remove the goods late at night. At ten o'clock the following night, Warren and a group of citizens ferried over to the island to set an ambush for Brown. When by midnight no one passed, they proceeded to the haystack only to find it had already been emptied of its contents. Proceeding to Negro Brown's cabin, they learned from his wife that five hours earlier, Brown, Fox, and Thompson had come and loaded the merchandise on a double sled. With the sled, Fox and Thompson had taken off in one direction while Brown had returned to Bellevue. With the aid of a lantern, Warren examined the spot more closely and found two packages containing pocketknives, razor-strops, spools, and a bolt of calico, which they had carelessly dropped. Collecting the articles, the party returned to town, frustrated that once again W.W. Brown and company had once again been one step ahead of them.

At first light, Hanby and Sublette followed the sled tracks. With little snow on the ground, they soon gave up and proceeded to the town of Elizabeth, hoping to obtain a clue as to the direction of the outlaws. No sooner had they pulled into town than they spotted Fox and Thompson coming from the opposite end. Realizing they had already hidden the goods and that further pursuit would be fruitless, they returned to Bellevue.

Meanwhile, Robert Reed, Elizabeth's deputy sheriff, had ridden to Galena to ask the storeowners to come to Bellevue to identify the goods Warren had recovered. After the merchants identified the goods as theirs, Brown and Thompson were arrested for burglary and larceny. The case eventually went to trial in Galena. Defending himself and his colleagues, Brown successfully argued that the offense charged was committed in Illinois and was therefore out of the Iowa Territory's jurisdiction. There was nothing to do but discharge the prisoners.

And so it went. Once again, Brown and his men had made a mockery of the justice system. Outlaws continued to come and go from Brown's Hotel. So too did the cycle of robberies and counterfeiting, arrests and trials, and exasperating acquittals—just as they had in Ogle County. And with each infuriating crime, and each miscarriage of justice, citizens' patience was fast approaching the tipping point.

# CHAPTER 8

# Colored Beans for Whipping

*The fight ended; the fire was put out, and the thirteen captured men were put under guard for the night . . . At sunset all was quiet and a gloom rested over our little village, for in the engagement some of our best citizens had fallen; and the house but a few hours before the scene of this bloody battle was now turned into a house of mourning.*

—Sheriff William A. Warren

In early January 1840, citizens of Bellevue were busy preparing for the celebration on the eighth of the anniversary of the Battle of New Orleans, the final major battle of the War of 1812. It was to be a lavish event at a brand new hotel on the corner of Park and Water Streets owned by Anson Harrington. Among the event planners was Brown's old nemesis, J.C. Mitchell, who successfully proposed that Brown and his men be barred from attending the patriotic celebration. Without the unsavory characters to spoil the event, everyone hoped it would be a memorable evening with a night of music and dancing.[1]

In fact, Brown's men had other plans that night. The evening of the ball, they were gathered in the back room of Brown's Hotel secretly plotting to rob Mitchell's house.[2] The instigator was James Thompson, who had long been itching to get even with Mitchell. Among the men in the hotel that night was Lyman Wells, Warren's informant. Upon hearing the plans, Wells made some excuse to be absent and hastened to Warren who was home sick and unable to attend the ball. When he heard of the plot, Warren penned a note of warning for Wells to convey to Mitchell. But instead of giving it directly to Mitchell, Wells went home and gave it to his wife before returning to the saloon.

Unaware of the note's contents, Mrs. Wells took her time primping for the ball. While she tarried, Fox, Thompson, Chicester, and Brown were breaking into Mitchell's house. Expecting no one home, they were surprised to encounter a thirteen-year-old girl, Jane Hadley, who had also been too sick to attend the ball. While Thompson stood guard in an upstairs bedroom over a terrified Hadley, the men proceeded to empty the house of all the furniture and valuables and place it on a wagon outside.

Assuming (incorrectly) that Hadley was Mitchell's daughter, Thompson suddenly realized an even better way of retaliating against Mitchell would be to rape her. The terrified girl tried to fight him off but within minutes, he had torn off her clothes and ravaged her.[3] After Thompson and the men left the house, the teenager ran, hysterical and nearly naked, to the ballroom next door. So overcome with terror was she that she was unable to speak. But just a few moments earlier, Mrs. Wells had arrived belatedly with the note for Mitchell, who at once grasped the situation. He led Hadley to a bedroom where she recovered sufficiently to describe the robbery and the subsequent sexual assault by Thompson. Apoplectic with rage, Mitchell borrowed a pistol from Tom Sublette and stormed off in search of Thompson.

Meanwhile, Thompson, who was fully expecting Mitchell to come after him, was now in the street stone drunk. It was a clear night and the moon was full. As he roared curses at Mitchell in the frosty air, he suddenly spotted him about a hundred yards off coming rapidly down the street toward him. With a pistol in one hand and a bowie knife in the other, Thompson started toward Mitchell. As they converged, Thompson raised his pistol and fired first. In the intense cold, the gun misfired. So close were they that Thompson managed to slash Mitchell's hand with his bowie knife. Mitchell fired back, striking Thompson in the heart. He fell back dead, his pistol still clenched in his hand and his bowie knife in the snow three feet away.

By the time Mitchell got back to the ballroom, the guests, who had heard the shots, already knew what had transpired on the street. He immediately surrendered himself to Deputy Hanby—chiefly for protection from the gang that would soon appear. Hanby alerted the women to depart for their homes as he did the men to prepare for retaliation by

Thompson's friends. Apart from Hanby, the only men with arms were Anson Harrington and John Ball, who resolved to stand by Mitchell at all costs. The other men ran home to get their weapons, leaving Mitchell with a tiny force to protect himself against the gang. Just then, the guests heard Brown and his men marching up the street, swearing and howling like a band of savages, "Revenge! Revenge!" At the sound of Brown's men, all the guests flew off in every direction, leaving shawls, cloaks, and bonnets behind. With his wife, daughter, and two sisters, Mitchell and the other men took cover upstairs. Hanby rushed out to stop the approaching mob but Brown and his men marched right past him into the ballroom. Finding the lower floor deserted, Brown started upstairs, ordering his men to follow. He got to the second step when he saw Mitchell at the head of the stairs with a pistol trained on him, warning that if he advanced one more step he would be a dead man. Knowing that a second attempt to ascend would be fatal, he called to the women to come down as he was about to set the house ablaze. When no one descended, Brown and his men began firing their pistols up through the floor.

Just then, Sheriff Warren, who had been summoned when Thompson was shot, arrived on the scene. Ordering the men to disperse, Warren said he would take custody of Mitchell and hold him accountable for whatever crime he may have committed. Somewhat mollified by Warren's assurances, Brown agreed to stand down. As they were leaving, Brown swore that if Mitchell were not arraigned in the morning, he would hold Warren personally responsible.

Upstairs, Warren found Mitchell had taken a stove and slid it near the head of the stairs, intending to push it down had Brown's men attempted to ascend. The three men, still with pistols in hand, looked as pale and anxious as the women. When Warren informed them that the gang had dispersed and that there was nothing more to fear, Mitchell's two sisters fell back into their chairs emotionally exhausted from the terrible ordeal. Hanby came up and whispered to Warren that Brown was at the door and wished to see him. For once the duplicitous Brown was deadly serious, cautioning Warren to station sentries around Mitchell's house as his men were drinking heavily and he had no idea what they would do. Expecting the worse, Warren told Hanby to organize a posse of the best men in town headed by Henderson Palmer, a man whom Brown's men not only respected but feared. Thus ended a night marked not by celebration and revelry but terror and bloodshed.

At nine o'clock the next morning, several armed guards escorted Mitchell to the courthouse to shield him from any potential attack by Brown's men. The coroner had already confirmed Thompson had died from a ball to the heart and Mitchell was arraigned on murder charges. Bail was denied. With no county jail, Hanby took Mitchell to a room in the courthouse and placed him in irons under heavy guard, mostly to protect him from Brown's men. The Board of County Commissioners was notified to meet at once to make financial arrangements for Mitchell's safekeeping. But after determining there weren't sufficient funds to pay for his guards, the commissioners decided to place him in his own house, believing the presence of his family and the secure nature of his dwelling would discourage the bandits from molesting him there.

But Brown's men were now dangerously idle. Normally the men were busy chopping wood for their boss on the government island opposite Bellevue. That winter, however, they had harvested all the timber, more than one thousand cords. Now that the wood business had ceased, Brown's men fell back on their old habit of gambling and drinking cheap whisky. And the more they drank, they angrier they became over the death of their good friend Thompson. Since Mitchell had been justified in shooting Thompson, they reasoned, no honest jury would ever convict him—let alone one of the town's most prominent men—of murder. (Indeed, two months later, Mitchell would be tried for manslaughter and acquitted). They began to plot an assault on his house.

With his cover still intact, Lyman Wells was privy to the entire plan. After the meeting, he rushed to Warren with news that the Long brothers, Chichester, Baxter, and Fox planned to storm Mitchell's house and kill him. Brown was ignorant of the plot. In response, Warren placed volunteer guards at Mitchell's house.

When the gang noticed the increased guard, they realized they would be unable to break into the house undetected. With Mitchell unable to leave the house, they decided the foolproof course of action would be simply to blow up the entire house. Wells voiced his opposition to the idea, saying it would result in the loss of too many innocent lives. By now, however, Wells could see the men were too drunk to reason with so he volunteered to apply the torch in the hope he could get to Warren in time to avert a disaster. Before he could get to Warren, however, the men, fired up as they were by liquor, decided to put their plan into action immediately. Breaking into Moss's store, they stole a tin containing fifteen pounds of gunpowder. By the time they arrived at Mitchell's with the powder, it was late and all the guards had all been relieved except Aaron Harrington, who was reading idly in the back of the house by a lantern. Easing around one side, Fox placed the keg in the cellar stairway. Wells, who was to lay a trail of powder from the cellar to the outside, now had to think fast to avoid a catastrophe. Fox had given him a small bottle containing three pounds of gunpowder with which to lay the powder trail. As he laid the trail, Wells set the bottle on the top step of the cellar but left a gap the rest of the way to the bottom of the stairs where the keg was. In this way, he had ensured the flame would never reach the keg. He and Wells then returned to their comrades to tell them of their success in placing the keg in the cellar and laying the train without detection. The news occasioned the passing around of a bottle of whiskey, which was repeated in rapid succession until the whole party—except Wells—was completely soused. By now, it was two o'clock in the morning and deathly still.

When it came time to decide who would light the fatal match, no one came forward. Since they had executed the whole affair, Wells and Fox argued it was more than fair that another person should touch it off. Still no one volunteered. Finally, they agreed to cast lots among themselves. The task fell to Chichester. With no hesitation, he crept to the house, lit the powder trail, and dashed off. After a few moments, there was a dull pop made by the remaining powder in the bottle exploding. Looking for the cause of the disturbance, Harrington came rushing around the house with a lantern. Seeing no one around, he supposed someone had attempted to vandalize the house and fled. For good measure, he called for additional guards, unaware that he and the occupants had been nearly blown to bits.

It wasn't until the following night that Wells managed to get word to Warren about the failed plot. At first, Warren refused to believe him, thinking such a plan too heinous even for Brown's men. Irked by Warren's doubt, Wells complained he would no longer risk his life to pass information if he had no trust in him. He suggested Warren go to Mitchell's cellar to see the powder tin for himself; he could also ascertain from at Moss's store if a can of powder was missing. They proceeded to the store where Moss looked for his can of powder and indeed found it missing. Harrington and Sublette then went to Mitchell's house where they found the keg in the cellar stairs.

Warren now wanted to arrest all of Brown's men, but to get a conviction he would need Wells on the witness stand. Even if Wells agreed to testify, it would destroy his usefulness as an informant, not to mention put his life in jeopardy. After weighing all the consequences, Warren wisely decided to keep the whole matter under wraps for the time being, not even informing Mitchell about the attempt on his life.

A few days before the powder plot, Warren had received a letter from Freeport deputy sheriff Tut Baker with a handbill enclosed. It gave a detailed description of two horses that had been stolen from Freeport in early fall. The description answered so well to the two horses Brown had recently sold to Thomas Graham that Warren had little doubt they were the horses in question and sent a letter to Baker informing him of the horses' location. On receiving Warren's letter, Baker and the owner of the horses, Spencer, started straightaway for Bellevue.

Arriving about noon on the same day, they picked up Warren and rode to Graham's who lived about three miles north of town. Although Graham had purchased the horses in good faith, after hearing Spencer's description of them, he had no doubt they belonged to him. Harnessing the horses, the whole party now rode back to Bellevue to confront Brown.

As was his wont, Brown received the men courteously, saying he believed Spencer was mistaken in thinking the stock belonged to him. The men from whom he purchased the horses were farmers from Missouri, decent, honest men who knew the horses since the time they were colts. Only a fool, he said, would attempt to sell stolen horses so close to home. Just an hour before, the horses were virtually in Spencer's possession, requiring nothing more than an oath to establish his title. So eloquent was Brown, however, that, according to Warren, "the delusion of ownership vanished before the logic of Brown's little speech."[4] When Graham acknowledged Spencer as the owner, Brown sternly warned him not to give up the horses without due process, saying if he did, he would not be responsible for the loss.

Moss, who, strangely enough, was also present as Brown's legal adviser, said that he too believed Spencer was the rightful owner of the horses. Pulling Brown aside, Moss advised him not to press the issue as it could awaken the community's simmering hostility toward him and his gang, especially as two of his men—Aaron Long and John Baxter—had stolen the horses. Better, he said, to bring the two to justice and thereby gain the community's good will.

Yet, this time Brown held fast to his position, declaring he was prepared to go to court to recover the horses. Knowing Long and Baxter would lie for him on the witness stand, he was confident he could make a strong case for ownership. Brown also knew that for Spencer to undertake an action of replevin would be costly, as he would be required to post bond for twice the value of the disputed horses.

In the end, the matter went to court and once again Brown triumphed. Outraged by the injustice, Baker denounced Brown in court as one of the worst criminals in the region, vowing to return one day and hang him and his men. The threat brought Fox and several others to their feet with pistols drawn, demanding a "retraction of his words or blood." Baker and Fox had known each other since their boyhood days in Indiana, where their fathers were successful farmers. Eight years Fox's senior, Baker had left home in 1832 for the lead mines at Galena where he acquired a reputation as a successful entrepreneur. For a moment, Baker stared fixedly at his old childhood pal gone bad. Scanning him disdainfully from head to toe, he blared, "I know you, Fox, and a more honorable upright man than your father don't live. But you are a degenerate son of a noble sire, unworthy of bearing his honorable name. Were I armed, I would not fear a host of such scoundrels. As it is, take my life if you wish. I retract nothing!" Everyone in the courtroom froze. Then Fox lowered his pistol on a level with Baker's breast, saying, "Baker, I can pay you the same compliment you have done me. Your father was an upright man but he has raised a son who is a disgrace to his name and nothing but your low cunning has saved your neck from the halter until now." Fox and his confederates then stormed out of the courthouse. Realizing that further attempts to recoup the horses would be useless, Baker and Spencer decided to go back to Freeport. On the evening of their departure, Graham took Spencer aside and told him he was satisfied the horses were his and if he would pay $50—the amount Graham had put down—and give his indemnity for a note he had executed to Brown for $150, he might take the horses back. The arrangement being satisfactory to all, the papers were drawn up and the horses returned to Spencer.

Even though Spencer had won out in the end, in citizens' minds, the trial reaffirmed just how vulnerable they were as long as Brown and his gang were in their midst. In March 1840, Bellevue residents began selling their property at a loss with the intent of moving to a safer town. Concerned by the sudden exodus, Warren and twenty-four of the town's leading men signed a pact to get rid of the Brown gang once and for all. Among the signatories were Cox, Harrington, Moss, John and Tom Sublette, Henderson Palmer, and James Kirkpatrick.

Two weeks later, on March 25, they rode to Dubuque to confer with Prosecutor James Crawford and T.S. Wilson, the district judge of the Territory, as to how to put their pact into action. The consultation was remarkably similar to the one that would be held between Ogle County residents and Judge Ford a month later in Oregon. Both Crawford and Wilson were all too familiar with the Brown gang for just a few days before the meeting, Fox and another bandit had been arrested for robbing a traveler on the road from Dubuque to Bellevue. The two had gotten off with an alibi, even though the victim had identified them in court as the robbers. Wilson's advice to Warren: draw up a warrant for the gang's arrest on charges of horse stealing, robbing, counterfeiting, and any other suspected crimes.

That same day, with Anson Harrington swearing to the warrant, Prosecutor Crawford filed charges against Brown, Fox, Long, Birch, Baxter, and twenty others. Armed with his warrant, Warren proceeded to Brown's Hotel to make the arrests.

After four frustrating years, a showdown was finally approaching.

When he arrived at the hotel, Warren called Brown out on the porch to read the warrant aloud. As he began to read, the outlaws instantly surrounded Warren, hissing and gnarring angry threats. Ever respectful of Warren, Brown urged his men not to harm him for the good Sheriff was simply doing his duty. Better, he said, to take their anger out on the man who filed the warrant against them: Anson Harrington. As soon as the men heard Harrington's name, Warren said, "With a bound and yell which I shall never forget, for they were more like demons than human beings, they left me alone with Brown and went in pursuit of Harrington."[5]

By some means, Brown had gotten advance notice of the warrant and had already warned Harrington who had taken refuge across the Mississippi. By urging his men to go after Harrington, whom he knew to be gone, Brown was likely protecting Warren by trying to control a situation that was spiraling out of control. Once his men found Harrington gone, Brown warned Warren, they would return doubly enraged and he had no idea what they would then do. As Warren equivocated, Betsy came running into the room. Taking Warren by the arm, she led him to the back door saying, "Run for your life. They are coming and will kill you!" Needing no further urging, Warren bounded off. Even Betsy was so frightened she took shelter at Moss's house.

When the men returned to Brown's, they continued to fuel their anger with whiskey. Brown looked on anxiously, knowing he was fast losing control over them. The following evening, Warren sent J.T. Sublette to Brown's with a note requesting a meeting. Fearing a bloody showdown if Warren attempted to arrest his men, he agreed to surrender on the condition that the others named in the warrant be unmolested.

That evening, Warren held a meeting at Moss's store with the signatories to the secret pact to discuss Brown's reply. Brown's offer, they unanimously agreed, was unsatisfactory. They needed to execute the warrant for all the men, not just Brown. Realizing they would now need more men to make the arrests, Warren and Cox set off into the countryside in opposite directions to recruit as many men as they could to assist in the arrest. Warren hoped a show of men from all parts of the county might induce Brown and his men to change their minds and submit peaceably. Although the meeting was supposed to be secret, they had not adjourned three hours until Brown knew all about it. It was the final week of March and the date for the arrests was set for April 1.

Over the next several days, Warren and Cox canvassed the countryside, laying out the dire situation in Bellevue. Those who could not travel to town wrote letters to Brown, urging him to surrender his men and allow the law to take its course. Others still considered Brown a persecuted man and refused to have anything to do with his arrest. In Illinois, all but one of the citizens of Sabula refused to participate, fearing retaliation by Brown. In the end, however, enough men agreed to participate that Warren felt confident he could execute his warrant.

At 9 a.m. on April 1, Warren rode back into Bellevue with his recruits. Cox and his volunteers were already gathered about four blocks below Brown's Hotel. He had ordered all the saloons in town closed. In front of the hotel hung a red a flag on which was written "Victory or Death." Beneath the flag, Brown's men were marching, drunk and belligerent, challenging the posse to "come, if they wanted hell." What they didn't know was that most of the posse were men who had served in the Black Hawk War and would not be easily intimidated. As they planned to approach the hotel on foot, one member of Cox's party mounted Warren's horse to take it to his stable in the upper part of town. As he passed the hotel, the outlaws pelted him with rocks and shouted threats. The tension in the air was palpable. Suddenly, out of nowhere, Anson Harrington started marching with several of his men toward the hotel. For a brief moment, it appeared the two groups would clash until Brown came rushing out of the hotel ordering his men to stand down.

After consulting with Cox as to the best way to bring in Brown's men without bloodshed, Warren decided to proceed alone to the house so as not to provoke them. He would then read the warrant and demand surrender.

Timorously, Warren walked down Front Street to the hotel. By now, all the residents on the street had vacated their homes and an eerie quiet prevailed. On the hotel porch, Brown received Warren and allowed him to read the warrant. As Warren read the names, Brown called up each person, stating to them the object of his visit and asked his silence while he read the warrant. For the two men who, for four years, had respectfully stared each other down from opposite sides of the law, it had come down to this moment.

When Warren finished, Brown asked to know what he proposed doing. Warren replied, "To arrest them all, as I am commanded."

Brown countered, "That is, if you can."

"There is no 'if' about it. I have a sufficient force to take you all, if force is necessary. But we prefer surrender without force."

To diffuse the tension, Warren then asked to speak with Brown and his wife in private. He showed him letters from some of the leading men of the county, advising Brown to refrain from any violence and surrender to the law. Seeking to buy time, Brown replied that if Warren would get J.T. Sublette, H. R. Magoon, Jerry Jonas, and "old man Watkins" to come and make the same pledge, they would surrender. Warren agreed and returned to the posse waiting anxiously down the street.

After assembling the individuals requested by Brown, Warren returned to the hotel. When they were within twenty paces, however, Brown and a half dozen of his men suddenly appeared on the porch, guns in hand. Brown ordered his men to halt, saying he wished to talk with the sheriff directly. Once again, Warren walked up to the porch and once again Brown's men surrounded him. Taking Warren aside, Brown whispered the boys were too full of liquor to reason with and would no longer listen to him.

Suddenly, the men seized Warren, shouting to the posse he was their hostage and if they attempted to arrest them or fire any shots, they would kill him instantly. For fifteen tense minutes, they held Warren. A heavy silence hung over the hotel as each side awaited the other's next move. Then one of the men on the porch shouted to Brown that Cox was in the street organizing his men for an assault. Brown immediately ordered his men to their posts. Shoving Warren into the street, he said, "You go and stop them, and come back." Warren bolted from the hotel. Having tried every means to bring about a peaceful end to the standoff, Warren realized Brown's men were now so drunk they would never agree to surrender. As soon as he reached Cox, he ordered him to prepare for an attack.

Among the men who had gathered, Cox asked for forty volunteers for the assault. When the men stepped forward, Warren addressed them, stating that what they were about to engage in what was "no boy's play" and that, in all probability, some would fall in the fight. If there were any in the ranks who were not disposed to such danger, they had better step out. Yet, every man stood fast. This left a reserve of another forty men to be brought up if necessary. It was now about two thirty in the afternoon. Nearly four and a half tense hours had been spent negotiating with Brown to surrender peacefully.

News of the day fixed for the arrest of the gang had reached Galena, and now Captain Harris of the steamboat *Otto*, who had collected a few men, tied his boat at the upper end of town. Arriving too late to participate in the fight, they gathered in the street to watch the standoff unfold. Before Warren started his march, he gave the men strict orders not to shoot unless fired upon. Warren was still hoping against all hope that when Brown saw the posse approaching, he would wave the flag of truce and surrender.

The posse moved in double file. Not a single word was spoken. When they came within thirty paces of the hotel, Warren sounded "Charge!" In a flash, the forty men were at the perimeter of the hotel. From the hotel window, one of Brown's men fired, killing a blacksmith. Warren once again shouted for Brown to surrender. Climbing the stairs, Cox and Warren raised and pointed their pistols at Brown. Warren said, "Surrender, Brown, and you shan't be hurt." According to Warren, Brown, who was standing on the porch at the head of his men with his rifle raised, began to lower it with the intent of surrendering when it accidentally went off, striking Cox in the leg.

Now all hell broke loose. The sound of Brown's rifle going off was a signal to his men, who began firing from the upstairs windows, wounding several men below. The posse returned fire shooting into the house into the north windows on Front Street. One ball passed through both of Brown's jugular veins and he died instantly.

For fifteen minutes, the gun battle raged. Loyal to her husband to the end, Betsy stayed in the house reloading guns for the men. When the posse finally forced entry into the hotel, the bandits, many of whom had run out of ammunition, fled upstairs to the second floor. A hand-to-hand combat now ensued with bowie knives, pitchforks, and gun barrels. Finding it impossible to ascend the steps, Warren ordered the house torched on the south side. As soon as they saw the flames, the bandits began jumping from a shed at the rear end of the hotel. Several in the posse gave chase, capturing thirteen including Fox, the Long brothers, and Chichester; seven others had escaped. With the fight now over, the fire was extinguished and the captured men were put under guard for the night.

Among the men in the posse, four had fallen, including Henderson Palmer who had taken a ball to the head. One more would later die from his wounds. Several others were injured, one seriously. Brown and three of his men lay dead and several more were injured. Runners were sent to Galena and Dubuque for surgeons to dress the wounds on both sides.

At the sight of the blood-spattered walls and corpses of men who had died defending their community, citizens began to cry for vengeance. "Hang 'em all," they cried. Ropes suddenly appeared. Nooses were being adjusted around their necks when several men urged for calm, begging them not to do something in the heat of the moment they would later regret. Fox, Long, and the other prisoners, who just minutes earlier had been so defiant, now behaved in the most obsequious manner, pleading for their lives and begging for mercy.

After order was partially restored, someone suggested the fate of the prisoners be determined by a majority vote which only sparked a renewed clamoring for hanging. Quickly mounting a box, Warren asked for everyone's attention for Cox had a few words to say. The respected legislator then stepped up on the box. Pointing to the women and children hovering and sobbing around the lifeless bodies of those who had fallen in the fight, Cox declared they had "a higher duty" to perform that night than to hang the scoundrels. "Your duty is to them, first, and tomorrow, whatever a majority of the citizens may say shall be done. I pledge you my word that you shall not only have my sanction, but my help," he said. The effect of Cox's brief words was to calm a situation that threatened to spiral out of control. After placing the prisoners under heavy guard, they tended to the wounded and made preparations to feed the hundred plus volunteers who had eaten nothing since morning. While the men ate, Rev. Joseph Kirkpatrick arranged for the dead to be taken to their respective homes. Warren's men then went into Brown's Hotel, rolled out every barrel of liquor, and emptied them in the street. Under the circumstances, Warren did not want his men, who were already edgy, to get intoxicated. He also suspected that Brown's men may have poisoned the liquor. It wasn't until well after midnight that most people finally retired to their homes.

But with the disposition of the prisoners still undecided, Warren, Cox, Moss, Harrington, and several others rode to the house of Kirkpatrick's brother James, the county coroner, for counsel as to what to do with them. Warren was the first to speak. Holding up the arrest warrant, he called for the men to respect the rule of law and that he be allowed to bring the outlaws to answer to the charges set forth in the warrant. Four of the men agreed with his approach, but Harrington and Cox took the opposite view, arguing it was impossible to arrest them as they had no jail. Furthermore, even if they were to put them in a makeshift jail, the prisoners had friends throughout the frontier who could be expected to break them free and possibly seek revenge. Now that these desperados were finally in their control, the friends and family of the fallen demanded nothing short of death.

Cox and Harrington had made such a compelling case that Warren was at a loss to argue against it. Seeing further argument in favor of the law would be futile, he began to press for a lighter sentence. Then David Bates offered the following resolution: that tomorrow morning at ten o'clock, they would meet with citizens and let them decide the prisoners' punishment by a majority vote. Bates's resolution was unanimously adopted with everyone pledging to carry out faithfully whatever sentence was approved. At 4 a.m., the men finally retired.

At 8 a.m., a steamer from Dubuque pulled into the Bellevue wharf. Among the passengers were Prosecuting Attorney James Crawford and Sheriff Cummins. With them was Reverend Babcock, who had been arrested for robbing a store in Prairie du Chien. Hearing of the shootout at Brown's, they had come to claim the goods now in Brown's store, which were believed to have been stolen by Babcock. As Babcock was being led up the bank, Cox at once recognized him. Taking him by the hand, with a twist of irony, Cox said that Babcock was just the man he had been looking for. Others were about to carry Babcock off with the other prisoners, when he appealed to Cox for protection. Asking the men not to harm him, Cox turned to Babcock and said, "We will treat you well today, but, damn you, we will hang you tomorrow!" The Reverend was then thrown in trembling with the rest of the prisoners. Just then the ship's captain, an old friend of

Cox, appealed to him to release Babcock because his poor wife on board the boat was beside herself with grief. Cox finally agreed on the condition that he would never again set foot on the soil of Bellevue.*

At ten o'clock, the prisoners were brought in, their wan, haggard faces clearly showing they were expecting the worst. Acting as chairman of the meeting, Cox then read the following statement:

> *The people of Bellevue had met for the purpose of prevailing on these men to surrender to the law. The officer, who was in charge of the writ for their arrest, held out every inducement to them for a peaceable surrender, and the people here assembled had offered them, through him, their protection and a fair and impartial trial; all these offers they had indignantly refused; this refusal had cost them the life of their leader and some of their companions; in consequence of which, we, the citizens, have had to sustain the arm of the law in discharging that duty, are left to mourn the loss of some of our best citizens, and as the spokesman of this meeting I am directed to say to you that we will relieve the Sheriff of his duty, and take your cases into our own hands. What sentence the people here may pass upon you, I am not prepared to say: your fate is in their hands, and whatever a majority may decide upon will be carried out to the letter.*[6]

Chichester meekly asked permission to speak on behalf of the prisoners. In a low, trembling voice, he acknowledged they were guilty of the crimes charged and were willing to submit to whatever punishment called for by law.

Seeing that Chichester had created some sympathy for the prisoners, Harrington countered with an impassioned speech saying he was opposed to turning them loose to prey upon some other community. They were all desperate characters and were beyond reform. With such villains at large, no man's life or property was safe. Like others, he had come to Iowa to make it his home with the expectation of living with law-abiding, Christian people where the law was enforced and life and property were protected. "What has

---

*While the good Reverend never returned to Bellevue, he quickly returned to his life of crime, robbing trains in Missouri.

been our effort to bring these men to justice? Have we succeeded in a single instance? Their ability to provide an alibi in every instance when arrested had demoralized the country. The time had come for people to take the law into their own hands!" Heretofore, Harrington had shunned mob violence, but now he admitted the law was inadequate in the present case. Nothing short of the people taking the law into their own hands and making an example of the desperadoes would save them from future depredations. "To offer mercy to such men would only jeopardize the lives of others," he argued. "Fear alone makes them penitent today. Free them today and in six months you or someone else will pay the penalty for this clemency. Reformation in such men is impossible, and I, for one, am unwilling to turn them loose to prey upon *any* community. Upon your votes depend the character and standing of the people of Jackson County." Harrington closed his speech by proposing that they decide by ballot whether they should be hanged, or whipped and banished forever from the country. The proposition was put to a vote and approved. Before the ballot was counted, every man in the room was required to pledge to abide by the decision.

Two boxes were then produced, one of which was empty and the other contained white and colored beans that were distributed to the men. On approaching each person, the man with the beans cried out, "White beans for hanging, colored beans for whipping." When the teller approached a voter, he would select his bean and cast it into the box. Each time a bean was dropped into the box, the prisoners cringed, fearing it was an ill-fated white bean. The beans were then emptied from the ballot box, counted, and found to correspond with the number of persons casting them. All was still as death as the tallying then began. The result was then written down and presented to the chairman. Holding it in his hand, Cox called upon the prisoners to rise and hear the verdict. Before announcing it, he asked for another pledge from the citizens to abide by and carry into effect the wish of the majority. He then announced the verdict: "whipping—by three beans."

The decision sparked a loud clamor among the men. Harrington rose and attempted to address the chair who immediately called him to order, saying the decision was not debatable. Harrington explained, saying, "I rise now to make the vote unanimous." The motion was applauded and adopted all over the house. Chichester, who was standing near him, took him by the hand, sheepishly intoning, "I thank you."

Cox now proceeded to pass sentence on each of the prisoners. Enumerating the charges against each, he meted out a sentence varying from four to thirty lashes on the bare back. After being whipped, they were to be placed in skiffs with three days' rations and if caught again in the county, they would be hanged. Among those appointed to carry out the sentence was L.J. Hiffley. He was assigned to whip an Irishman named Connolly who, on the day of the gun battle, had been one of the men parading the streets with the red flag and shouting at the top of his voice, "To come on if they wanted hell." He received twenty-five lashes. In applying the lash, Heffley proved himself an expert, every stroke tearing pieces of flesh from his back. Twice during the whipping, Connolly fainted. Fox received the lightest whipping, owing to the intercession of friends who knew his otherwise good family in Indiana. About sundown, the thirteen were placed in skiffs and sent downstream. As they drifted away, the outlaws thanked the men of Bellevue for their light punishment—all except Connolly who was unable to sit up—promising never to return.

About two weeks after the incident, someone from Seawards Island went to Warren to say that Fox was on the island and wanted to see Warren alone. Fearing a ploy to exact revenge, Warren took several armed citizens along. When they arrived, Fox came creeping out of the thicket covered with dirt and in rags. He at once began to apologize for coming back and begged them to spare his life. He had come only to recoup his pocket-book, containing $400, which he had given to Mrs. Brown for safekeeping on the day of the fight. Begging Warren to cross the river and get it for him, he promised to leave immediately and never return. On informing Mrs. Brown of Fox's request, she confirmed she had the pocketbook and had never opened it. She also had a good suit of clothes belonging to Fox which Warren took to Fox along with some provisions. Warren's final— and somewhat misguided—act of kindness toward Fox was the last he and Bellevue's citizens would ever see of him and the rest of Brown's gang. Yet, Anson Harrington's prediction that, in sparing their lives, within six months someone else would pay the penalty for their clemency would prove prescient, deadly prescient. In fact, it would take less than three.

## CHAPTER 9

# The Murder of Colonel Davenport

*And know this, that if the good man of the house had known what hour the thief would come, he would have watched and not suffered his house to be broken through.*

—MATTHEW 24:43

William Fox never again set foot in Jackson County. Neither, in all likelihood, did John and Aaron Long or Robert Birch. From Bellevue, they went to Nauvoo. For the next five years, they used it as a safe haven from which to raid the borderlands, mainly Illinois and eastern Iowa. Then, in July 1845, while the Hodges were languishing on death row, they received a tip about a home where they could make a huge score: $20,000 in a Rock Island mansion belonging to Colonel George Davenport.

In the entire Mississippi Valley, few men commanded more respect and admiration than George William Davenport. Born in Great Britain in 1783, in his youth he went to sea and broke his leg rescuing a shipmate in New York Harbor. After recovering in a New York hospital, Davenport enlisted in the US Army where he served ten years, even fighting against his native country during the War of 1812. At the conclusion of the war, he went to work as a sutler, running supplies from St. Louis to Rock Island for the building of Fort Armstrong intended as a bulwark against the Sac and Fox. In 1822, Davenport established his own trading company, exchanging goods with the Sac, Fox, Winnebago, and Pottawattamie Indians. Davenport generously allowed them to trade on credit until they could conduct their winter hunt. He learned to speak the Sac language and enjoyed warm personal relationships with the Indians who regarded him as a man of integrity. So close was he with the Indians that his two sons, George and Bailey, had only Indians as playmates as children.[1]

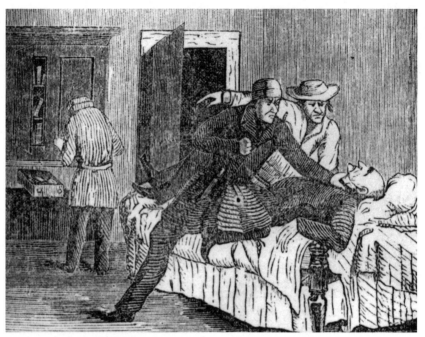

Edward Bonney's Depiction of the Torture of Colonel Davenport
*Source: Courtesy of the Abraham Lincoln Presidential Library and Museum*

When Davenport heard that his friends the Sac were being removed to Iowa, he traveled to Washington to advocate on their behalf with his former army commander, President Andrew Jackson. Being no friend of the Indians, Old Hickory had scant interest in assisting a tribe that had sided with the British in the War of 1812. When efforts to keep the Sac on their lands failed, Davenport purchased a few thousand acres—including the land on which Black Hawk's lodge resided, so that they might continue to live east of the Mississippi. Jackson refused to bless the agreement, warning that if they did not vacate the land signed over in the 1804 treaty, he would remove them at the tip of a bayonet. When the war against the Sac broke out in 1832, Davenport was appointed quartermaster in the Illinois militia with the rank of colonel. Yet, he remained a lifelong friend of Black Hawk, who in his autobiography later wrote, "He [Davenport] is a good and brave chief. He always treated me well, and gave me good advice."[2]

With the wealth he accumulated trading with the Indians, in 1833, Davenport built a large white two-story mansion on the western shore of Rock Island with a sweeping view of the Mississippi River. At his elegant home, he often entertained local businessmen to discuss various ventures. Of late, he had been discussing the possibility of building a rail line between Chicago and Rock Island. Several had liked the idea, promising some $20,000 toward the venture. Though money never changed hands, bandits got wind of the discussion, mistakenly believing a small fortune was locked away in Davenport's mansion. It would be yet another robbery that would go terribly wrong.

On July 4, residents of Rock Island were celebrating Independence Day at the courthouse in Stephenson. Feeling unwell, Davenport decided to stay home. His family objected to leaving the sixty-two-year-old man alone, as there was general apprehension about the recent spate of banditti attacks on the island. Dismissing any cause for alarm, Davenport insisted they attend the celebration and that he would be fine. "Go," Davenport said. "Go, and enjoy yourselves. I feel secure from all harm." Thus assured, his entire family, including the domestics, went off to the celebration. Unbeknownst to Davenport, John and Aaron Long and Robert Brown had been camping near Rock Island for several days patiently waiting for the time when the entire Davenport family would be attending the festivities.[3]

After his family departed, Davenport retired to his parlor to read the newspaper and gaze out at the rolling Mississippi waters from his bay window. A little after noon, he went out to his well for a pitcher of water. He had just set down the pitcher in the kitchen, when he heard a noise in the parlor made by the fall of a poker he used to prop up a rear window. As he reached for the parlor door, Fox and John Long burst through. Long cried out, "Seize him, Chunky!" Without a word, Fox produced a pistol and shot Davenport in the left thigh. Reeling backward, Davenport attempted to reach for something—his cane or a pistol on the mantel—as the two men pounced on him. Fox blindfolded him with his red silk handkerchief while Long tied his arms behind his back with hickory bark. For a moment, they left him while they went upstairs and attempted to open an iron safe in his bedroom. Unable to unlock it, they dragged the

Home of Colonel Davenport on Rock Island
*Source: Courtesy of the Abraham Lincoln Presidential Library and Museum*

bleeding Davenport into the hall and up the stairs and ordered him to open it. After he complied, they found about seven hundred dollars—far from the windfall they were expecting. Furious with disappointment, they dragged Davenport to another bedroom and threw him on the bed. As he lay bleeding and in pain, they threatened to kill him if he did not reveal where the money was hidden. Weakened by the loss of blood, Davenport pointed feebly to a dresser drawer in the room. In their haste, they opened only one drawer. Finding nothing, the two set upon him, beating and choking him until he fell unconscious. One of the men threw water on his face to revive him. When the colonel came to, they continued to beat him while demanding the location of the money. By now, Davenport had lost so much blood he was unable to speak and could only make vague gestures to a drawer they had failed to open. Again, they beat and choked him, pouring water over his face whenever he appeared on the verge of passing out. While Long and Fox debated whether to burn him alive in the house, Davenport fell backward and passed out. Thinking the old man was dying, the men fled with Aaron Long who had been standing guard outside. In addition to $400, they made off with Davenport's gold watch and chain, a shotgun, and a pistol.

The first to find Davenport were three men from Moline who were drifting down river in a skiff fishing. Upon hearing Davenport's cries of "Murder! Help! For God's sake!" one of the men, Benjamin Cole, wanted to rush to the house but his friends objected, believing it was probably an Independence Day prank. Hearing the cry a second time, Cole decided to investigate. On entering the house, they found blood spattered on the walls and floors with trunks overturned and objects scattered everywhere. Following the trail of blood upstairs, Cole found the battered Colonel on the bed pale and moaning in pain. Davenport asked why he had not come sooner and told him to fetch Dr. Brown who was at the celebration.[4]

In due course, Cole returned with Brown who administered first aid and sewed up a knife would in his left thigh. As he was being treated, Cole sent some of his party to Iowa who brought back Drs. Patrick Gregg and Witherwax. Later, at the trial, Dr. Gregg described Davenport's condition and the gruesome scene within the house:

> *The colonel was sinking fast from exhaustion, in great agony, and cold from head to foot. I examined the wound, and found that there had been a profuse flow of blood. The blood was everywhere. The house looked like a butcher's shambles—blood in the sitting room, in the hall, and along up the stairs; and in the closet by the safe was a pool of blood; and in the room below there was the same. On the door case of the closet containing the safe was the mark of a bloody hand. The left leg of his pantaloons and the bed clothes were saturated with blood. I observed contusions on his left arm and side, and he appeared as if he had been bruised or beaten.[5]*

When Davenport came to, he described his attackers. He saw three men but felt there may have been more. He described one of his assailants as small and slightly built and wearing a cloth hat and the other as tall and thin. As the evening wore on, Davenport groaned in pain and struggled to speak. Dr. Gregg tried to ease his pain by rubbing the wounded leg. Davenport's body then became cold and his breathing labored. Gregg held his right hand and felt his pulse which grew weaker and weaker. Davenport said he expected to die and was not afraid. Around 9:00 p.m., the colonel passed away. Just before he died, a gust of wind blew in from the casement window and extinguished the lamp by his bedside.[6]

At noon the next day, Davenport's funeral took place in a service conducted by his old friends, the Fox. They buried him on the premises in a beautiful spot under a large oak tree. At the head of his grave, the Indians placed a white cedar post and painted it with images of headless humans, symbolizing the many Sioux they had killed in battle. Brandishing a war club, Fox braves then danced three times around the grave from west to east. At each circumambulation, they intoned a prayer, gesturing toward the sun and the Northeast, the direction of the Sioux, beseeching them to open the gates of the setting sun and eternally protect their old friend.

The Davenport family immediately offered a reward of $1,500 for the arrest of the killers followed by a $1,000 offer from Governor Ford. Handbills were printed describing the gold watch and the amount of money along with a description of the men Davenport had provided. On the island, residents established a night watch while vigilantes fanned out into the surrounding countryside. A weeklong search produced not a single lead. With no other witnesses, and Davenport's description too vague to be of much use, residents feared the murderers would never be apprehended—until the plucky Edward Bonney joined the investigation.

Bonney first heard the news of Davenport's murder on July 8 while in West Point talking to Sheriff James Estes.[7] From the description of the men in the wanted poster, Bonney told Estes he strongly suspected William Fox and John Long, who were suspiciously absent the day they were to testify on behalf of the Hodges. The third person he guessed to be a bandit he knew only as "Bleeker," who had collaborated with Fox in the attempted robbery of Beach in Nauvoo just a few days before Davenport's murder. To facilitate Bonney's investigation, Estes sent a letter to the Rock Island County sheriff, suggesting he consult with the amateur detective as someone who had been instrumental in helping to solve the murders of Miller and Leisi.

Following his hunch, Bonney began to gather information on all the actual and would-be witnesses for the Hodges. He soon learned that Long, Fox, and Bleeker were known to frequent the house of Grant Redden on Devil's Creek about five miles from Montrose. On inquiring, it turned out that four men had been seen visiting Redden's on July 8 just before leaving for Missouri.

After the botched robbery attempt, the Longs and Fox had fled east in a panic. Reversing direction, they stole a skiff and drifted down the Rock River to Grant Redden's cabin on Devil's Creek. In Redden's wheat field, Fox cached the money and kept Davenport's gold watch, which he would later give to Robert Birch who was already at Redden's cabin when the others arrived.

Four days later, Aaron Long and William Redden went up to Nauvoo where they heard that Davenport was dead and saw a handbill giving a partial description of the murderers and the stolen items. Aaron rushed back to Devil's Creek to warn his partners, noting the description of his brother and Fox was "damned good." Fearing they might be traced to Devil's Creek, Fox dug up the money and stolen articles. He reburied the weapons further out into the prairie and distributed everyone's share of the loot. He tucked the gold watch and chain in his pocket and rode all night to Missouri with Birch and John Long. (Aaron rode a stolen horse to hide out at his father's house in Galena.) At sunrise, the three came to a farmhouse near the Des Moines River where they stopped for breakfast. Long purchased some beeswax from the cook, telling her he was a tailor who was setting up a business in the area.

After breakfast, they slipped down a ravine behind the house where they prepared to hide their money and the watch in the bluffs along the river. Long instructed Birch to lay the beeswax in the sun to soften it. Each then put money from their respective robberies—totaling around $800—into a glass jar. Taking the softened beeswax, Fox sealed the jar, as well as Davenport's watch, and buried them with $200 in silver tied up in a cloth.

They then rode into Macon County, Missouri, where Fox and Long stopped. Birch rode on another ten miles to inquire about a valuable race mare in Centerville he had admired. After learning of the mare's location, Birch returned to tell his partners. The following night the three rode to Centerville and stole the mare and two other horses. They took the horses to St. Louis, leaving them with Tom Reynolds, a stable owner, to fence. Crossing back into Illinois, they stole three more horses in Belleville then started east across the Wabash River to Owen County, Indiana.

Meanwhile, Bonney had met with Rockford County sheriff Joseph Knox who showed him a letter from a man giving a detailed description of twenty-five-year-old Robert H. Birch reputed to have been a felon since he was fifteen. A loquacious and sociable man "who could play the bar room dandy to perfection," Birch was known as "Brown" on Rock Island, and elsewhere by the aliases "Harris, Haines, Bleecher, and Bleeker." The previous month, Birch had partnered with Amos Hodges in the attempted robbery of Beach's store and was also wanted in connection with the robberies of McKinney, Mulford, and the Frink stagecoach. Having found no clues at Davenport's house, Bonney focused on anything that might link the murder to Birch.

While Bonney cast about for a lead in the investigation, a certain John Baker arrived in Montrose with a phalanx of beautiful bay mares for sale. Hoping Baker might be linked with Birch and the other bandits, Bonney ingratiated himself with Baker, who after several meetings took him for one of the bandits. At one point, Bonney dropped the names of Long and Fox. Baker said he knew them well but had not seen them for several months for he had been in the upper Missouri since the previous winter. In any case, he said, he had had a falling out with Fox over some property they jointly owned and no longer did business with him. Bonney suggested if he wished to see "some of the old boys," that he visit old man Redden. With that, the two parted ways and Baker rode off to Devil's Creek.

Two days later, Bonney ran into Baker and asked him how he had made out at Redden's.

"First rate!" Baker exclaimed.

"Did you see any of the boys?" Bonney asked.

"No, but I heard about them."

"What did you hear?"

"Why damn it, man," he whispered, "they are the ones who killed old Colonel Davenport!"

Grant Redden, it turned out, had divulged the entire story of Davenport's murder to Baker. Even though Bonney's suspicions were now confirmed, he still had no solid evidence to link the men to the crime, let alone enough to get a conviction in a court of law. Indeed, after nearly six weeks since Davenport's murder, all he had was Baker's second-hand testimony from Grant Redden. In his words,

> *I confess, that confident as I was in my knowledge of the guilty persons, I felt much disheartened in view of the present aspect of the case. The idea of attempting to pursue and arrest four desperate robbers and murderers, who were constantly committing their deeds of darkness, and escaping from point to point under cover of the night, and changing their names with every change of the wind, with no other track than the one left in their flight from old Redden's, and that already one month old, certainly gave little prospect of success.*[8]

Returning to Rock Island, Bonney met with the authorities to discuss a different approach. It was concluded that the only way to solve the case would be to pose as one of the banditti and infiltrate the gang. While Bonney supported the idea, he declined to take on the assignment, deeming it too dangerous for a man with a wife and several children to support. Already since the Hodges' execution, he had received death threats. Moreover, he was known to some members of the gang and might easily be discovered. However, when no one else competent could be found, Bonney accepted on the condition that the state would, in the event of his death, guarantee to protect his family and provide for the education of his children.

Thus began Bonney's risky assignment—part bounty hunter, part undercover operative, one-man vigilante—and one of the first of his kind in the United States. Confidential letters were sent to various authorities alerting them to Bonney's investigation. Since Bonney would be posing as a counterfeiter, Judge Wilson, an official at the Miner's Bank of Dubuque, accompanied him to the bank where he obtained sets of unsigned bank notes with which to gain the banditti's confidence. Bonney planned to show some of the notes to the outlaws and obtain their agreement to pass them once he returned from Cincinnati where he would print more and have them signed.

The following day, Bonney took a stagecoach to Galena in search of a man named Millard, who, an informant had told him, was in the possession of Davenport's gold watch. After a few days floundering about the city, he realized he had been duped and boarded a steamer bound for St. Louis. Soon after embarking, a young man in his early twenties approached Bonney addressing him by name, saying he remembered Bonney from Loomis's Tavern in Nauvoo. At first, Bonney did not recognize him. When he introduced himself as Granville Young, Bonney recalled hearing of him when he was in search of Thomas Brown in St. Louis.* They then repaired for a few drinks in the ship's saloon. Even with the alcohol, Young remained on his guard, so Bonney retired for the evening. The next day, Bonney met Young in the saloon and the two went for a walk. Producing the Miners' Bank bills from his pocket, Bonney asked if he could detect they were bogus. Carefully examining them, Young pronounced them very good, though the paper, he thought, looked thinner than that issued by a bank. Bonney said he wanted to put a few thousand of the bills into circulation around Galena. In view of their high quality, Young offered to buy all of them for twenty-five cents on the dollar. After some haggling, he agreed to pay fifty cents with money he would raise in Nauvoo. Young said that he had just come through old man Redden's with two stolen horses that he sold for next to nothing in Prairie du Chien. While in a store there, he noticed a large amount of gold in the merchant's drawer while he was exchanging a large sum of money. After studying the store for several days, Young broke in at dusk. He was opening the desk drawer when the owner entered through the front and caught him red-handed. Bolting out the back, Young raced for the river with the merchant hot on his heels. Near the riverbank was a house owned by some girls he knew. Bursting into the house, he cried out for them to hide him. Telling him to

---

*Young later said he had run with "the united banditti" referring to a gang led by John Murrell, a legendary outlaw operating on the lower Mississippi.

squat in the corner, Big Maria sat over him, throwing her long dress over his head. When the irate merchant arrived, the girls told him that Young had passed out the back door. Young hid out until 9:00 p.m.—presumably not under Big Maria's dress the entire time—when he made his way to Galena and caught the steamer where he now was.

Now Young wished to "raise a sight" in Nauvoo but said he could no longer trust Return Jackson Redden after a job they had done. When Bonney asked him to explain, Young told of how he, Redden, and a Gentile thief named William W. Louther went up the Illinois River. Stopping at Pekin, Young and Redden visited an old Mormon who, as it turned out, had a large amount of gold in the house. Redden had quickly concocted a story that Brigham Young was in need of gold to purchase materials for the Holy Temple he was building that could not be bought with anything but gold or silver. After purchasing some of the gold with a phony hundred-dollar bill, they learned the old Mormon had another $1,700 dollars in specie in another part of the house. When Louther returned from upriver, the three returned to the old man's house to steal the rest of the gold. While crawling into a window, Young accidently put his hands on the face of someone sleeping. Astonishingly, neither of the two persons in bed awoke and Young was able to make off with $240 in gold. Afterward, Redden proposed they should separate for a while and lay low to which Young agreed. But the next night, Redden returned to the house alone and stole the remaining gold as well as the counterfeit bill they had passed. He later buried the loot and refused to share it with his partners. Thus betrayed by Redden, Young refused to have further dealings with the scoundrel.

Young, however, could work with Aaron Long, but the latter would not work without William Fox who was traveling with John Long. Wishing to steer him to the subject of his purpose, Bonney asked if the Longs and Fox could raise money to purchase his bills. Indeed, said Young, though Aaron would not reveal how much money they had gotten from Davenport. Just after selling some stolen horses in Fort Madison, Young had run into Fox, Birch, and the Longs who said they were going to Rock Island "to rake down" an old man for thirty or forty thousand dollars. Young had proposed to accompany them but they had refused, saying they had to share the booty with a man who had tipped them off as to the money and its location.

According to Young, the outlaws had first learned of Davenport's money from a man who used to work for the colonel and was intimate with the entire family. About two weeks before the murder, the employee went to Davenport's on the pretext of a cordial visit to assess the situation of the household and the best mode of entry. He found that the four men in the family were well armed and slept upstairs, and the money was in a safe in Davenport's chambers.

Bonney told Young he had to go to Cincinnati to have the bogus bills printed, after which he wished to take an extensive tour of the country to meet some of Young's associates. Thinking it a good idea, Young said he knew "all the boys" operating in the south and west as well as around the lead mines at Galena and could give him four hundred names if he wanted. After Bonney asked for some contacts in the St. Louis area, Young proceeded to recite a long list of men in Illinois and the St. Louis area whose houses served as stations for Fox, Long, and Birch when they traveled. "They are of the *right stripe*," said Young. "Tell them you are a friend of Granville Young."

At Nauvoo, the two parted. Young went to Grant Redden's where he was later arrested as an accomplice in Davenport's murder. Bonney stopped at Loomis's Tavern, a favorite haunt of the banditti, to speak with the owner. Loomis said at the bluffs south of Rock Island, called Robbers' Camp, two bloodstained coats were found buried under branches and leaves. In a pocket of one of the coats was a pair of kid gloves. Loomis believed he could identify the coats as belonging to John Long and Fox and the gloves as the property of Birch.

It had been an extraordinary bit of sleuthing on Bonney's part. Not only had he confirmed the identity of the murderers, he had learned how they were able to "get up the sight" at Davenport's. He had also learned of the location of other bandits and station houses, as well as their modes of operation and geographic range. He now needed to hunt down Davenport's killers on the run somewhere in the northwest frontier.

## CHAPTER 10

# The Hunt for Davenport's Killers

*No other person could be found who was considered competent to the task, and the visage of the venerable and lamented Davenport—his grey hairs clotted with blood, and his frame distorted in the agonies of a terrible death, cried aloud for vengeance and justice.*

—EDWARD BONNEY

Based on what Granville Young had said, Bonney returned to the Davenport residence to speak to his son George about recent visitors to the house just before the murder. After narrowing down the list of possible suspects, they concluded the man who had passed information to the bandits as to the location of the safe was John Baxter, a friend of the family and long-time resident of Rock Island. Baxter had dinner at Davenport's in May and moved to Jefferson, Wisconsin, shortly after the murder. With yet another suspect added to a list of accomplices, now scattered throughout the Mississippi Valley—the Reddens in Iowa, Baxter in Wisconsin, and Granville Young in Nauvoo—Bonney decided to focus on capturing Davenport's killers: Fox, Birch, and the Longs who were believed to be traveling together and hiding out in Missouri.

On August 23, Bonney arrived in St. Louis vexed to learn that the confidential information he had given the Montrose sheriff had been leaked to the *Qunicy Whig*, which the St. Louis papers had promptly picked up. Concerned the articles would alert the outlaws, he asked Sheriff Reuben Knox to pass information to the press contradicting the earlier reports. Since the Dubuque bank bills would be of little value in Missouri, Bonney obtained several blanks from the State Bank of Missouri. He then called on Tom Reynolds, the livery stable operator whose name he had gotten from Young. At first, Reynolds was wary of Bonney, disavowing any knowledge of Young, the Longs, Fox, Birch, or any of the other outlaws Bonney mentioned. To set him at ease, Bonney rented a horse and carriage and invited him to go for a ride in the country where they could talk privately. Once out of town, Bonney reached into his pocket and produced the blank notes. Reynolds was greatly impressed, praising them as "the best imitation of genuine bills I ever saw." Though his main business was in stolen horses and occasional bogus gold, he expressed interest in passing several thousand dollars of the bills. At any one time, Reynolds had twenty horses in his stable and never had an owner come to claim his horse. After modifying the horse's appearance, usually by shearing the mane and docking the tail, he put them on a steamboat bound for the southern markets. Reynolds complained that business was slow of late, though just a few days earlier, Long, Fox, and Birch had come through with three good horses they had pinched in upper Missouri. The three had subsequently bolted after seeing an article in the *Chicago Democrat* containing West's disclosures at Oliver's trial implicating them in several robberies on the Rock River. The article also reported they were being sought in connection with the Davenport murder. While he did not know Birch and Long very well, Reynolds had known Fox a long time. He was a clever man who was always "flush" and had recently stashed $2,000 dollars in the bluffs along the Des Moines River.

Having learned all he could about the killers from Reynolds, Bonney bid farewell, promising to return with a wad of bogus bills. Before leaving town, he purchased three sets of handcuffs and set out for Springfield to obtain letters of requisition for several states. At Edwardsville, he chanced to run into Governor Ford on his way from Springfield to St. Louis. During a long conversation with the Governor, Bonney updated him on the murder investigation. When he finished, Ford looked at him solemnly and remarked, "[Y]ou are placing your own life in jeopardy in this adventure."

Upon arrival in Springfield, Bonney was miffed to find the requisition letters to several state governors had not been prepared. Unaware precisely in what states the outlaws were—or would be—he obtained a slew of blank requisitions with the State of Illinois seal with Governor Ford's signature. Armed with his official documents, he set out by stagecoach for Clark County in southernmost Indiana to find Birch.

Bonney's hunch was that Birch had holed up with his father just as Aaron Long had. Granville Young had told him that Birch's father, John, lived in the hamlet of Marshall in Clark County. At the county seat of Jeffersonville, Bonney paid a call on Sheriff William P. Bennett. Bennett, it turned out, was all too familiar with the troublesome Birches, noting that John Birch was a boyhood pal of Owen Long, the father of the Long brothers, while the two were growing up in Asheville, North Carolina. Known locally as "Old Coon," John Birch was one of the shrewdest outlaws in the Northwest, having eluded capture for years.

Mounting their horses, Bennett and Bonney rode to the Birch cabin located deep in the heart of a dense forest. When they had ridden to within a half mile of the place, Bennett halted and allowed Bonney to proceed alone. After following a narrow path through the woods, Bonney came to a clearing in the center of which stood a derelict log cabin. The broken front door was wide open. Inside he could see a wretched-looking old man standing at the foot of his bed being dressed by an old woman and a young girl. Bonney introduced himself as *Tom Brown*, an associate of Granville Young and the Longs. He then displayed several of his bank notes, saying he was on his way to Cincinnati to have them printed and wished to do a little business. Old Coon took the bait instantly, offering to buy the notes "if the price was fair." Could he, Bonney asked, also purchase horses with the money and have them delivered in Louisville or St. Louis? Easily, Birch replied, as he had the protection of several associates, one of whom was none other than Mr. Arbuckle, clerk of the Marshall Court. "They can't hurt Old Coon as long as he is Clerk of the Court," he boasted, suddenly revealing how it was that he had eluded Sheriff Bennett for so long.

Old Coon then began to reminisce about the gang's exploits, lamenting at one point how a group of irate vigilantes in Texas had hanged his son John "like a dog." Robert, on the other hand, was too smart to be caught, though he had not seen him in eight years. The remark fell on Bonney with a thud as he realized his hunch had been wrong. Promising to return to Old Coon's with some of the bank notes, Bonney rode off, arriving back in Marshall around midnight.

The next day, he departed for Terre Haute, not before informing Bennett of the court clerk's outlaw ties. In Terre Haute, Bonney called on Deputy Sheriff Marvin Hickox, who said that two men, one named Fox and the other Shack Phips, had just been arrested in Clay County in southwest Indiana on charges of horse stealing. "Shack" was short for John Mashach Phips, who had come to Marion, Indiana, in 1833 with his father Jesse and his brothers Eli, Shadrach, and Mathew, all of whom were outlaws.

Suspecting it to be the very Fox he was hunting, Bonney and the Sheriff rode at once to the Bowling Green jail where the two were being held. By the time they arrived, however, both men had already been released on bail posted by their fathers. Fox had been seen leaving town immediately after speaking with his father. Examining the stolen horses, Bonney immediately recognized one as fitting the description of the valuable race mare Reynolds had boasted of in St. Louis.

With his leads having gone cold, Bonney turned to local officials in the hope of developing a new one. Shack Phips, it turned out, lived in neighboring Owen County, a remote and sparsely populated area whose residents were outlaws incestuously linked to one another through inter-marriage, much as the Driscolls and Brodys had been. Phips, for example, had married a daughter of the Widow Long, who was the sister-in-law of Owen Long and mother of Aaron and Hiram Long, first cousins of Aaron and John. Phips and his wife now lived with the Widow Long. Fox was staying there when he was arrested. With this information as his only lead, Bonney set out for the "Den of Thieves in Owen County"—with Fox's stolen horses in tow.

The next day, Bonney found the Widow Long, besmeared with dirt and dressed in tatters, in a miserable shack deep in the woods. Even more repulsive was the cabin's squalid interior:

> *The furniture consisted of crippled chairs, half a dozen three-legged stools, two miserable bedsteads of which were made of rough poles with the bark still on; an old rickety cupboard; a table made of a slab of timber, roughly hewn; a couple of iron kettles, half a dozen broken plates, as many knives and forks without handles, and a few tin cups.*[1]

Mother Long eyed Bonney suspiciously. When asked if Phips was at home, she curtly replied he was out and said nothing more. Shack's wife Mary was also wary, inquiring if Shack owed him any money. All it took was for Bonney to say he was "an intimate friend" of William Fox to put the molls at ease. Shack's wife then went outside and made a cooing call to her husband who was hiding in the woods. Upon seeing Bonney, Shack began fulminating that he was an honest and hard-working man whom the people of Bowling Green were trying to ruin. He insisted he had bought the horse in good faith a few days earlier. After paying full value, Shack was dismayed to have the owner turn up the next day claiming the horse was stolen.

Just then, a rumble of thunder signaled the approach of a summer storm. Bonney hastened outside to bring his horses under shelter and asked Shack to help him. When they had gotten out of earshot of the women, Bonney whispered to Shack that these were the horses stolen by Fox, which he intended to spirit out of the country before their owners found them. All he needed was for Shack to find someone to testify that Bonney was the rightful owner. At the sight of the stolen horses, Shack dropped his guard, saying he could find "plenty of people in the neighborhood who will testify to anything," but that Fox had wanted all of the horses destroyed in a barn fire to eliminate the evidence against him. All except the race mare thought to be the fastest quarter horse in the country and worth more than $1,000.

By now, Shack was confiding wholeheartedly in Bonney, even recounting the story of how he and Fox came to be arrested. A few weeks earlier, Fox, Birch, and John and Hiram Long had come to the Widow Long's with four horses they had stolen from a farm in the Rock River Valley. Shack bought one of the horses. The mare Fox had planned to keep, leaving Hiram Long to negotiate the purchase of the remaining two. With old charges still against him, John Long decided not to linger and left with Birch on the afternoon of the third day. Fox had planned to head out in the morning but that evening a posse from Bowling Green rode in, arresting Shack and Fox and confiscating the horses. Fox had specifically instructed the men to stay off the main trails with the stolen horses until they crossed the Wabash River. But after traveling fifty miles, the men returned to the main trail, thereby allowing themselves to be tracked easily. Of the four, only Hiram Long had managed to avoid arrest. For two weeks now, he had been hiding out in the woods, too frightened to go home. Every two days, he moved to a different location, returning to the same spot each morning to receive provisions from Shack. Bonney suggested the next time Shack took food to Long to inquire as to Fox's whereabouts so that he could deliver his prized mare.

Bonney and Shack went back inside the cabin. As the supper hour was near, Mary told Shack to put more salt on a rotting piece of venison they had been eating for more than a week. Even though he had not eaten since breakfast, Bonney could not bring himself to touch the putrid fare. Instead, he sampled a few balls of cornmeal—aptly called *dodgers*—rolled in the Widow Long's grimy hands that had the consistency and taste of mortar.

Shortly after dinner, such as it was, three raffish-looking men entered whom Shack introduced as his cousins who were spending the night. Meeting so many people began to put Bonney on edge for fear of being exposed. In his pockets were the Rock Island County arrest warrants, letters of requisition from Governor Ford, and the handcuffs, any of which, if found, would have led to his immediate death. When bedtime came, Bonney took a place in the corner of the cabin, placing his firearms within close reach.

At dawn, the three strangers left and Widow Long reheated the previous night's vile meat. A few hours later, while sitting on the porch, Bonney heard the shrill cry of what sounded like a turkey issuing from the woods. It was young Hiram "whistling for his grub." Taking some food, Shack promptly went off in the direction of the sound. When he returned, he said that Hiram had approved of Bonney's plan and wished to speak with him but dared not come out into the open. Walking several yards into the woods, Bonney found the twenty-two-year old sitting nervously on a log. He was struck by the young outlaw's almost feminine beauty, consisting of long eyelashes, lustrous auburn hair, and delicate porcelain skin. Hiram said Fox was staying with his father in Wayne County and would pay dearly for Bonney to deliver the mare. With this revelation, Bonney politely took his leave, promising to return and share some of the counterfeit bills he would print in Cincinnati.

Back in Bowling Green, Bonney met with two of the owners of the stolen horses from Belleville who agreed to allow him to pose as their owner while he was in town. The race mare he left with Deputy Hickox to await the arrival of its owner.

Before departing, he had one more call to make: Fox's lawyer, a shrewd and unscrupulous man named Williamson. After Fox's arrest, Williamson had written to Tom Reynolds in St. Louis, asking him to send a famous horse jockey named Myers to come and claim the horses in order to spare the horses the gruesome fate Fox had in mind. Claiming to be a friend of Fox and the rightful owner of the horses, Bonney asked Williamson to get word to Fox that it was now safe to return and stand trial as there would be little repercussion. Williamson could not have been more delighted by the news, promising to convey it immediately to Fox.

By now, everyone seemed to have swallowed Bonney's elaborate deception hook, line, and sinker. Fox was happy to be getting his prized mare back, Williamson satisfied there would be no charges against his client, even townsfolk were pleased to see the rightful "owner" had recovered his horses. Once outside town, Bonney returned the horses to their owners and boarded a stagecoach for Indianapolis.

Among the passengers in the coach was the son of the late governor of Kentucky, John Adair. When they stopped for breakfast, Adair mentioned to Bonney he had heard that a man had just passed through in pursuit of Davenport's murderers and was closing in on them at that very moment. To Bonney's exasperation, Deputy Hickox had confided the news to Adair whose loose lips now not only threatened the investigation but Bonney's life as well. To silence Adair, Bonney tried to shame him for divulging secret information to a total stranger such as himself. Yet, Adair refused to see the harm, giving Bonney no choice but to disclose his true identity. Incredulous at first, Adair finally acknowledged his imprudence and promised to be more cautious in the future. Since the other passengers had overheard Adair, Bonney asked that they pledge themselves to secrecy, hoping he had nipped the entire matter in the bud.

In Indianapolis, Bonney met with Thomas B. Johnson, former US marshal of Iowa Territory. Confident he would be able to arrest Fox at his father's, Bonney asked Johnson to take custody of Fox to allow him to pursue the rest of the killers. Early the next morning, the two set out for Centerville, the seat of Wayne County, arriving in the evening. Wayne County sheriff David Gentry indicated John Fox, the father, lived in a cabin nine miles southwest of town and that a neighbor had reported having seen William there for the first time in nine years. Though coarse and illiterate, John was considered an industrious and successful farmer and was not suspected of any criminal activity whatever.

Though Gentry was itching to arrest Fox, Bonney persuaded him to wait for his signal before doing so as he first needed to glean information from him as to the location of both Birch and Long as well as the money Fox had stashed on the Des Moines River, a portion of which he believed was Davenport's. There was just one problem: Fox had seen Bonney at the Hodges trial and would recognize him on first sight.

Leaving Gentry at Centerville, Bonney started alone on horseback for Fox's house. When he arrived, John Fox said that William was not at home. After conversing briefly with the old man, Bonney left a note for William to the effect that he had met with his lawyer and supported his plan to summon Myers to claim the horses, which were now in his possession. The note went on to say that he was in a hurry to get to Cincinnati and would be taking the next stagecoach out of Centerville. He signed it "Thomas Brown." Bonney was hoping that the note would prompt Fox to hasten to Centerville before he departed.

Sure enough, at about ten o'clock that night, Fox pulled up to Bonney's tavern with a horse in tow. "Is there a gentleman stopping by with you by the name of Brown?" he asked the owner. Having already been instructed by Bonney, the owner replied that Brown had gone to the stage office for a coach to Cincinnati—thus to allow Bonney time to get to his room. He then went after Fox telling him that Brown was actually in his room and would meet him there.

Meanwhile, Bonney rushed upstairs to his room and threw himself on the bed pretending to be asleep. A few minutes later, the owner brought Fox to the room, dimly lit by a single candle. As Fox entered, Bonney yawned and slowly turned toward him. When he caught sight of Bonney, Fox became startled.

"This is not Mr. Brown!" he exclaimed.

"Not exactly," replied Bonney.

"Is it not Mr. Bonney?"

"That's it, when I am home. I am Brown when traveling," Bonney said, extending his hand, which the bewildered Fox took.

Explaining he was on his way to Cincinnati to print up some "rag currency," Bonney had but a brief moment to speak. He then related the same plan he had related to Williamson: that he had recovered Fox's horses and spoken to Reynolds and Williamson, and that Fox could return to Bowling Green and safely stand trial.

Swayed by the confidential nature of what he heard, Fox shed any suspicion of Bonney. Still, had not Bonney been involved in the arrest and trial of the Hodges? he asked.

"Certainly I was!" he declared in an effort to appear consistent. "They were charged with murder, which I oppose under all circumstances. There are ways enough for us boys to get money without killing men for it. I have no doubt you are as much opposed to murder as I am." Fox agreed wholeheartedly with Bonney, having no idea he was being sought for Davenport's murder.

Outside the tavern, Johnson and Gentry were waiting with a large posse for the signal from Bonney. But to give it now would prevent Bonney from obtaining information about Birch and Long. While Fox was saddling up his horse, Bonney slipped off to tell Johnson of an ingenious twist to the plan. Since Bonney was spending the night at Fox's, they should arrest Fox at his home the following morning. They should also arrest Bonney on a phony charge. With Bonney alone in jail with Fox, he would then be able to ferret out the location of Birch, Long and the money.

The next morning, while awaiting the posse's arrival, Bonney pretended to prepare for his departure to Cincinnati. But when the posse failed to show, he realized he needed to change plans once again. He remarked to Fox that, it being Sunday, there might not be a coach operating. Fox suggested in that case he wait another day. With so much time to pass and confident that he enjoyed Fox's full trust, Bonney decided not to wait until they were both in jail to query him.

As they sat idly in the hotel room, Fox began a rambling account of his exploits. Robbing houses was a far less risky way to make money than counterfeiting or horse stealing. The money was good and it was easy to get away as residents were invariably too frightened to resist or give chase. In Bellevue, Iowa, he had been caught with William Brown and had been subsequently "whipped nearly to death" and released. (Recall he had received the lightest punishment.) He boasted he had committed the robbery for which Bliss and Dewey were convicted, the Haskel robbery, the attempted robbery of Beach in Nauvoo, the robbery of the Troy Grove peddler, and the Frink stagecoach robbery in which they failed to get any gold.

Seizing the opportunity, Bonney pointedly asked why, given that Long and Birch were with him in St. Louis, were they were not arrested with him? The two, it turned out, had left the Widow Long's for Ohio just a few hours before the posse arrived to meet with Norton Royce (the counterfeiter whom Governor Ford had admonished from the bench) somewhere along the Ohio River. Once they hooked up, they planned to send a letter to Fox telling him where to rendezvous. The letter would arrive at the home of Jesse Ray who lived in Lawrence County in southern Indiana. Ray had got up a sight for Fox—a neighbor's home containing about $800. Ray had learned about the money when he went to his neighbor's rotting log cabin to repay a loan. Taking the money, the old man then hid it under his bed. Every Sunday, Ray and his wife attended church, during which time Fox planned to rob the house before heading to Ray's to share the loot and pick up the letter from Birch.

While Fox talked, Bonney was frantically jotting down in his notebook all the names and locations of the bandits. For a brief moment, he was nearly exposed when the word "Reward" in the notebook caught Fox's eye.

"What is that, 'Reward'?" Fox asked.

"Only a reward offered for some runaway negroes," Bonney replied nonchalantly. In fact, the reward in question was that offered for the capture of Davenport's murderers.

Satisfied with Bonney's answer, Fox continued to recount, in minute detail, his long litany of crimes. By sundown, there was still no sign of the posse and the two retired for the night.

In the morning, Fox offered to accompany Bonney to the stagecoach house in Centerville. Upon arrival, Bonney took a room at the hotel; Fox had his horse taken to the stable while he went off to visit a friend down the street. Looking down from the window of his room, Bonney was surprised to see Johnson and Gentry in the street below poised to arrest Fox. Just how they knew Fox would accompany Bonney to Centerville was unclear though they likely had been watching them all along. After Bonney discussed the modalities of the arrest with the sheriff, it was decided that when the moment was right, Bonney would signal from his room for them to come up and arrest Fox on charges of stealing the race mare. To maintain his cover so he could arrest Birch and Long, Bonney would also be arrested for counterfeiting.

When Fox returned to Bonney's room, he was sitting near the window and gave the signal. There was a knock at the door. When Bonney opened it, Johnson rushed in with several men ordering them to arrest and search Fox and Bonney. Assuming they were dealing with two of Davenport's killers, the posse proceeded to rough them up, including Bonney, whose true identity was unknown to them. When word got out in the circuit court across the street of the arrest of "two blacklegs," a gaggle of lawyers suddenly appeared at the door each offering to represent the prisoners for a fee. All the while Fox stood there pale and motionless, too stunned to utter a word. Sheriff Tom Johnson placed iron manacles on him and whisked him off to Indianapolis. After his long rampage of stealing and killing across the northwest frontier, William Fox had been nabbed at last.

On the morning of September 10, Bonney's stagecoach pulled into Columbus, Ohio. A check of all the hotel registers turned up nothing. He then walked down High Street to the Union Livery Stable and hired a carriage to take him to Berkshire in Delaware County, John Driscoll's old hunting ground. There was only one tavern in Berkshire owned by a man named Van Sickle. Initially leery of Bonney, Van Sickle said that Royce had stayed at the hotel for several weeks before departing definitively for Illinois. Long and Birch had gone to western New York, a claim so improbable it indicated that Van Sickle was covering for them. Using a more oblique approach, Bonney said he had a "fine mare" in Indiana on which he had wagered $500 in a race set to take place on October 1. To ride her he needed John Long, who had ridden the mare in several previous races. Having heard the outlaws speak glowingly of the mare, Van Sickle began to lower his guard, saying Long and Birch were traveling under the aliases *Henderson* and *Bleecher* and might still be at Dresden on the Ohio Canal about sixty miles east. Conspiratorially displaying his phony bills, Bonney said he was on his way to Cincinnati to have them printed up. At the sight of the bills, Van Sickle now completely dropped his guard, saying Royce was not in Illinois at all but in nearby Marion County and was expected to arrive that very evening.

Sure enough, Royce rode in at dusk. Introducing himself as a friend of Fox, Bonney told Royce he had possession of his horses. When the time was appropriate, he displayed the banknotes, saying he was looking for Long and Birch to help move some of his bogus green when he returned from Cincinnati. Alas, Royce lamented, had he known their whereabouts he could have made some serious money on two good sights. Royce's aunt had recently sold her home for $2,200 in gold but had since left the state. Another missed opportunity was a merchant who had passed through Berkshire with $1,800 in a trunk. Nonetheless, a promising sight still remained they could hit as soon as the pair turned up. An old Jersey farmer named, he thought, Blackman or Black, lived on a farm with his family in a remote part of Marion County. Ten days earlier, Long and Birch had gone to Blackman's house with the intent of robbing him but unexpectedly encountered a religious revival camp nearby. Deeming it too risky to proceed with the robbery, Long nonetheless approached Blackman's house asking to spend the night. As the house was full of preachers, Blackman had turned him away, though not before Long had scoped out the cabin's interior. The three had subsequently arranged to meet Saturday at midnight and rob Blackman the following night. After the robbery, they planned to ride all night, hide the next day, and ride again until they were safely out of the "zone of suspicion." When Bonney offered to participate in the robbery, Royce declined, saying it was an easy job and he already had enough men.

Without knowing the location of Blackman's house, Bonney would be unable to arrest them there and suggested they all reconnect when he returned from Cincinnati. So keen was Royce to obtain Bonney's bank notes, he offered to meet him at a place of his choosing. Bonney had just one problem: he could not forget how Miller, Leisi, and Davenport had all been murdered when the robbery went bad. If a similar scenario played out at Blackman's, it would certainly lead to the death of one or more of the family. He had to find a way to short-circuit the robbery without jeopardizing his pursuit of Long and Birch. All night he tossed and turned over his dilemma, unable to sleep. By morning, he had come up with a solution.

To deter Royce from going to Blackman's, Bonney offered him a chance to catch a bigger fish: a sight he had raised that would yield a whopping $80,000: The South Bend Bank of Indiana. To break in one had only to tunnel beneath the floor to the vault, making the level of risk no greater than robbing Blackman but the payoff much higher. All he needed was five men and since Fox had already signed on, Royce, Birch, and Long would neatly round out the number. Royce immediately took the bait, adding that most sights usually yielded far too little for the risk and effort. Bonney proposed that Royce round up Long and Birch while he would pick up Fox after his trip to Cincinnati. They would all meet up next Saturday in Adrian, Michigan, on the Indiana border before proceeding to South Bend. As the two parted ways, Bonney exclaimed, "Tell the boys Tom Brown is on hand!"

In the morning, Bonney boarded a stagecoach to the Columbus courthouse where he presented the letters of requisition from Governor Ford and obtained arrest warrants for Long and Birch. Concerned that Long and Birch might still attempt to rob Blackman—with or without Royce—Bonney went to the tax office where he got Blackman's address. He also confirmed that a religious camp revival had recently taken place in the northwest part of Knox County.

After informing Sheriff Thrift of the planned robbery of Blackman, the two rode north to intercept Long and Birch should they be heading to Blackman's. They rode sixty miles through Mount Vernon, Frederick, Middlebury, and Mt. Gilead, stopping at hotels, livery stables, and JPs. Finding not a trace of the outlaws, they then searched for Blackman's cabin to warn him of a possible robbery attempt but with no luck. Around and around they rode in search of Blackman or the robbers. After three days of fruitless searching, Bonney concluded the two outlaws were not in the area.

Concerned that the thieves might be suspicious when Bonney showed up in Adrian without Fox, the next day he drafted the following handbill:

*On, or about the 10th day of September, a man by the name of William Fox was arrested near Bowling Green, having in his possession three stolen horses. He gave bail for his at the appearance at the next term of court in the sum of eight hundred dollars, and left the country.*

*A few days afterwards a man calling his name Jack Brown, made his appearance, proved a claim upon the horses, and took them away. In a few days the real owners of the horses appeared, but nothing could be heard either of them or of Jack Brown, who is supposed has gone to Cincinnati. The public would do well to be on the lookout, as a gang of horse thieves are (sic) in our midst. – Wabash Enquirer.*[2]

Bonney had the article printed on a piece of paper, which had writing on the back to make it look as if it had been cut from a newspaper.

Before setting out for Adrian, he sent a letter to Sheriff Johnson, instructing him to proceed with Fox to Springfield. Little did Bonney know that the previous day, Fox had bribed Sheriff Johnson and was once again on the loose. As it turned out, Johnson had never placed Fox in jail but confined him in an upper room of Browning's Hotel with a simple pair of light handcuffs for restraints.

On September 17, Bonney and Thrift took a stagecoach north in the direction of Adrian hoping to intercept Long and Birch. Knowing the boys liked to bet on the horses, they stopped at a racetrack in the hamlet of Little Sandusky on Lake Erie. Sure enough, they spotted Birch in the crowd wearing Davenport's gold watch and chain. Assuming he was on his way to join up with Royce and Long, they made no attempt to arrest him.

About fifteen miles outside Sandusky, Bonney spotted Royce walking along the trail, a portmanteau draped over his shoulder. Halting the coach, Bonney beckoned Royce aboard. They rode in stone silence the entire way. When the coach stopped for a rest at Howard's Hotel, a deeply suspicious Royce pulled Bonney aside to ask who Thrift was and why Fox was not with him. Calmly, Bonney replied he did not know Thrift and would explain Fox's absence when they reached Perrysburg near the state line. Despite his caution, Royce apparently trusted him enough to say that Long and Birch would be meeting him at the American Hotel there.

When they arrived in Perrysburg, Bonney pulled Royce aside to explain that after leaving Berkshire he had gone to Cincinnati where in a reading room he had chanced to see a newspaper article indicating authorities were searching for a horse thief named Jack Brown. Handing his fabricated news article to Royce, Bonney said that with the law hot on his heels, it would have been too dangerous to return to Indiana to fetch Fox. As it was, he had hurriedly printed the bills before skedaddling out of town.

The elaborate story worked. Royce's suspicions completely dissolved and he confided that Long and Birch had agreed to delay the robbery of the old Jersey farmer whose name he now recalled was not Blackman but *Wilbourne*. When the boys heard they would be robbing a bank with their old cohort Tom Brown, they were delighted, saying they hadn't seen since him since he fled Nauvoo when the Hodges were arrested.

Bonney then repaired to his room to await the arrival of Long and Birch. At 11:00 p.m., he was about to retire when a messenger arrived from Little Sandusky with news that they had been arrested. At five o'clock on the day Bonney had left Sandusky, a coach from the southern line had arrived containing two passengers fitting the description of Long and Birch. When Sandusky sheriff Dickerson checked the manifest, he found the names *Henderson* and *Bleecher*. He immediately raised a posse and traced them to the Railroad House where Birch was at the bar drinking. When Birch saw the posse enter, he frantically ripped the gold watch from his side and threw it over the bar. A body search of him produced eight dollars, some silver, a box of percussion caps and bullets, and the bowie knife he had waved in the face of Mrs. Mulford. Long was arrested in his room. In his possession was found Miller's silver watch and the pistol used to shoot Davenport. The two were taken to the courthouse and placed in separate rooms. Neither Birch nor Long was informed as to the reason for their arrest and neither was cooperative, refusing to answer any questions.

When Bonney arrived in Sandusky to take custody of them, he informed them they had been arrested on charges of murdering Davenport. At this

Long became belligerent, denying so much as ever hearing of Davenport or Rock Island. He then tried to bribe Bonney into allowing him to escape. When that failed, he warned Bonney that if he tried to bring him back to Rock Island to stand trial, his many friends along the way would surely kill him before he arrived.

Meanwhile, when Sheriff Thrift heard the news of the arrest of Long and Birch, he hastened to the American Hotel in Perrysville and arrested Royce. A search of Royce produced a pistol and a $10 counterfeit bill, astonishingly little for a man who had once been a major counterfeiter. Even though it was not enough to keep him in custody, they planned to hold him long enough for Bonney to get to Rock Island and hunt down the remaining suspects in the Davenport case.

On the morning of September 20, Bonney and Thrift set out for Detroit with a morose Long and Birch in iron manacles. After overnighting, they boarded a train to St. Joseph, Michigan. As they waited for the train to embark, the jailor took Bonney aside to warn him that overnight he had heard Long telling one of his partners that at the earliest opportunity he and Birch planned to seize their pistols and kill them. If that failed, he was confident they had plenty of friends between Chicago and Rock Island who would prevent them from ever reaching their destination.

As the train rumbled toward Detroit, Long waited for an opportunity to overtake Bonney. With Bonney on his guard, Long turned to threatening him in the hope of getting released. After a time, he finally sank back, sullen and quiet, in his seat. Later, Birch offered to bribe Bonney $10,000 to release him.

At dusk, the train pulled into Marshall where they hired a stagecoach to St. Joseph on Lake Michigan. From there, they boarded the steamer *Champion* for Chicago. As the steamer drifted toward the Windy City, Birch, complaining of seasickness, began to hector Thrift to go on deck. Since Birch was manacled and could not flee except by jumping overboard, Thrift saw no harm and finally relented. Once on his own, Birch broke into the captain's office and stole Bonney's portmanteau. Thinking it contained all the evidence, he hurled it overboard into the lake. Among the items in the coat were Miller's silver watch and Birch's bowie knife.

Fortunately, the key piece of evidence, Davenport's watch, was still in Bonney's possession.

In Chicago, the prisoners were temporarily placed in jail. A journalist from the *Chicago Democrat* came to interview the prisoners, telling them of the arrest of Bridge, Oliver, and McDowell and of West's testimony at their trial. Hearing this, Birch became wildly distraught, fearing that if he were sent to Rock Island he would certainly be lynched, not for the murder of Davenport—which he continued to deny—but for his many other crimes. For his part, Long remained perfectly calm, insisting he had nothing to fear because he was innocent.

Bonney now faced the toughest part of his return journey with the prisoners: 180 miles across the prairie wilderness where Long's friends could be lying in wait. Adding to his fears, the day the *Champion* docked in Chicago, a stagecoach had departed south carrying passengers who had been on the steamship and would certainly be spreading the news of the capture of Davenport's killers. To delay the news, Bonney had orders rushed by mail coach to detain the stagecoach at Dixon until he had gotten past the town. As a precaution, Bonney put extra irons on the prisoners and requested Chicago deputy sheriff Wisencraft to accompany him in the Frink and Walker stagecoach.

In Naperville, they stopped to speak with Judge Thomas who advised him to stay off the main trails, even if it meant going out of his way to get to Dixon. Not wishing to linger in the wilderness any longer than necessary, Bonney disregarded the advice. If attacked by outlaws, he and the Sheriff had resolved to fight their way through, failing which, they would put the prisoners to death rather than allow them to escape.

At midnight, they reached Little Rock sixty miles east of Dixon. Complaining of fatigue, the drivers wanted to halt until morning, but Bonney ordered them to push on. They were now entering the heart of banditti country, expecting any moment to see outlaws leaping out of the prairie tallgrass to attack them. A few miles south of Little Rock two men on horseback came out of the wilderness and rode up alongside the coach. Inside, Bonney's carriage was lit by a lantern and the curtains were closed. Unable to see inside, for a moment they eerily fell back before advancing on the coach again. The two men followed the coach until dawn when they disappeared.

At 9 a.m., they reached Dixon where the mail coach was waiting to accompany them to Rock Island. At midnight on the twenty-sixth, they finally reached Rock Island where they remanded the prisoners to the custody of Rock Island County sheriff Lemuel Andrews. Worn out from the exhaustive manhunt, Bonney took a much-needed rest on Rock Island, leaving the capture of the men still at large to law enforcement. For his efforts, the State of Illinois later reimbursed Bonney $135 in expenses, $200 for the capture of Long, and $100 for Birch.

Within days of Bonney's arrival, Sheriff Joe Johnson arrested Aaron Long at Sand Prairie outside Galena. Aaron was baling hay at his father's farm when the sheriff arrived. He denied any involvement in the Davenport murder, but a search of his house turned up bloodstained trousers hidden at the bottom of a box. At the same time, John Baxter was arrested at the house of his brother-in-law, Berry Haney, in Madison, Wisconsin. Baxter made a full confession to the arresting officers, not only of his involvement in the Davenport murder but in the robbery of the Knox and Drury office on Rock Island the previous summer.

Two weeks later, Davenport's gun and pistol that Fox had buried were found on Grant Redden's property. As luck would have it, a Dr. D.H. Rousseau of Fort Madison had an extensive practice in Devil's Creek bottom near Redden's. In the border of a pond that had partly dried, the son of one of his patients had found a pistol and shot gun which he took to the doctor, who, having read a of description of them, suspected they were the weapons used in the murder of Colonel Davenport.[3]

As a posse of irate citizens prepared to arrest Redden, Sheriff Estes tried to persuade them to wait, concerned it would undermine the investigation. Brushing Estes aside, the posse rode to Redden's house, seized the old man, his son William, and Granville Young and placed them in the Fort Madison jail. Soon after, Young was transferred to Rock Island to stand trial for the Davenport murder.

On September 28, Sheriff Millard arrested John Long in Jo Daviess County, Illinois. In Long's possession were letters from his brother and other members of the gang, which left no doubt as to his connection with them in several other robberies.

Thus ended what had been an extraordinary manhunt, for it had begun with frustratingly few clues and ranged across several states, yet ended in the capture of all but one of the killers in less than three months of Davenport's murder.

# CHAPTER 11

# Confessions and Trials

*Public hanging as a legal sanction was introduced as a "conspicuous symbol of indignity intended to deter and shame; hanging often produced "a slow and agonizing death," the embarrassing manifestation of which—twitching, kicking, choking, loss of bowel and bladder control—were readily visible to sizeable gatherings. All execution techniques spawn macabre death scenes, but the spectacle of a dangling corpse is the most degrading of all.*

—RICHARD STACK, *Dead Wrong*

Robert Birch was not in Rock County jail very long when he agreed to testify against his confederates in exchange for a reduced sentence. In his first confession, Birch tried to conceal his involvement in the Davenport affair by substituting the name of Tom Brown for himself. After contradictions began to appear in his story, he eventually made a full confession of the details of the murder and their flight to Widow Long's. One of Birch's revelations was the precise location of the money Fox had secreted in the Des Moines bluffs. When Bonney, Sheriff Estes, a heavily manacled Birch, and several Lee County residents went in search of it, they found everything exactly as Birch had described—the woman who had sold Fox the beeswax, and the ravine where they halted—all except the money, which had already been carried off.

When he heard Birch was in the Rock County jail, Mr. Mulford came to identify him as the man who had robbed him. Recalling Mulford's imperturbability during the robbery, Birch remarked that in his long career of crime Mulford was the only man whom he had been unable to intimidate. In a desperate bid for clemency, Birch said that if he lived, he would return his money.

As the date of Birch's trial neared, he became increasingly anxious. Convinced he would get the death penalty, he began to make more disclosures. The first meeting to plan the Davenport robbery was held in Joseph Smith's old council chamber in Nauvoo. In addition to Birch, those in attendance were William Fox, John and Aaron Long, Return Jackson Redden, Amos Hodges, O.P. Rockwell, John Ray, and William Louther.[1] All along, Birch said, he had been against robbing Davenport for, contrary to the wild assertions of Fox and Baxter, he believed there was very little money in the house. Nor did they abuse the old man as alleged but had thrown water on his face in order to keep him alive and reveal where the money was hidden. During the struggle, John Long had killed Davenport but his gun had gone off accidentally. As they were fleeing the scene of the crime, Long and Fox wanted to finish off the old man but Birch, of course, opposed it. He believed they could find Fox in Niles or Adrian, Michigan, at the house of Tom Brown who had participated with the Hodges and Artemus Johnson in the murder of Miller and Leisi. He also said that Return Redden had murdered Ervine Hodges to keep him from talking.[2] To top it off, Birch offered to disclose all he knew about the criminals operating in the region.

Since some of Birch's claims were consistent with the known facts of the various cases, the Rock Island Court subsequently issued a warrant for the arrest of Return Jackson Redden for the murder of Ervine Hodges. At that moment, however, Hancock County was being rocked by violence between Gentiles and Mormons. Gentiles were torching Mormon homes in the countryside and Mormons were retaliating with lethal force. In such a volatile environment, authorities concluded that the only way Redden could be taken was by stealth. Lyman E. Johnson, an excommunicated Mormon who had served as Redden's lawyer and was related to him, was asked to coax Redden to a Nauvoo landing where he could be arrested. On October 25, 1845, Redden was waiting at Nauvoo's upper stone house wharf to meet with Johnson to discuss arrangements for bailing his father and brother out of jail. As he waited, Sheriff Kimball, armed with an arrest warrant, attempted to take him into custody. When Redden resisted, the passengers and crew of a nearby steamer, the *Sarah Ann*, rushed to Kimball's aid. An even larger number of Mormons who had had seen the struggle came to Redden's assistance brandishing canes, whips, and bricks. As the two sides clashed, Kimball was injured and Johnson was struck in the face with a brickbat.[3] When the dust finally settled, Redden had escaped.

Three days later, authorities met with Brigham Young for assistance in arresting Redden. Hoping to divert them, Young said Redden had fled to Michigan. But that same week in the *Sangamo Journal*, William Smith, who had been excommunicated from the church, charged that Redden was at large in Nauvoo and being protected by Young.[*]

To return to Davenport's killers, the fall term of the Rock Island circuit court opened on October 6, 1845, with Judge Brown presiding and T.J. Turner as state attorney. The same day, the grand jury handed down indictments against John Baxter, William Fox, John and Aaron Long, Robert Birch, and Granville Young for the murder of George Davenport. Grant and William Redden were charged as accessories before the fact. Being without counsel, the accused were assigned defense counsel by the state.

Four days later, Young, Baxter, and the Longs were brought into court. As their names were read in the indictment, each pleaded "not guilty." The Longs and Young then requested a change of venue, but the court denied it on the grounds that sufficient notice had not been given the state's attorney. The court then proceeded to empanel a jury for the trial of the Longs and Young, which took three days.

The prosecution's first witness was Patrick Gregg, one of the three doctors called to the scene shortly after the assault on Davenport. In minute detail, Dr. Gregg gave a description of the attack as Davenport had related to him just before he died. He then described the gruesome scene he found upon arrival:

> *The blood was everywhere. The house looked like a butcher's shamble—blood in the sitting room, in the hall, and along the stairs, and in the closet by the safe was a pool of blood, and in the room below there was the same.*[4]

---

*Return Redden was never apprehended for the murder of Ervine Hodges. In 1848, he followed the Mormon exodus to Utah where he continued to pass counterfeit money and steal horses. In 1877, he was indicted for the murder of two cattle rustlers.

Gregg also testified that while Davenport's body was badly bruised, the gunshot wound had killed him. Ben Cole, the first on the scene, also testified to the carnage he found when he entered the house.

In a last ditch effort to save his life, Birch became one of the principal witnesses against Young and the Longs. During his testimony, he said that John Long had told him that he and his brother Aaron, Fox, and a man known as Lee or Little Brown had robbed Davenport. Davenport's son George then testified that the man who shot him was small and slim and wore a cloth cap—a close description of Fox. He described the guns stolen from the house, which he later identified as those found at Grant Redden's. He also identified the gold watch and chain Birch had thrown over the bar as his father's.

At one point in the proceedings, John Long was brought before the jury and his boots and heels were examined. Dr. Gregg said that he had measured small bloody tracks at the house, which appeared to be the same size as Long's boots. Several Rock Island merchants testified to having seen the Longs purchasing liquor and other items the day of the crime.

Grant Redden confirmed the Longs had stayed with him the night of July 6 or July 8—he could not remember exactly which—though they never mentioned a word about Davenport.

The jailor testified that he heard the prisoners saying they would kill Bonney as soon as they could break out. Several more witnesses testified after which the prosecution rested its case. On Friday, the evidence was closed, closing arguments were made, and the jury retired. The jury was not gone more than two hours when they returned with a verdict of guilty of murder in the first degree against all three.

In the morning, the three condemned men appeared before Judge Brown for sentencing. After an impassioned but unsuccessful plea for clemency by the defense, Brown sentenced the three to be hanged on October 29 between 10 a.m. and 4 p.m. Upon hearing his sentence, John Long clownishly bowed and thanked the judge.

While Young and the Longs sat on death row, a certain Silas Haight from Keokuk, Iowa, visited them, promising to save them from hanging if they but follow his instructions. An agent in the counterfeiting division of the treasury department, Haight had known ties to the banditti and was reputed to take payoffs from counterfeiters to look the other way. In view of their hopeless situation, the condemned men instantly agreed to Haight's proposition. Haight went directly to Fort Madison where, with the testimony of several of the old Nauvoo gang, got four indictments against Bonney, three for counterfeiting and one for the murders of Miller and Leisi. Armed with the indictments, Haight obtained a letter of requisition from the governor of Iowa ordering Governor Ford to arrest Bonney on the day of the execution of Young and the Longs. Haight then set about seeking a stay of execution for the condemned to get a new trial or at least buy them enough time to engineer an escape.

Governor Ford had no intention of obeying the requisition, declaring he would never surrender Bonney to the Iowa authorities on the basis of testimony provided by the "so-called witnesses." In a long letter of reply to Iowa's governor, Ford laid out the facts of the Davenport case, demanding the governor recall the requisition.

Meanwhile, upon hearing of the requisition, Bonney turned himself in to Sheriff Estes at Fort Madison. Just before he left, he stopped by the Rock Island County jail and told the prisoners he would not be present on the day of their execution. Knowing fully well the case against Bonney had been fabricated, Estes refused to arrest Bonney, telling him to go wherever he pleased.

As it turned out, Haight's chief witness against Bonney was Bill Hickman, one of the last Mormons to leave Nauvoo now wanted for several larcenies in Lee County.[5] Hickman had also helped put up money for the lawyers for the Hodges' defense. Somehow, to the complete ignorance of the officers of the court, he had appeared before the grand jury to produce the Bonney indictment. When Estes learned it was Hickman who had provided the testimony against Bonney, he set out to arrest him.[†]

By this time, the day of execution had arrived. People had started to gather the night before to witness the hanging and by morning the streets were thronged, prompting the sheriff to issue patrols. For the site of the

---

†Bill Hickman was never brought to justice for the many crimes he was alleged to have committed, including murder. After serving in the Utah legislature, he died in Wyoming in 1883, leaving behind thirty-six children he had fathered with ten wives.

gallows, a residential section of Rock Island was chosen, a decision later denounced by some as inappropriate. At about one o'clock, the prisoners were marched from the jail around the courthouse to the scaffold. Out of fear the banditti would attempt a last minute rescue, 130 armed guards surrounded the prisoners. John Long was nattily attired in a dress coat and pantaloons, black cravat, and black hat, a sign he was expecting to be rescued. In the lead wagon, a band played a funeral dirge written by a local composer who was conducting the band. After they ascended the twelve-foot high scaffold, the sheriff proceeded to read the sentence:

> *That upon that day they be taken from the jail and hanged by the neck until dead; that the body of John Long be then delivered into the hands of Dr. Gregg, of Rock Island for dissection; that of Aaron Long to Dr. Egbert S. Barrows, of Davenport; and that of Granville Young to Dr. Reuben Knox of St. Louis.*[6]

The arms of the criminals were then untied. Each was then permitted to make a final statement as Reverend F.A. Haney introduced the men to the assembled crowd. Speaking first in a tremulous voice, Aaron Long had only to say he was innocent as he had been outside the entire time of the robbery. Granville Young briefly appealed to his friends to save him.

John Long then gave a rambling speech that lasted nearly an hour. He acknowledged his own guilt while insisting on the innocence of his brother and Granville Young. The true murderers of Colonel Davenport, he declared, were Robert Birch, William Fox, Theodore Brown, and himself, and if death was meted out to any other person for that murder it would be unjust. Fox, he said, had shot the colonel entirely by accident. He himself had brought up the pitcher of water but for the wounded man to drink. He then launched on a long tirade against Bonney, accusing him of many crimes, including being accessory to the murders of Miller and Leisi for which the Hodges were wrongfully executed. Shall Bonney be allowed to escape and a boy like Granville Young be punished? he asked.

Long described how he attempted to live above the station in life into which he was born. Being too proud to work, he took to robbing and

Edward Bonney's Depiction of the Execution of Young and the Long Brothers
*Source: Courtesy of the Abraham Lincoln Presidential Library and Museum*

counterfeiting for a living, joining a gang of counterfeiters under William Bridge (now in irons in the Ohio penitentiary) in 1840. He claimed the robbery for which he was about to be executed was the first robbery he ever committed that was attended by violence of any kind. Normally, his victim was as safe with his pistol to his breast as if guarded by a justice of the peace himself. Although arrested many times for robbery, he always managed to escape. Lynch law, he argued, actually made robbers and murderers of honest men and that it was owing to the frequency that men took the law into their own hands and administered punishment upon innocent men that so many murders abounded throughout the West. Fox, for example, had always been an honest man until unjustly punished with a band of horse thieves in Bellevue, Iowa, in 1840. "Will not those persons who are advocates of this summary method of administering justice take into serious consideration the reflections of this malefactor?" he pleaded.[7]

While he waited on death row, Long said he had reflected on his life from his infancy to the present time and had concluded that the period of his life during which he was most happy was when he led an honest life. Veering wildly, his philippic once again turned to Bonney whom he accused as being a gang chief who must be arrested. He then cried out to his confederates to come to his rescue and to kill Bonney.

Long's long tirade had likely been an attempt to stall the proceedings long enough to be rescued. But no outlaws had appeared and now all hope was lost, and Long knew it. As a final request, Long asked his friends present to take his body and that of his brother to his parents so that they might look upon the mortal remains of their only children. During his entire harangue, Aaron and Young stood silent and motionless, too terrified to speak.

At the request of the prisoners, Dr. Gatchell offered up a prayer to the "Throne of Grace," after which Psalm 139 was read. The arms of the condemned men were untied and they were permitted to pass around the scaffold shaking the hand of each person present. Their arms were then bound behind their backs, the ropes adjusted around their necks, and caps drawn tightly over their faces. As the cap was being drawn over John Long, he was gazing into the distance, still hoping for a last minute rescue. At 3:30 p.m., with a single stroke from the Sheriff's axe, the drop opened. John Long's body dropped motionless; Young twisted and struggled spasmodically for a few minutes before he died.

But the rope attached to Aaron's neck had snapped and he fell with a thump on the boards beneath the gallows.[8] Shaken and disoriented, he was led back to the scaffold. As the rope was being refastened around his neck, he insisted he was innocent and pleaded that his life be spared. A few onlookers cried out, "Let him go!" Others countered, "Let the law be fulfilled!" "Murder!" "Make haste!" One of the witnesses, a priest, admonished, "[Y]ou will soon be joining your brothers."

Amid the clamor, someone circulated a rumor that a rescue of Aaron was in progress and they were all in danger of being attacked. Seized with panic, men, women, and children suddenly went flying in all directions.

When calm was finally restored, they found that no outlaws had appeared and no one had been hurt except the breaking into pieces of one wagon by the rushing crowd. Picking up their hats, shawls, chairs, they returned to the perimeter of the scaffold. The plank on which he stood was knocked from under him and his last cries were hushed in the spasmodic efforts of a dying man.

But their punishment did not stop there. In a ghoulish sequel, all three bodies of the hanged men were donated to Dr. Gregg for dissection and study. Gregg later buried Aaron Long. He traded Granville Young to another doctor for a barrel of rum. The skeleton of John Long he kept on display in the hospital steward's office at the Rock Island Arsenal. When Gregg died, his widow gave Long's skeleton to Dr. Charles Kalke of Chicago, who in turn passed it back to the Arsenal in 1940. John Long's skeleton remained on display at the Rock Island County Courthouse until it was transferred to the Hauberg Museum at Black Hawk State Park in Rock Island. On September 14, 1978, John was buried in Dickson Pioneer Cemetery on Rock Island. As one historian put it, finally "retiring from his unexpectedly active death." [9]

Four others remained to be tried for Davenport's murder: John Baxter, Robert Birch, and William and Grant Redden, the latter two charged as accessories before and after the fact.

Like Birch, a portion of Baxter's confession had been calculated to minimize his role in the crime. During his testimony, he claimed to have met with the Longs, Birch, and Fox in late June while they were eating dinner at Bald's Bluff with their pistols and knives laid out on the table. John Long had wanted to rob Davenport that same night but Baxter urged them to wait until July 4 when the whole family would be out of the house and they would not have to hurt anyone. On the morning of the fourth, Baxter had spoken with Bailey Davenport who confirmed that the entire family would be attending the public dinner on the Island. He then went into the woods where the boys were hiding to give them the green light. Baxter said he never wanted the old man murdered and offered to turn state's evidence, promising to live an honest life if given a second chance.

Despite having been merely an accessory, the jury found Baxter guilty of murder and sentenced him to hang on November 18.[10] While he was awaiting sentencing, his lawyers submitted a writ of error on an unknown technicality to the state supreme court, which reversed the judgment and ordered a new trial.

Meanwhile, the Reddens' trial came up. On a Wednesday afternoon, after the pleading of the lawyers and charge of the judge, the jury retired to weigh the evidence and render a verdict. Of the twelve jurors, ten were in favor of conviction, the other two voted against. The following day, one of them yielded to the majority. The jury was unable to change the lone holdout's mind, resulting in a hung jury. A new trial was schedule for the following May.

In February 1846, Baxter and Birch were retried. The first to be called was Birch, whose lawyer moved for continuance on the grounds that the summons for trial was wholly unexpected and that he was not prepared with witnesses and so forth. The judge approved the motion and Birch was returned to jail. The court then proceeded with the trial of Baxter.

Baxter's lawyer, Mr. Wells of Galena, requested a change of venue to Warren County where the case finally came up for trial in November of 1846, Judge Norman H. Purple presiding. In court, Wells moved that the irons of the prisoner be taken off but Judge Purple rejected the motion. Wells then protested the shortness of time that had elapsed since the court had ordered an extra term for the trial of the accused prisoner, stating that at least twenty days should have elapsed, whereas only eight days had passed between the time of ordering and convening of the extra term. Considerable discussion followed, but it was finally overruled and the court proceeded to empanel the jurors. Little difficulty was experienced in obtaining a panel, and by the middle of the afternoon, the court began hearing the evidence. The principal witness on behalf of the prosecution was a man by the name of Johnson to whom Baxter had made a free confession of his participation in the crime. By Friday evening, the examination of witnesses was closed, counsel on both sides made their closing arguments, and the jury retired. After two days of deliberation, the jury found Baxter guilty of murder. In pronouncing the sentence, Purple launched on a long-winded chastisement of Baxter for his role in the murder, the peroration of which was

> *The sentence of the law and the sentence of the court is that you be taken from this place to the jail of the county of Warren, from thence to the place of execution, and that on Wednesday, the ninth day of December next, between the hours of one and four o'clock p.m. of said day, you be there hanged by the neck until you are dead, and may God Almighty save your soul.*[11]

After two appeals, John Baxter managed to get his death sentence commuted to life in prison.

A week after Baxter's trial came that of Birch. Birch filed for a continuance until June 1847 and another continuance after that. After several delays, he took a change of venue to Knoxville County where he escaped on March 22, 1847.[‡]

After two continuances, the Reddens' trial came up in May 1846. Grant pleaded not guilty as an accessory to murder and was acquitted. After his release, old man Redden rode the Mormon Trail to Salt Lake City, if not to find redemption then a fresh start. William pleaded guilty and received one year in the state penitentiary, three weeks of which was in solitary confinement and the rest in hard labor. With end of the Redden trials, the spring term of the circuit court in the Illinois counties came to a close.

A final bizarre twist in the saga of Davenport's murder was the trial of Edward Bonney himself. At the time, only one grand jury was in session in the District of Illinois in Springfield. A member of the Nauvoo gang named A.B. Williams had charged Bonney with counterfeiting. In this, the gang was not shooting blind, for while he lived in Nauvoo,

---

[‡]Birch disappeared into the frontier, resurfacing a decade later as an associate of Jacob Snively, founder of Gila City in the Arizona Territory. He went on to become the city's first postmaster in 1858. Two years later, he followed Snively to New Mexico where the two discovered gold on Bear Creek. A mining camp soon sprang up around the claim named Birchville in his honor. When the Confederate Army invaded New Mexico at the start of the Civil War, Birch volunteered for the Arizona Rangers. He died shortly after the end of the war, never having faced justice for his myriad crimes. See Dan L. Thrapp, *Encyclopedia of Frontier Biography: In Three Volumes*, Vol 1, pp. 114–115.

Bonney had acquired a minor reputation as a passer of the long green. He had once stood trial in Indiana for counterfeiting but was acquitted. Bonney first heard the news from Judge T.J. Turner while passing through Rushville on his way south, still in search of Willian Fox. Aware of the critical role Bonney had played in the arrest of Davenport's killers, Turner warned him not to go to Springfield where a warrant for his arrest was outstanding. To make matters worse, Silas Haight had succeeded in turning public opinion against him as well, persuading many Rock Island residents that the Longs and Young were innocent men who had been wrongly executed.

Confident the spurious charges would not stick, Bonney went straight to Springfield where he met with Governor Ford. Ford advised him to focus on Fox and let the indictment await his return. Fearing such action would appear as an attempt to flee, Bonney persuaded the governor to have the US marshal take him into custody while Turner went to Rock Island to secure signatures for his $2,000 bond. Two weeks later, Turner returned to Springfield with the bail money, a portion of which was posted by Governor Ford, Turner, and the clerk of the Supreme Court. On January 8, Bonney was released in time to enjoy a sumptuous dinner with Judge Turner at the American Hotel where a celebration was in progress marking the anniversary of the Battle of New Orleans.

A few days later, Bonney set out for Centerville in search of Fox. By now, the gang had learned of his pursuit of Fox and had forewarned him. When he reached Centerville four days later, Sheriff Gentry told him that since his escape, there had been no sign of Fox. In Ohio, Bonney learned that Fox had crossed the Ohio River and gone south. Realizing the trail had gone cold, he returned to Rock Island.

Shortly after, Bonney met with Judge Brown, who had presided over the trial of Davenport's murderers, Brown showed him a long, threatening anonymous letter he had received from a gang member, part of which read,

*To the Honorable Judge: If I should use the word honor in connection with a name that is as black in the eyes of the world as the devil himself. You damned old stack of carrion. I find in looking over the news*

*that you have passed sentence on two innocent men, Aaron Long and Granville Young; and I cannot say that John Long was guilty of the crime for which he was hung. True he was in the crew who killed Davenport; yet, he did not kill him. I am the man who shot Davenport; and beware, sir! Since things have gone as they have, I'll be damned if you don't share the same fate as the Colonel. The pistol that closed the scene with him, will have the honor of conveying a bullet through your infernal, old, empty skull . . . And this man Bonney, will come up missing when least expected. I knew where the chap was on the 19th of October; he knew it best to be absent on that day; and well the pup knows me, and intimately, too. You can inform him that he will see me again and only once more; then I am inclined to think his eyesight will fail.*[12]

The letter was postmarked Columbia, Adair County, Kentucky. Bonney believed the letter aimed to support John Long's gallows confession and intimidate the court and people of Rock Island. While the postmark corresponded to the last trace Bonney had of Fox, the letter did not correspond to Fox's handwriting. Bonney showed the letter to Birch, who was still in jail at the time and identified it as the hand of Hiram Long. Hiram and William Fox were never heard from again. As for Thomas (or Theodore) Brown, his identity remained a mystery.

In April 1846, at the opening of the Lee County Circuit Court, Bonney traveled to Fort Madison to face the charges against him. Since the banditti had provided the testimony, no one showed up in court to serve as witness save their lawyer Haight. Still, the prosecuting attorney filed for continuance in October on the assurance from Haight that he would deliver plenty of witnesses to support the charges. When the witnesses again failed to appear, another continuance was filed for June. By this time, Bonney was too ill to appear in court and another continuance was filed for October 1847. When witnesses failed to appear, the indictments against him were finally dismissed.

One indictment—for counterfeiting—was still pending against him at Springfield, which came to trial in December 1846. Governor Ford was in attendance to vouch for Bonney. By now, the jury was aware the charges had no merit, and that it was merely an attempt by the gang to avenge Bonney's role in the Davenport investigation. After acquitting Bonney, the ten-member jury submitted a long letter to the judge, charging Haight with gross misconduct and requesting he be dismissed as an agent of the US government.

After his trial, Bonney abandoned the search for William Fox.[§] Two years later, he ran for justice of the peace in DeKalb County but was defeated, never having attained the official law enforcement status he sought. He was later a stagecoach driver for Frink and Walker. When the Civil War broke out, Bonney enlisted in the army as a private in 1862. Discharged with a disability in December 1863, he died two months later in Chicago.

§William Fox was never brought to justice for the Davenport murder and disappeared into the frontier.

## CHAPTER 12

# Hell's Cave

*It is a very curious cavern . . . I could not help observing what a very convenient situation this would be for a hermit, or for a convent of monks . . . I have no doubt that it has been the dwelling of some person or persons.*

—CHRISTIAN SCHULTZ, *Traveler*, 1807

While Governor Ford was trying to suppress the civil war between Mormons and Gentiles in Hancock County in the late summer of 1846, another, more bizarre conflict was brewing two hundred miles to the south. What was intended to be a short-lived vigilante action in Pope County would explode out of all proportion into a full-blown war that plunged several counties, particularly Massac and Pope, into a state of total anarchy. The War between the Regulators and the Flatheads, as it was called, lasted an astonishing five years. Even more astonishing, at a given point, the war became so utterly convoluted as to make it virtually impossible to distinguish which side were outlaws and which vigilantes.

That vigilante uprisings elsewhere in Illinois had been relatively short-lived and contained suggests there was something different about the Flathead War. Yet, details about it are scarce and what exists is shrouded in myth and inaccuracy. What we do know is that the war had roots, deep roots that stretched back nearly fifty years to an enormous cavern in Pope County, Cave-in-Rock, that opened onto the landscape like a festering wound. Perched on a limestone bluff overlooking the Ohio, Cave-in-Rock (hereafter referred to as "Cave") was 55 feet wide and 160 feet deep with a small arched opening. Early travelers had remarked on its unusual size, one Englishman praising it as "one of the finest grottoes or caverns I have ever seen."[1]

As outlaws and petty criminals began moving across the frontier after the American Revolution, they found the Cave a perfect lair for their operations. It had a commanding view up and down the river and was obscured by small trees and shrubbery. A natural opening in the rear ceiling of the Cave allowed for large open fires or easy escape. And it was sufficiently high as to prevent flooding in all but the worst conditions.

The Cave's first criminal occupant was a thirty-year-old counterfeiter named John Duff. Born John Michael McElduff, he had served on the Revolutionary War's western front before settling on southern Illinois's black bottoms in 1778.* Just when Duff began minting bogus coin is unclear for he seems to have been a legitimate businessman and officer of the court while in Kaskaskia.[2] At any rate, by 1790, Duff was using the Cave as headquarters for a bristling "coining" operation. He also minted

Cave-in-Rock, Outlaws' Lair
*Source: Courtesy David Wilson*

*The black bottoms were lands periodically subject to flooding by the Ohio River. The land was thus very productive and many people purchased or squatted on them while making their homes higher up.

ten miles upriver at his home—called "Duff's Fort"—in Caseyville, Kentucky, and at the mouth of the Saline River where he obtained his silver and lead. So prolific was Duff that it was said the caves along the river were filled, Captain Kidd-like, with chests brimming with bogus silver and gold coins.

Shortly after his arrival, Philip Alston and his son Peter arrived, having been driven out of Logan County, Kentucky, for counterfeiting.[3] Duff and Alston joined forces, coining mainly the Spanish silver dollar and five-dollar gold pieces.[†] Their ingenious operation consisted of die made of two iron plates the size of a dollar bill welded together along the long edge. In each plate were two disc-shaped depressions 1.5 inches in diameter with a cavity leading outward. Clay was pressed into the depression and cavity of each plate to form one side of a genuine coin and the straw-like stem used to fill it. The two parts of the clay mold were joined together and sealed. The hot silver-lead mixture was then poured into the clay stem. Coining was slow, tedious work. The molds often shattered and each coin needed to be filed to eliminate signs of home manufacture. Although bills were easier to manufacture, most people preferred the tangible value inherent in precious metals. Once minted, Duff employed three men to get the coins into circulation.[4]

A few years after Duff had been operating, several irate settlers who had been burned by his specie, came after him. (Philip Alston had already moved on, leaving his son behind to work with Duff.) When they arrived at Duff's Fort, his wife was washing laundry near the river in a large, heated iron kettle. Duff upset the kettle and with a stick rolled it to the water's edge. When it cooled, he lifted it over his head and waded into the Ohio. The river was quite low and he was able to make most of his way across by wading. Before he reached the Illinois shore, his pursuers had reached the bank and began firing at him. Although several bullets struck his makeshift helmet, he dashed unharmed into the woods.

With citizens now onto Duff, it was only a matter of time before the authorities caught up with him. One day, Duff was mining silver near

†The Spanish dollar was the standard coin until 1793 when the government set up its own mint. It was valued at eight *reales* and was often cut up into pieces for small change, a practice that gave rise to the term "bits," two bits being a quarter dollar.

Saline with his devoted slave Pompey and his three passers, when soldiers from Fort Massac took them by surprise. As the soldiers had only four manacles and were unsure as to whether to convict a slave, all but Pompey were placed in irons. Returning downriver to the Fort with their captives, the soldiers stopped to eat at the Cave. After stacking their arms, they went ashore, leaving one soldier to guard the prisoners. Casting about for some means of escape, Pompey found a file on board and passed it to Duff, who began to sing a death song while he filed away at his chains. Once he removed the shackles, he freed the other prisoners who overtook the guard and tied him to a tree. Seizing the stacked arms, they rushed the soldiers in the Cave who, having no side arms, were forced to surrender. The hapless soldiers were then shackled, thrown into the boat, and sent drifting downstream.[5] When the Fort's commander, Captain Zebulon Pike, father of the famous explorer, learned what had happened, he vowed revenge for his humiliating defeat. In the meantime, Duff and his companions made their way up home upriver to the Saline to live—and coin—another day.

While Duff continued to churn out coins, in 1797, a new type of criminal made his appearance at the Cave, a bloodthirsty "river pirate" named Samuel Mason. Like Duff, the burly Mason had served in the war (with two of Duff's brothers) under the distinguished George Rogers Clark, who had liberated the Illinois country from the British. Mason had probably first seen the Cave when Clark's forces landed at the old French Fort of Massac just a few miles below it.[6] After the war, Mason moved to East Tennessee and, with no work, began robbing the cabins of black families on Sunday while they were attending church. The year 1786 found him living on the Ohio River at Red Banks, Kentucky, where he robbed passing travelers and flatboats on the lower Ohio.

While Mason was living at Red Banks, one of his daughters ran off to Diamond Island with a bandit named Hardin Kuykendall whom Mason disapproved of. Kuykendall carried a set of "devil's claws" in his waist pocket, which could rip the side of a man's face with a single blow.[7] Mason, who preferred to use proxies to do his killing, probably engaged his eldest son Thomas to kill her suitor. Already Thomas had assassinated the constable of Red Banks for recovering two slaves his father had stolen as well as two other men who had crossed him.

Around 1796, Mason moved his operation down to Diamond Island but was not there long before he was driven off by vigilantes. At nearly fifty years of age with a wife and four children, he took refuge in the Cave.

Mason was many things—a horse thief, robber, slave trader, highwayman—but above all he was a river pirate. With the increase in settlement and trade came a virtual flotilla of sundry craft booming downriver: keelboats, scows, arks, broadhorns (so called for the two oars projected from either side of the bow), barges, and the most common and prized quarry of all, the flatboat.

First designed in 1781, the flatboat became the most important means for transport of cargo or travel into the interior. The Ohio flatboat has been described as "an oversized raft" but some were actually far larger and more commodious. They could run as large as 125 feet and could carry as many as 18 people, 13 head of stock, and a wagon. One end had a low roof to provide shelter and sleeping quarters. Flatboats could haul as much as $3,000 in cargo consisting of livestock, corn, whiskey, flour, wheat, potatoes, and hay.

The modus operandi of Mason and other river pirates was to station one or two men or women at a prominent place on shore to hail passing flatboats. When flatboats came ashore, the decoys would ask to be taken aboard, claiming they needed to purchase goods or they were lost and wished to be taken to some settlement further down the river.[8] Once on board, the pirates overtook the crew and plundered the boat or led it down river into the hands of their confederates. Another tactic involved boat wrecking. Under one pretext or another, the pirates managed to get aboard a flatboat and run it aground where their confederates were waiting to attack. If they found a boat tied along the bank, they bored holes in the bottom or dug out the caulking from the flooring. When the crippled boat began to sink, the pirates rushed to the scene to seize their booty. Yet another ploy was to pose as an experienced pilot able to steer flatboats through the eight miles of dangerous currents between Walker's Bar at the horseshoe bend to Hurricane Island. Once in control of the craft, outlaws drove the boats aground into the hands of their associates.

Keelboats and Flatboats on the Ohio
*Source: Courtesy of the Abraham Lincoln Presidential Library and Museum*

If outlaws could not entice the boat to shore, they attacked it outright in canoes. However, the boat was obtained and the crew was usually murdered. Even women and children were not spared, though women were sometimes kept as concubines. The boat was then taken down to New Orleans and sold, the men returning with cash via the Natchez Trace.

As settlement of the frontier grew, flatboat trade on the Ohio increased rapidly. So, too, did the number of river pirates on the Ohio from Red Banks to Fort Massac called "flatheads" after a species of catfish found in the river. Flatheads plied the creeks of southern Illinois which were capable of sustaining flatboats many miles from their mouths at the Ohio River. Before the land was cleared for agriculture in the 1830s, these creeks were fringed with thick tangled grasses called cane breaks that made ideal hideouts for river pirates. From these creeks, pirates waged regular attacks on flatboats. After murdering the crew and passengers, they towed the boat upstream, plundered the cargo, and destroyed the craft or sent it downriver to sell.

Of all the river pirates, Mason's reputation was legendary. The naturalist John James Audubon, who was living in Kentucky at the time, later wrote,

*The name of Mason is still familiar to many of the navigators on the lower Ohio and Mississippi. By dint of industry in bad deeds, he became a notorious horse stealer, forming a line of worthless associates from the eastern part of Virginia (a state greatly celebrated for its fine breed of horses) to New Orleans and had a settlement on Wolf Island, not far from the confluence of the Ohio and Mississippi, from which he issued to stop flatboats and rifle them . . . His depredations became the talk of the whole eastern country.*[9]

After two years at the Cave, Mason decided to move on, fearing, perhaps, it would be overrun by regulators as Diamond Island had.‡ Or he may have left because that summer two men appeared who had the distinction of being America's first serial killers: the Harpes.

By the time they reached the Cave in late May or June of 1799, Micajah Harper, known as Big Harpe, and Wiley Harper, Little Harpe, had already butchered at least eleven people, including two children.[10] Born in North Carolina in late 1760s, the Harpes were likely first cousins and not brothers as some have suggested.[11] Twenty-six-year-old Big Harpe looked every bit the homicidal maniac he was. He was a huge, filthy man with enormous limbs and an unusually large head crowned with dark, curly hair. His grimy face was etched in a ferocious scowl. Two years younger than his cousin, Little Harpe was small and wiry with "fox-red hair." During the Revolution, their fathers, who had emigrated from Scotland, had fought on the side of the Tories. Big Harpe and Wiley likewise fought in several battles against the British including the Battle of Kings Mountain in 1780, though they would have been no older than teenagers at the time.[12] They were also part of a Tory gang that took

‡Mason and Peter Alston moved to the Natchez Trace in the Mississippi Territory. In 1803, Mason was arrested along with Wiley Harpe and Peter Alston by Spanish authorities for crimes committed in Spanish Territory. At the time of his arrest, the Spanish found twenty human scalps in Mason's luggage. While being transferred to American authorities, Mason was shot in the head while attempting to escape. When Mississippi territorial governor William A. Claiborne put up a large reward for the recapture of the three outlaws, Harpe and Alston brazenly brought in Mason's head in an attempt to claim the reward money. Whether they had killed Mason or he died from his head wound has never been determined, though on February 8, 1804, Harpe and Alston were hanged for the murder of Mason. Their heads were cut off and displayed on a pole as a warning to other outlaws.

advantage of the war's havoc by raping, stealing, murdering, and burning and destroying property, especially farms of patriots.

After the war, to avoid persecution by patriotic Americans, the Harpes took refuge in the Cherokee settlement of Nickajack in eastern Tennessee. In Nickajack, the Harpes lived as backwoodsmen, subsisting crudely off the land and clothing themselves with leather hunting shirts and moccasins made from the untanned skin of animals they killed. They stayed in Nickajack for ten years during which time they accompanied their Indian hosts on marauding expeditions of settlements in Tennessee, Kentucky, and North Carolina. During one such rampage in North Carolina, Big Harpe kidnapped two women—Susan Wood and Maria Davidson—to be his "wives."[13] In December 1794, the Harpes heard that Captain Andrew Jackson was planning to sack Nickajack; they fled to the Cumberland Mountains where Susan gave birth to a child, possibly her second.

The year 1797 found the Harpes settled in a log cabin outside the young town of Knoxville on a small tract of cleared land on Beaver Creek. Here they committed the first of their many murders: Moses Doss, a member of their gang who ran afoul of the cousins when he made a pass at one of the women or objected to the way they were treated. While at Beaver Creek, Little Harpe met and married a teenager, Sally Rice, a daughter of a nearby Baptist preacher. Together they cultivated a small plot to create the image of hardy settlers while they pursued their true crafts: stealing horses, sheep, and hogs, and razing barns. After they were caught stealing a neighbor's horses, they fled to Crab Orchard, Kentucky. While on the run, they stopped at a "groggery" on the banks of the Holston River. At the bar, they met a man known only as Johnson whom they believed had put the posse on their trail in Knoxville. Days later, Johnson's body was found floating in an eddy of the river, his torso ripped open and stuffed with stones.

Following the Wilderness Road into Kentucky, they arrived in Knox County in early December 1798. In the dense forests around the Cumberland Pass, the Harpes then embarked on a killing spree. Near the Pass they killed a solitary peddler named Peyton and stole his horse and a few of his wares. In Lincoln County, they shot two traveling Marylanders in the back of the head and stole all their valuables, including the clothes off their backs. When one of the victims who had been wounded attempted to flee, Big Harpe split open his head with a tomahawk he carried in his belt.

A few weeks later, the Harpes stopped at an inn run by John Farris near the Rockcastle River. In the morning, they set out with one of the guests, William Langford, whose bulging purse of silver coins they had noticed when he generously paid for their breakfast. Days later, a group of cattlemen driving their herds to Virginia spotted Langford's blood-stained body in the woods along the trail. A local merchant, Captain Joseph Ballenger, quickly organized a posse that apprehended the Harpes in the woods near Crab Orchard on Christmas Day. After Langford's horse and other property were found in their possession, the party was taken to a two-room log jail in Logan's Station, the men placed in one room and the women in the other. On January 5, an indictment was handed down against all five for the murder of Langford and they were taken to Danville to await trial in the spring. As the Danville jail was little more than a log hovel and the trial not for a few months, to secure the facility the jailor put extra locks on the doors and bolted the men's feet to the floor with "horse locks." Four men were hired to guard the prisoners. Despite these measures, the Harpes managed to break out in mid-March, leaving the women behind to face trial for murder.

While awaiting trial, Susan and Betsy each gave birth to a child. That the accused women, described as "spinsters" in court records, were now mothers who had been coldly abandoned by the men created a great deal of sympathy for them with the jury and they were eventually acquitted. When the seemingly forlorn women said they wished to return to Knoxville and start life over, Danville citizens generously took up a collection of clothes and money and sent them and their newborn infants on their way on an old mare. But when the women had gotten some distance from town, they abruptly changed course and turned south along the Green River. A few days later, they traded their horse for a canoe and drifted downstream—to rendezvous with their husbands at the Cave.

Meanwhile, the decomposed bodies of Peyton and the Marylanders had been discovered and suspicion immediately fell on the Harpes. The governor of Kentucky, James Garrard, authorized Captain Ballenger to form a new posse to hunt down the killers—this time into other states if necessary. On April 10, Ballenger unexpectedly ran into the Harpes near the headwaters of the Rolling Fork. Such was their fear of the killers that they froze in their tracks, thereby allowing them to escape into the impenetrable cane breaks.

Having lost the trail, one member of the posse, Henry Scaggs, went to enlist the help of a seasoned backwoodsman, Colonel Daniel Trabue. When Scaggs arrived, Trabue was in his yard awaiting the return of his thirteen-year-old son John whom he had sent to borrow some flour and beans from a neighbor. The boy had taken his small dog. While they were talking, the dog came limping into the yard badly wounded. Suspecting young John had been kidnapped by the Harpes, they immediately sent out a search party. Fifteen miles southwest of Trabue's farm, the party found where the outlaws had killed a calf and fashioned moccasins from its skin but no trace of the boy. It wasn't until years later that someone passing along the trail accidentally discovered the boy's cut up remains in a sink-hole near the trail. The Harpes had butchered the boy when they emerged on the other side of the cane breaks while fleeing Ballenger's men.

Entering northern Tennessee near Fort Blount, Big Harpe spotted a little girl walking merrily home along the trail and slaughtered her. When the child's body was found in the woods the next day, seven soldiers from the Fort took off in search of the killers. To elude their pursuers, the Harpes hid in Mammoth Cave for a few weeks until the soldiers lost the trail and abandoned the search.

On April 22, terrified citizens appealed to the governor for more help in capturing the Harpes. The governor promptly issued a statewide proclamation offering a $300 reward for their capture. The proclamation described Micah as thirty or thirty-two years of age with black hair and an "ill-looking, downcast countenance." Wiley was said to look older than his cousin, "very meager in his face . . . and has likewise a downcast coun-tenance." Before the warning could be circulated, however, the Harpes had butchered two more men. One of the victims named Stump was living alone in the wilderness when he saw the Harpes approaching. Eager for company, he went to greet them with his violin and a turkey he had just shot. Stump's body was later found in the Barren River with the by now gruesome Harpe trademark—gutted and stuffed with stones. The Harpes then continued west along the river valley toward the Cave to rendezvous with the women. Twelve miles above the Cave, they slaughtered a party consisting of at least three people camped near the mouth of the Saline River on the property of another pirate, Billy Potts.

By now, Captain Ballenger had lost the Harpes' trail and he abandoned the chase. Determined to cleanse western Kentucky not only of the Harpes but outlaws altogether, a Captain Young organized a group of vigilantes in Mercer County, "The Exterminators."[14] Starting in Mercer, the Exterminators undertook a massive sweep of the countryside. As they moved west, more men joined the Exterminators, and by the time they reached the Ohio River two hundred and fifty miles away, they had succeeded in driving all the outlaws from western Kentucky—right into southern Illinois.

As a result of Young's raid, the Cave was now crowded with outlaws, including the Harpes who had reunited with the women and children in late May or June 1799.§ While Susan, Betsy and Sally were waiting for their men to arrive, they had worked for Sam Mason, hailing flatboats at Diamond Island.

Once at the Cave, the Harpes joined with other outlaws in attacking flatboats coming down the river. The first boat to come along landed a quarter-mile above the Cave at the foot of a small bluff to make some repairs. While several men worked on the boat, a young couple hiked to the top of a cliff to take in the view. As the two lovers sat on the brow of the cliff gazing out over the river, the Harpes emerged from the forest and pushed them off. Although they fell forty feet to the sandy beach below, miraculously, they escaped unharmed.

The next flatboat they attacked consisted of two large families intending to settle in Smithtown. The Harpes killed all the passengers save two, who were taken hostage. Anxious to display their brutality to their fellow outlaws, they stripped one of the captives and tied him to a blindfolded horse on the bluff above the Cave. With the naked man tied

§Young's raid was probably the same one that had driven Mason from Diamond Island, which was part of Kentucky.

to its back, they then frightened the horse into running headlong over the bluff, falling more than a hundred feet to the rocks below. So horrified were the other outlaws by the depravity of the act that they drove the Harpes from the Cave.

During the two weeks the Harpes were at the Cave, the bodies of Peyton and the two Marylanders had been discovered and Kentucky authorities had now launched an aggressive manhunt for the Harpes. The trail of their subsequent murders gives a clear indication as to the direction in which they departed—as well as their audacity—for they had returned to their old killing grounds in eastern Tennessee. In mid-July, they killed a farmer named Bradbury fifty miles west of Knoxville. A week later on Black Oak Ridge, they murdered a boy who had been sent by his father to borrow a fiddle. He was found shot in the head, his brains splattered across an oak tree. In Knoxville two days later, they killed William Ballard and dumped his stone-filled corpse into the Tennessee River. When the body surfaced a few days later, people refused to accept the Harpes were behind it, believing even they would not be so daring—or foolish—to return to Tennessee.

Leaving the women temporarily behind, Big and Little Harpe crossed the Emery River where they came across James Brassel and his brother Robert on the crest of a mountain west of Knoxville. When the Harpes asked if they had any news, the Brassels related the stories of the recent spate of murders around Knoxville. When they finished, Big Harpe suddenly seized James and began tying him up, accusing them of being the killers. Realizing that he and his brother had fallen into the very maw of the Harpes, Robert jumped from his horse and dashed into the woods. After running for ten miles, he came upon a small party of men he persuaded to return with him to rescue his brother. By the time they reached James, however, it was too late. Robert could scarcely recognize his dead brother as his throat had been slit and his face beaten beyond recognition.

While Robert was organizing a larger posse, the Harpes had rejoined the women and were now moving north to the Kentucky line. Along the way, they killed a man named John Tully and hid his body under a log. Kentuckians were mystified as to the perpetrators of the murder, believing Young's vigilantes had driven the Harpes from the state for good.

Colonel Trabue thought otherwise. When informed of Tully's murder, he sent an affidavit to the governor to alert the entire state that the Harpes had returned and were on a killing rampage. The affidavit was published in the *Kentucky Gazette* on August 15, 1799, and in several other papers in Kentucky and Tennessee. To make sure the word got out, Trabue sent runners, one north and the other west, to alert residents that the Harpes were at large in the area. No one was precisely sure where. Settlers feared only the next murder would indicate that.

While Trabue was dispatching his messengers, the Harpes were traveling up Marrowbone Creek about twenty-five miles south of Trabue's home. Coming upon an isolated cabin in the woods, they received permission from its owner, John Graves, to spend the night. In the morning, the Harpes slayed Graves and his thirteen-year-old son by splitting their heads open with Graves' own axe. When buzzards were spotted circling over the house a few days later, neighbors found the bodies of John and his son lying heaped like trash against the brush fence surrounding the house.

From Graves' house, the Harpes traveled north to Russell County to visit Susan's father Robert. After a brief stay, they set out west toward Russellville. Along the way, they came across a black boy, walking to a mill with sacks of grain and flour. When the boy's body was found several days later, it appeared he had been swung by the feet and his skull smashed against a tree. Further along the trail, the body of a little girl was found. Eight miles beyond Russellville, they laid low by taking cover in a cave for two weeks. While there, they spotted two brothers and their families and a few black servants preparing to make camp for the night. At daybreak, the Harpes returned to the camp with two Cherokee renegades. While everyone was still asleep, they slaughtered the entire party save one brother who managed to escape. He ran half-naked eight miles to Drumgool's Station in Logan County where he alerted Sheriff William Stewart. Stewart immediately organized a posse of a dozen men to track down the Harpes. Believing the outlaws were traveling south, the posse took off toward the Tennessee line.

The elusive Harpes, in fact, were moving west. A few miles outside Logan County, Big Harpe began to complain that the constant crying of the children would sooner or later lead to their capture unless something wasn't done about it. Once before, he had threatened to kill the infants but the women had refused to allow any harm to come to them. This time, in a fit of rage, Big Harpe snatched who he thought was his nine-month-old daughter. Holding it by its feet, he swung the tiny infant headlong into the side of a maple tree shattering its skull. The child was, in fact, Sally's daughter.

While Stewart's posse was combing the south in search of the killers, the Harpes were in a rented cabin on Canoe Creek near the salt licks of Henderson County. John Slover had seen his new neighbors but suspected nothing, confident Captain Young had swept the area clean of outlaws a few months earlier. One day, as Slover was returning home with a bear he had just killed, he heard the snap of a gun misfiring. Turning in the direction of the sound, he recognized his new neighbors brandishing firearms. Slover quickly reeled and raced home to alert his friends. Everyone refused to believe it was the Harpes, thinking they would not be so stupid as to return to Henderson. While the men debated the identity of the murders in their midst, the Harpes killed another man returning from the salt licks with a sack of salt.

A few days later, Slover returned with General Hopkins and several of his men to surveil the Harpe cabin. Knowing they were being watched, the Harpes were neatly attired in clothing they had stolen from their victims. So differently did they now appear from the day Slover had encountered them that he did not recognize them. After several days' spying on the Harpe cabin and seeing nothing amiss, General Hopkins withdrew.

The Harpes then rode to Steuben's Lick fifteen miles south where they had left their wives and children. On the way, they met James Tompkins who invited them to share his meager fare. Over a dinner devoid of meat, Big Harpe inquired why his host had no venison when deer were so plentiful in the area. Tompkins lamented he had no powder for his musket. Then Big Harpe poured some from his powder horn into Tomkins' teacup, an act of generosity that would repay him in a most unexpected way.[15] After dinner the Harpes continued on, having left their host unmolested. A mile down the trail, they stopped near the farm of Silas McBee. As

McBee was a justice of the peace and had been active in fighting outlaws, the Harpes were intent on murdering him. Only the frantic barking of McBee's dogs prevented them from doing so.

From McBee's, they turned northwest in the hope of spending the night with old friends from Knoxville, the Stegalls. The nature of the Stegalls' relationship to the Harpes was unclear, though just days earlier Mrs. Stegall had put up the Harpe women and children for the night. When the Harpes arrived, a Major William Love was there waiting to see Mr. Stegall on business. Long before, the Harpes had warned the Stegalls never to address them by their real names in front of a stranger. The major was thus ignorant as to the identity of her visitors. With only one spare bed in the loft, Mrs. Stegall assigned it to Love and the Harpes. After the Lieutenant fell asleep, he began to snore loudly. The snoring so infuriated Big Harpe that he took his axe and, with a single blow, shattered Love's skull as he lay. In the morning, the Harpes went downstairs and asked Mrs. Stegall to make breakfast for them. Unaware Love was lying dead upstairs, Mrs. Stegall said it would take her some time to prepare as she needed to tend to her sick baby. The men suggested that she place the baby in the cradle and let them rock it. After breakfast, Mrs. Stegall went to check on her baby as it had been quiet for some time. There lying lifeless in the crib was the infant, its throat cut from ear to ear. Before she could respond, Big Harpes slayed her with the same butcher's knife used to kill the baby. After gathering some bedding and clothing, they set fire to the house.

Stealing Stegall's gelding and Love's mare, the men rode a short distance and halted, hoping to ambush McBee when he saw the house ablaze. While lying in wait for McBee, the outlaws halted two passing men, Hudgens and Gilmore, who were returning from Robertson's Lick with sacks of salt. The Harpes accused them of murdering the Stegall family and burning the house and took them into custody. While marching them along, Big Harpe purposely dropped behind and shot Gilmore through the head, killing him instantly. Hudgens tried to escape but was overtaken by Little Harpe who snatched his gun and pistol-whipped him to death. The murderers then returned to their hiding place to await McBee.

As they waited in the bushes, five men returning from Robertson's Lick, having seen the flames coming from the Stegall cabin, went racing past to alert McBee. The Harpes made no attempt to overtake them, figuring they would return with McBee. As it turned out, when McBee heard about the fire, he took a short cut to rouse a neighbor. When they arrived at the Stegall house, Moses Stegall was in front aghast at the carnage before him. Three case knives were found embedded his wife's charred body, one so deeply even the fire had not burned the handle.

Realizing such a depraved act could only have been committed by the Harpes, Stegall and McBee rounded up a posse of a half dozen seasoned backwoodsmen who had fought in the Revolution and Indian wars, including James Tompkins who had hosted them earlier. Provisioning for several days, on August 21, they struck out in the direction of the salt licks. After riding several miles, they came upon a clearing where the Harpes had scattered a herd of buffalo in order to erase their tracks. Dividing the posse, they were able to locate the Harpes' tracks and regained the trail the next day. Fording Pond River, they came upon the still-warm bodies of several dead dogs, killed, they presumed, to prevent their barking. Realizing the fugitives were nearby, they approached cautiously. A mile down the trail McBee spotted the Harpes on a hillside some distance away talking to a stranger. Alerting the other vigilantes, McBee raced forward on his horse. Realizing they had been detected, Big Harpe hurriedly brought up two horses for his wives and children. But when he saw how rapidly the posse was advancing, he took off on Love's grey mare, leaving the women and children behind. Little Harpe, who was on foot, took off in another direction. As the posse approached, McBee spotted one of the men dart behind a tree; in the heat of the moment McBee fired, striking who he thought was Little Harpe in the arm and leg. As he drew nearer, to his horror McBee realized he had shot a local resident, George Smith, who had been accosted by the Harpes and had fled in a panic when the posse appeared.

By now Big Harpe, having dashed off on Love's fleet grey mare, was well out of sight. Only Tompkins, who was riding a fine Virginia bay mare, *Nance*, was able to close the gap between them and Harpe, with John Leiper close behind. Two miles along the trail in Muhlenberg County, Tompkins caught up with him in a copse of woods along a creek bottom. Holding his fire, Tompkins called for Harpe to surrender as escape was impossible.

"Never!" Harpe shot back. When Leiper arrived, his horse was failing fast and his ramrod had gotten stuck in the wet barrel when he fired at the Harpes the first time. Leiper said, "Let's exchange horses and give me your gun and shot pouch and I'll bring him down if I can overtake him." They dismounted and exchanged weapons and horses. Leiper raced off and after passing through the woods, came within sight of Harpe as he was ascending a slope. Harpe warned him "to stand off or he would kill him." Leiper replied, "One of us has to die, and the hardest fend off." At that moment, Leiper spurred his horse to within ten feet of Harpe, threw his leg over the horse's mane and jumped to the ground. Harpe attempted to shoot but his gun snapped. Leiper fired back, striking Harpe in the leg but failing to bring him down. Leiper fired again, striking Harpe twice in the back with the very powder Big Harpe had given Tompkins the previous day. Harpe disappeared into the cane breaks but moments later he emerged slumped in his saddle, weak from loss of blood and without his hatchet. Leiper rode up and pulled him from his horse. As he lay on the ground writhing in pain, he asked for water. Taking pity on a dying man, Leiper removed his shoe and descended to the river to fetch some water. In his final minutes, it was said Big Harpe confessed to having killed eighteen or nineteen people, regretting none, save the murder of his own child.** (The total was closer to forty.) While Leiper was at the creek, Stegall, Tompkins, and the others rode up. Whether out of simple revenge or fear that, in his final moments, Big Harpe would reveal something about their relationship, Stegall seized a knife and slashed Harpe's throat from ear to ear. He then proceeded to sever his head, leaving his body to be devoured by wild animals on what would forever be known as "Harpe's Hill."[16] Slinging the head over his saddle (some accounts say that Susan was made to carry the head by its hair), Stegall returned to Robertson's Lick, where he lodged the skull in a tree as a gruesome warning to other outlaws. There the head remained on display for several decades. An old crone finally pulverized the skull in the hope it would cure a member of her family of fits.

In late September, Susan, Maria, and Sally were tried in Russellville as accessories to the murder of Major Love and the Stegalls and acquitted.

---

**Strangely, he still did not know it was Sally's baby he had murdered and not his own.

Miraculously, Wiley Harpe had vanished into the wilderness, eventually making his way back to the Cave. It was late summer in 1799. By this time, most of the outlaws had moved on. It may have been because that June, Captain Zebulon Pike, who had vowed revenge against John Duff, had dispatched three Shawnee Indians and a French Canadian backwoodsman who assassinated him and his slave at his home in Caseyville.[††] Whether Pike had also swept the Cave is unclear, though for the next decade, it remained mostly free of outlaws.[‡‡]

In 1809, while passing down the Ohio from Pittsburgh on a flatboat, a petty thief named Jim Wilson was overtaken by a terrific storm.[17] Steering his boat under a cliff, he noticed the yawning mouth of Cave-in-Rock. So taken was he with the spaciousness of the natural shelter that the following spring he returned with his wife, five children, two slaves, and his friend, William Hall, a counterfeiter. His boat was loaded with provisions, stores, liquors, and arms that Wilson had stolen from the Fort Pitt warehouse the night before his departure. The imaginative Wilson transformed the great Cave into a tavern (read: whorehouse) and inn for travelers. At the water's edge, he planted a sign advertising his abode as "Wilson's Liquor Vault and House for Entertainment." Wilson's novel sign soon attracted the attention of other outlaws passing downriver into the frontier, and river piracy resumed with a vengeance.[§§]

The disappearance of so many cargo boats over the course of the next year prompted Pittsburgh shippers to put up a large reward for information as to the location of the robbers. Seeking to make some fast money, in the spring of 1810, Kentuckian John Waller and several companions set out down the Ohio on a flatboat in a dangerous hunt for the river pirates. After drifting several days, one evening the adventurers were

---

[††]For years after Duff's death, treasure hunters scoured the caves around Caseyville in search of the counterfeiter's reputed buried coins. One party from Arkansas, who, after several days' searching, was seen digging up a box not far from Duff's Fort near the mouth of the Tradewater River and disappeared shortly after.

[‡‡]Wiley Harpe subsequently worked his way to the Natchez Trace where he joined up with Samuel Mason and Peter Alston. Harpe was with Peter Alston when the two tried to submit Mason's head to claim the reward money and were captured and hanged in 1804. Harpe's head was displayed on a stake alongside Alston's.

[§§]Over time, the Liquor House name changed to Cave Inn or Rock Cave Inn, then Cave Inn, from which emerged its final name, Cave-in-Rock.

lured siren-like by Wilson's sign and the presence of several females on the bank gesturing them to land. Once ashore, Waller and his men were quickly overcome by the pirates who gave them an ultimatum: join them or die. Waller and his men joined, though only to buy enough time until they were able to escape. Returning with reinforcements, they destroyed the outpost on Hurricane Island, decapitated Wilson, and delivered his head in Pittsburgh to claim the reward.

Waller's gruesome harvesting of Wilson's head may have discouraged other outlaws from inhabiting the Cave, for several years after no reports emerged of criminal activity there. Then, in 1820, Merrick, Roswell, and their father William Sturdevant arrived from New England by way of Madison County, Illinois, with a large contingent of followers. The Sturdevants hailed from a multiple generations of counterfeiters that stretched back to the late eighteenth century. With such pedigree, Roswell was considered the best counterfeiter of his day. Consisting of coins and bills, his counterfeiting operation was set within sight of the Cave just downriver in a two-story fortified log blockhouse strategically located on a bluff overlooking the Ohio in southern Pope County (today's Hardin County). Although Sturdevant did not live in the Cave, he used it as a place to exchange his specie, selling $100 for $16 in good money.[18]

Like William Brown, Roswell cultivated the image of a model citizen to ward off any suspicion. Educated, genteel, and articulate, he treated everyone with warmth and civility. Sturdevant's one rule was that his men never pass counterfeit money in their home state. So when counterfeit money began flooding the local economy, no one had the slightest suspicion as to its source, even though Merrick was arrested in 1821 for passing counterfeit bills in Golconda.

Whether out of hubris or carelessness, in 1822, Roswell began allowing his associates to pass counterfeit money in Pope County. Though several of his men were arrested and tried for counterfeiting, in every case they were acquitted, thanks to a confederate who was able to infiltrate the jury. After a slew of bogus bills turned up in Shawneetown, residents of Pope County finally formed a small group of Regulators to drive the Sturdevants from the area for good. Among the Regulators were some of the most prominent men in the community like attorney

John McLean (who was Captain), Dr. William Sim, Hugh McNulty, and John Raum, all of whom would later lead the Regulators' fight against the Flatheads.

Armed with an official warrant, the Regulators rode to Sturdevant's stronghold ten miles outside Golconda. When he saw them approaching, Sturdevant sounded a horn summoning dozens of reinforcements from among his many confederates in the Cave and its environs.[19] Having heard the horn and knowing they would soon be outnumbered, Regulators made haste. While five Regulators stormed the main gate, two managed to slip into the rear of the compound and made their way to the second floor undetected. There they found the proof they needed for a conviction: a complete counterfeiter's workshop with benches, engraving tools, and vials of liquids for mixing ink. Taking Roswell and Merrill into custody, the Regulators withdrew before his reinforcements appeared. Yet, in their haste to avoid an encounter with Sturdevant's men, they failed to collect the counterfeiting paraphernalia needed as evidence. Ergo, when the prisoners were arraigned, the case against them was dismissed.

An entire year passed before Regulators again attempted to take the Sturdevants at their fort. This time they came in force—some twenty strong. Yet, when they arrived, they discovered they were still grossly outnumbered. As they attempted to retreat, one of the Regulators was shot and killed. A few days later the posse returned, this time with forty men who rushed the fort and broke down the gate. Finding a howitzer cannon trained from the top of the stairway leading to Sturdevant's house, the Regulators retreated and called for reinforcements. As they waited for more men to arrive, the Sturdevants slipped off in the night and disappeared, never to return to Pope County.***

If the Regulators thought they had cleansed Pope County for good of its criminal element, they were sorely mistaken. For that same year, just two miles below the Cave, a highwayman named James Ford was setting up a most deadly ferry service across the Ohio. Since 1799, Ford had been living five miles south of the Cave on the Kentucky side of the Ohio River near the former Shawnee village of Tolu.[20] Six feet tall and weighing three

***Roswell later turned up on the Natchez Trace where he worked as professional gambler.

hundred pounds, he was as large as the sterling reputation he had shaped over the years as a pillar of the community. He was a justice of the peace, active in community affairs, and generous to the poor. He had served as a captain in the calvary of the Livingston County Regiment, called the Cornstalk Militia because many of its men lacked weapons and trained with cornstalks.

Just when—or why—the civic-minded Ford took up with slave traders, highwaymen, and river pirates is unclear. Certainly, by the time he set up his ferry service, he was already robbing passing flatboats on the Ohio. Ford's Ferry ran just below the Cave from Crooked Creek to the mouth of the Anthony Creek in Pope County on the Illinois side. Clients were charged 12½ cents a head to cross, 25 cents for a horse, and $2 for a wagon a team, though many paid a much higher price—their lives. To draw clients to his ferry, Ford used his considerable influence to have the access road improved, which he named Ford's Ferry Road and which still exists today. On the Illinois side, with his own money he built a new road, the High Water Road, which was not susceptible to flooding. He deliberately chose hilly, wooded country for his route so that travelers could be robbed unobserved. At taverns and crossroads, Ford placed signs advertising his ferry service had the best roads leading to it. To run the ferry, he chose brigands from the Cave—later called Ford's Ferry Gang—and elsewhere who were well dressed, appeared educated, and could win the confidence of emigrants crossing into the frontier. He then stationed watchmen in Nashville and every six miles along the way to the ferry to "facilitate" emigrants' passing.

What emigrants didn't know was that Ford had set a lethal trap. When watchmen in Nashville spotted trains carrying rich cargoes of horses and slaves, they would ride to the next station and inform the man there and so on down the line until news reached Ford. He would then dispatch a team to meet the emigrants on the way and offer them safe passage. Sometimes his men would pretend to be strangers who claimed to be heading for Illinois. They would chat with the emigrants and assess if they were worth robbing and to what extent they would resist. Only the most prosperous were singled out for robbery so as not to attract undue suspicion to the ferry. If the traveler appeared to be carrying considerable money, they were usually robbed and murdered. To dispose of the bodies they slit the bellies of their victims, filled them with stones, and dumped the weighted corpse in the river. Sometimes the bodies were disposed of in caves along the river. If the victims had any livestock they were then penned on Hurricane Island—which Ford owned—until they could be resold. Wagons were usually destroyed to eliminate any evidence. When the job was done, Ford and his men would meet at the Cave, divide the spoils, and discuss plans. In the Iroquois language, "Ohio" means "the beautiful," but for emigrants and merchants who had the misfortune of using Ford's Ferry, it was more like a river of death.

In some cases, emigrants were permitted to cross to the other side where they were encouraged to stay at Potts Inn run by Billy Potts, made famous in a ballad by Robert Penn Warren. The large and attractive inn ironically was known to serve excellent food. If the traveler was alone Potts would encourage him to take a drink from the fresh spring near the hotel. When the unsuspecting traveler bent over to drink, Billy would put a tomahawk to his head or a knife to his back.[21]

Ford also partnered with Gallatin County resident John Hart Crenshaw who bred, traded, and kidnapped freed slaves at his lavish antebellum plantation manor near Shawneetown.[22] Ford's role was likely in using his ferry to transport kidnapped blacks out of Illinois into Kentucky, a slave state—the underground railroad in reverse. Although Kentucky passed a law in 1833 restricting importation of slaves, it was widely ignored.

For a long time, Ford was never suspected in connection with any of these crimes, quietly serving as a justice of the peace, surveyor, and executor of estates. In 1825, he became sheriff of Livingston County, evidence of just how much trust he continued to inspire and which allowed him to handle crime investigation. Whenever Ford's men were suspected of a crime, Ford would urge them to leave the area for a while. He would then claim he had run the miscreant out of town, thus appearing to satisfied residents as a most fearless and effective justice of the peace.

Devious though Ford's operation was, it was only a matter of time before local residents would link the disappearance of so many travelers to Ford's Ferry—if only indirectly. By 1826, as more and more travelers disappeared along Ford's Ferry Road, emigrants were being advised to take alternate routes. In time, suspicion fell on two of Ford's men whose income was out of all proportion to their jobs, ferry operator Vincent B. Simpson and Henry Shouse. Whether it was for this reason or not, Ford began setting up additional ferries up and down the river, though his flagship ferry remained the most important.

At the height of his operation, Ford made a crucial mistake. In January 1829, he purchased a slave named Hiram from Simpson for $800. Although Simpson had assured Ford that Hiram was a good blacksmith and of sound health, the slave died shortly after the sale. Seeking compensation for the loss of labor, Ford filed suit against Simpson for $1,000 in damages, claiming Hiram was neither healthy nor a blacksmith. For three years, the acrimonious case dragged through the courts. Even though it was eventually dismissed, Ford claimed victory as he felt he had proved in court that Simpson had defrauded him.

But Ford's victory would prove to be pyrrhic. For the ferry operator knew every detail of his criminal activities and was soon overheard threatening to turn state's evidence in retaliation for the bitter court battle and the public shame he had endured. Ford might have felt sufficiently insulated from any accusations Simpson might make, but that he did not fire his ferry operator indicated he was apprehensive. Each side knew too much and each was eyeing the other, anxiously waiting for the other's next move. The next move came indirectly from Ford.

One morning, Henry Shouse approached Simpson at Ford's Ferry and tried to provoke the ferryman into a fight. Suspecting a ruse, Shouse quietly withdrew. A few days later, Shouse accused him of threatening to expose not only Ford's operation, but the identity of all the robbers, counterfeiters, and murderers in the area. A fistfight ensued but was inconclusive. A week later on June 30, 1833, Simpson rode down in his boat to the Cave for reasons that are unknown. Upon his return, he stopped at Shouse's home at Cedar Point on the Illinois side—mostly likely to kill him. When he entered Shouse's yard, someone fired from an upstairs window hitting him in the back. He died the next day.

Given the well-known acrimony between Ford and Simpson, Regulators immediately suspected Ford of being behind the murder. At some point, perhaps after talking to the aggrieved Mrs. Simpson, they became convinced he was the gang's boss and decided he had to go. Three of the Regulators rode to Ford's house on the pretext of conferring with him about the Shouse trial. Along the way they ran into him and asked him to accompany them to Simpson's to discuss testimony for the grand jury the next day. When they arrived at Simpson's it was dark. Inside, Mrs. Simpson was preparing supper for several men. As Ford sat at the table with his back to the wall, one by one the men disappeared until only Ford was left alone in front of a lone flickering candle. One of the Regulators then asked him to read a letter and held the candle near, not so that Ford could read it, but so the shooter could see his mark in the darkness. As Ford read the letter, a shot rang out and a bullet pierced his heart. His massive frame crumpled onto the floor and he died moments later. Simpson's son had pulled the trigger. Ford had become so corpulent in his later years that it took the coffin maker two days to make his coffin.

A final bit of poetic justice occurred at his funeral. As his coffin was being lowered into the ground, a thunderstorm came up. As slaves were lowering the coffin into the grave, a lightning bolt struck nearby causing one of the slaves to lose his grip. The coffin fell at an angle headfirst whereupon it became stuck. With the rain falling in sheets and the men unable to extricate it from its position, they hurriedly filled in the hole and ran for cover. For years after, locals quipped how, when old James Ford died, he had "landed in Hell headfirst." As Ford had always acted through intermediaries, Regulators were never able to prove his involvement in the Ferry Gang.

Shouse was later captured in Arkansas and convicted for the murder of Simpson. While waiting execution in 1834, he decided to reveal to Judge Wiley Fowler all he knew concerning the Ford's Ferry gang. Though the judge took copious notes, he showed them to no one. He later destroyed the record saying, "No good could come of its publication. It would cast a shade upon the reputation of some of Livingston County's most esteemed citizens."[23] On June 4, 1834, Shouse was hanged, the first—though by no means the last—legal hanging in Pope County.

## CHAPTER 13

# Honest Men and Rogues

*That which at first was merely a war between honest men and rogues, is converted into a war between honest men alone, one party contending for the supremacy of the laws, and the other maintaining its own assumed authority.*

—GOVERNOR THOMAS FORD

With the breakup of the Ford's Ferry Gang, peace returned to Pope County. Just why isn't entirely clear, though those who hadn't already been killed or driven out by Regulators had likely moved deeper into the frontier to more lawless places like the Natchez Trace. That Illinois was still part of the lawless frontier became painfully evident in the early 1840s when yet another crime wave erupted in Pope and Massac Counties. Some of the criminals like the Cheatam Lynn gang were probably newcomers to the Illinois frontier. Others were children of the earlier highwaymen, river pirates, and counterfeiters who, considerably less bloodthirsty than their fathers, confined their criminal activities to horse stealing, robbery, counterfeiting, and the kidnapping of freed slaves.[1] Just as in Ogle County, some crimes went unsolved while convictions for others went unobtained as barns burned, witnesses were intimidated, and gang members infiltrated juries.

The outlaws might have gone on unmolested for years had it not been for two incidents that had particularly outraged settlers. For years it had been a common practice for slave owners to come to Illinois (an abolitionist state) to free their slaves or for freed slaves to relocate there. One such slave was Elijah Morris and his wife Junetta who, in the late 1830s, had emigrated from Tennessee to Pope County with their ten children.

As required by law, they appeared before Circuit Clerk John Raum (one of the Regulators who ousted the Sturdevants) and presented their freedom papers. Just outside of Golconda Elijah found work on the farm of Sam Blair and quickly earned the respect of locals for his honesty and industry. It looked as though the Morrises had embarked on a new and better life when around midnight on October 10, 1844, six masked men burst into his cabin and abducted Katherine, Martha, David, and James. The children ranged in age from six to twelve years.

Black kidnappings had been a persistent problem in Illinois for years. Abductees were often lured on a trip south on a flatboat or sent on an errand. At some prearranged point along the Ohio or Mississippi River, they would be seized by traffickers and forcibly taken into the interior where they were sold back into slavery. Others were seized while working in the fields and brought back to Kentucky or another slave state. The law did little to discourage such kidnappings, making no provision for criminal conviction apart from a fine.

Involving as it did innocent children, the Morris kidnappings sparked a firestorm of public fury. Search parties were organized and the countryside combed, but after several days, not a single trace of the kidnappers was found. A large reward was then put up and handbills of the missing children were circulated in neighboring cities and towns. Some time passed when a response came from St. Louis indicating the children had been sold in the open slave market there and could be found on the Mississippi farm of a Mr. Dorsey. Pursuing the lead, Pope County sheriff William Rhodes and Elijah set out for Mississippi.

Finding Dorsey at his farm, Rhodes asked if he had purchased four "colored children." Dorsey admitted he had but that he had paid for them in good faith and thus had title to them. If he had been deceived, he would need sufficient proof to relinquish his property. Seeing that the children were working in the fields, Rhodes proposed that he and Elijah wander into them and if the children were his, they would certainly recognize their own father. If they did not, then Elijah obviously had no claim. Dorsey agreed and the men took off in the direction of the children. They walked slowly, pausing now and then to look at some crop so as not to attract the attention of the children too easily. While they were still some distance from them, one of the children called out, "La! Yonder comes Mr. Rhodes. Yes, and Papa, too!" Dropping their hoes, the children ran to embrace their estranged father. When Rhodes asked whom he had purchased the children from, Dorsey produced a bill of sale showing the seller to be one William H. Vaughn, a respectable farmer who lived at the mouth of Big Bay Creek in Pope County.[2]

When Rhodes returned to Pope, he immediately arrested Vaughn who claimed ignorance of the entire affair. When summoned before the grand jury, he finally allowed that he had purchased the children from Joe Lynn and other members of the Lynn gang but had played no part in the abduction. The Lynns, Joseph and Cheatham, were well-to-do farmers in Pope long suspected of trafficking in kidnapped slaves. In return for his testimony, Vaughn was let off with a scathing rebuke by Circuit Court judge Walter B. Scates. Deeply shamed, Vaughn returned to his farm and family with the intent of going straight. Two weeks later, after drinking from a bottle of whiskey, he dropped dead, poisoned, it was widely believed, for betraying his accomplices. Of the four other men Vaughn had named, all were later convicted and sent to prison for eight years. Even though justice had prevailed in this instance, the abductions were an unnerving reminder of just how endemic crime in the county was.

The Morris kidnappings were still fresh in the public mind when the brutal robbery of an old farmer, Henry Sides, occurred in the spring of 1846. Several years earlier, Sides had emigrated from Tennessee to Pope County with his wife and daughter to free his sixteen slaves. As some of his slaves were married to slaves owned by others, the good Sides went so far as to also purchase their freedom so as not to separate the families. He generously built living quarters for them so that they could work his farm.

One of Sides's neighbors back in Tennessee named Dobbs subsequently brought his own slaves to Pope County where he freed them and bought some land for them to work. A short time after returning to Tennessee, Dobbs passed away. Dobbs had bequeathed his entire estate to his former slaves and named Sides as executor. After his estate was liquidated, $2,500 was forwarded to Sides in two boxes containing silver half dollars. With not a single bank in Pope County, Sides decided to keep the money at home secreted in a bag of seed cotton in the bedroom loft until he could distribute it to the beneficiaries.

As soon as word got out Sides was in possession of a hefty sum of money, a large party of armed robbers broke into the house at midnight. At the sight of the robbers, the black servants fled. When Sides refused to turn over the money, the robbers set upon the couple and began beating them senseless. Helplessly looking on was their servant, a lame young black woman, who was mostly spared, it was thought, for the sake of her baby. Just before he passed out, Sides finally revealed the location of the money. The robbers tossed the coins into a pillowcase and set fire to the house with the now unconscious couple in it. After their departure, a heavy rainstorm came up and extinguished the fire. Though their lives had been miraculously spared, seventy-year-old Mrs. Sides had lost an eye as a result of the heavy blows she had received.

It was then that all the pent up fear and frustration of settlers who had endured nearly a half century of river piracy, murder, counterfeiting, and robbery was suddenly unleased in a great tidal wave of righteous anger. On July 23, 1846, at the Golconda courthouse, irate citizens gathered to formulate a strategy to deal with the worsening crime in the county. Thus was born the "Pope County Regulators." Their mission started out innocuously enough: not to inflict summary justice on "Flatheads" but to hunt them down and bring them to trial in a formal court of law— quasi-regulating, if you will. A steering committee of a dozen or so prominent men was formed that included Dr. William Sim (who had first tended to the injured Sides couple and had been one of the Regulators in the assault on the Sturdevants more than a decade earlier), Circuit Court judge Wesley Sloan, and Sheriff William Finney. The committee's role was to formulate plans and strategies that would be implemented by a hundred-man militia. Their first task: to find the Sides's assailants.[3]

When the committee went to the Sides's house to interview the family for clues, one of the black servants said he had found a homemade butcher knife in the yard next to a button that had become detached from the owner's clothing. When the knife was shown to Jesse Davidson, a blacksmith, he identified it as one he made for one Ned Hazel. When questioned by the Regulators, Hazel said he had sold the knife to his brother Dan.

Under questioning, Dan Hazel professed ignorance of both the knife and the Sides affair. Convinced he was lying, Regulators offered Hazel immunity if he would simply name his accomplices—but to no avail. As several members of Hiram Green's gang had also been arrested in connection with the Sides case, one night the Regulators took one of them out with Hazel. The two suspects were separated out of sight, though still within earshot of one another. Taking a hickory stick, one of the Regulators proceeded to loudly whip a tree while another Regulator cried out in mock agony. Hazel was then led to the site of the whipping where he could see worn hickory switches as well as several fresh ones ready to be applied to him. Still, he refused to talk.

With no confessions forthcoming, the suspects were put in cramped quarters that served as a makeshift jail. Being the height of summer, they soon began to chafe from the heat and agreed to plead guilty if a special session of the court were held. But when brought before the grand jury, they once again claimed ignorance of the robbery. All, that is, but the nineteen-year-old Ahab Farmer, who offered to testify in return for immunity from prosecution. But when his case finally went to trial, Farmer instead pleaded not guilty and requested a change of venue for him and his confederates to Johnson County in the hope that friends would rescue them during their transfer. Even though his request was granted, to their frustration, they would be kept in their miserable Golconda quarters until the trial. As the next court session in Johnson County was not until September, and the jail little more than a ramshackle log cabin, each night five or six Regulators volunteered to stand guard.

All this time, confederates of the prisoners had been slipping into town at night to assess the strength of the guard. Realizing they would be unable to break them out without some kind of distraction, they decided to set fire to several places in Golconda as a distraction. While they were enlisting recruits for the plan, one of them suddenly had second thoughts and hastened to town to alert the Regulators.

If the informant was expecting to be received with open arms, he was sorely disappointed. Some days earlier, the guards had noticed him visiting the prisoners and lamenting the sorry state of their conditions, a sign he was sympathetic—if not indeed one of them. So when he arrived in Golconda, he was immediately seized and thrown in with the rest of the prisoners for several days. Before he was released, he was tarred and feathered. With the information he had provided, the Regulators rounded up several plotters and whipped them. Others were ordered to leave the country and the county commissioner was forced to resign merely for having expressed sympathy toward the prisoners.

With the investigation stalled, the Regulators told the prisoners that they were only concerned with recovering the money, not the attack on the Sides. Assuming he would be released if he cooperated, Hiram Green offered to show where it was hidden. There was the added hope of being rescued en route to the money. Under heavy guard, Green led them to the mouth of Big Bay Creek about ten miles outside town. Wading into four feet of muddy water, he reached under a rock and produced the pillowcase filled with the silver coins.

In his desperation to be released, what Green hadn't considered was that in producing the stolen money he had now confirmed his guilt in the robbery. With enough evidence now to go to trial, the Regulators put all the prisoners in a wagon and headed for the Vienna courthouse. As rumors were in the air of an attempted rescue on the way, the prisoners were heavily chained and guarded by an army of over a hundred Regulators. Of the nine men put on trial, six were sentenced to ten years in prison, four of whom would die there. Upon his release, Dan Hazel returned to his farm and went straight. Hiram, not so.

Had the Pope County Regulators disbanded then and there, their actions would have met with public approval and the terrible War that engulfed southern Illinois might never have occurred. But their success in catching the robbers and recovering the Sides's money now emboldened them to undertake a righteous cleanup of the county.

Meanwhile, inspired by the success of the Pope Regulators, Massac County decided to do some regulating of its own and invited them to cooperate in a massive "campaign against crime." Responding to the invitation, seventy-five Pope Regulators rode to the Massac capital of Metropolis in a massive show of force. As a great stampede of horses came down the road, farmers and citizens looked on with assurance. Little did they know that with the formation of the Massac Regulators they were witnessing the beginning of a five-year reign of anarchy.

Massac County was different from Pope in two important respects. Massac citizens had little faith in their legal institutions, believing they were invariably subject to the machinations of the outlaws, particularly the courts. In addition, few people in Massac were considered competent to serve on juries. Indeed, when the county was formed in 1843 out of parts of the Pope and Johnson counties, of the thirty-two cases on its first docket—mostly for counterfeiting—only one had resulted in a conviction.

In August 1846, Massac Regulators, assisted by the old Kentucky Regulators, rounded up the Lynn gang, one of the most notorious counterfeiters and horse thieves in the county. Although the Lynns were armed and ready to fight, when they saw the large number of Regulators approaching they immediately surrendered. Regulators seized clan patriarch Cheatham Lynn, his sons Young and Matthew, and county magistrate William Turner. Young and Turner were taken to Tennessee Island where Turner was given a "cording" which "caused his tongue to hang out quite far."[4] Cording employed ropes bound tightly over the arms around a prisoner's body. A spike was then inserted into the ropes and twisted until the ribs and sides were crushed in by force of the pressure. Small wonder then that Turner's tongue had hung out. After being served in the same style, Young confessed to counterfeiting and indicated the location of his molds. After recovering his paraphernalia, the Regulators released the men on the condition that they leave the country. The first Massac roundup had been an unqualified success.

But the methods of the Massac Regulators has gone far beyond those of their Pope counterparts who had operated strictly in terms of a *posse comitatus*, acting in concert with the law but refraining from dispensing justice themselves. Massac Regulators, however, had realized confessions and valuable information could be extracted from Flatheads simply by giving them a little incentive to talk. In addition to cording, another mode of torture was to take suspects to the Ohio River and hold them under water until they confessed. Others were strapped across logs and their bare backs whipped mercilessly with hickory switches. Some were tied standing to trees and made to hold weights until they fainted.

As violence increased, so too did opposition to the Regulators and their methods. According to one resident of Massac,

> *Soon both counties were divided, rather the citizens of each county, those who condemned the new method were known as "flatheads"—a term of reproach not confined to real criminals by no means, but all who disapproved or predicted trouble from the violent methods of the Regulators . . . "Liberty of speech" was at a discount, a word of sympathy for the hunted or disapproved might stamp him a "flathead." Refusal to join in a raid might lead to suspicion. Excitement grew to fever heat, and for a time we had a sort of French Revolution, nobody was beheaded, but suspects were plenty and hunted down in a way that had to be stopped. It finally grew into personal quarrels, and men ordered to leave their homes who were only suspected of disapproval of ways of dealing . . . If half the stories of cruelty told was true, it proves the Regulators had lawless men among them.[5]*

Refusal to join in a Regulator roundup led to suspicion even of innocent men who were arrested or ordered to leave their homes. If opponents could not be coerced to support the Regulators, then they had to be forcibly disposed of. As far as Regulators were concerned, anyone who disapproved of their actions simply had to be a Flathead, an enemy, someone to be driven from the country by whatever means possible. Among the honest men opposing the draconian measures of the Regulators were Sheriff John Read, Judge Walter B. Scates, and pretty much everyone else in Massac County law enforcement whom the Regulators accused of being Flatheads. To make matters more confusing, some outlaws actually felt safer going over to the side of the Regulators to avert their wrath.

As a result of the commingling of sides, by late summer of 1846, the opposing groups had reached the state where all good men were not Regulators and all bad men were not Flatheads. Each side claimed to be the honest party and denounced the other as opponents or "rogues." And each side was using violence in the name of the law. Caught in the middle of all the chaos were four thousand law-abiding residents of Massac County.

As the conflict between Regulators and Flatheads deepened, Massac County elections had come up in August and the issue of vigilantism was high on voters' minds. Sheriff Read was running on the pro-law enforcement Whig ticket. His Democratic opponent, Elijah Smith, was a Regulator who had lost many bids for elected office, including to Read in the previous election.[6] Determined to thwart Read's bid for reelection, several days before the election, Regulators rounded up two bandits, one of whom was Young Lynn, and coerced them into falsely accusing Read of passing counterfeit money. Armed with the testimony of a known counterfeiter, the Regulators proceeded to arrest Read just a few days before the election. Runners were then sent to various precincts to report that Read had been arrested for counterfeiting. At the same time, Regulators ran 150 families out of the county in an effort to cut into the political base of anti-Regulators.[7] Despite the heavy-handed chicanery, when the vote was tallied, Read had won by a margin of 3 to 2. The anti-Regulators had prevailed.

With the political defeat of the Regulators, residents of Massac were hoping the entire vigilante affair had been brought to an end. But the Regulators merely redoubled their efforts. They tried Read in court for counterfeiting but, thanks to a vigorous defense by his lawyer, Richard Nelson, he was acquitted. Unable to convict Read, Regulators named Elijah Smith as their "sheriff." With support from friends and kin from Paducah and Smithland, Kentucky, they rounded up suspects and tried and punished them as they saw fit. Some were whipped, others tarred and feathered and ordered to leave the country. Others were tortured into confessing to crimes or revealing their confederates. Regulators even beat several strangers passing through on the belief that anyone unfamiliar who looked like a vagabond must be guilty of something. As Governor Ford observed, "they committed actual violence by whipping a considerable number, and threatening summary punishment to everyone, rogue or honest man, who spoke against their proceedings."[8]

When one criminal was tortured at length into accusing Sheriff Read, the county clerk, and Judge Scates of being members of a gang of robbers, the Regulators ordered them to leave the country. Fearing for his life, in early September, Read briefly disappeared. Governor Ford, unaware of the circumstances of his departure, declared the Office of Sheriff of Massac vacant for failing to appear and ordered a new election.[9]

Wherever he was, Read had no intention of conceding defeat. Instead, he asked Governor Ford to send the militia to prop up the legally constituted authority of Massac. Ford, who was preoccupied with the Mormon war, instead dispatched Brigadier General John T. Davis to assess the situation and call out the militia if necessary. (He also rescinded the election order for county sheriff.)

Davis arrived in Massac in late September and proceeded to call representatives of the two parties together. Each side pointed an accusatory finger at the other, the Regulators insisting they were acting in the name of law and order, and the Flatheads accusing them of arbitrary violence and using vigilantism to settle personal grievances. In the atmosphere of anger, recrimination, and confusion, they were both half-right. Despite the rancor on both sides, Davis brokered an agreement whereby the Regulators agreed to disband in favor of a twelve-member committee of Flatheads and Regulators that would investigate crimes in Massac. A few days later, three of the Lynn boys were ordered out of the country and a referendum was set for the expulsion of dozens of others. Several Flatheads acknowledged their criminality and agreed to leave as well. Claiming victory, on October 3, the Regulators held a barbecue in honor of General Davis. The *Sangamo Journal* triumphantly announced, "The War in Southern Illinois is terminated."[10]

But all the celebrating was premature. For no sooner had Davis left Massac than violence broke out anew, partly over the return of those who had agreed to leave. Then, in early November, Regulators went to the house of an old man named Mathis whom they suspected of counterfeiting. The old man was taken outside and tied to a tree to be whipped. When they approached his wife, an unusually brawny woman, she leveled two of the Regulators with a frying pan. One of the Regulators then pushed the barrel of his rifle into her breast, threating to "blow her heart out" if she continued to resist. When she tried to push the gun barrel away, it went off, wounding her in the thigh. She was then stuck several times in the head with a gun barrel before finally succumbing. Her husband was hauled away.

Mrs. Mathis subsequently filed charges against her attackers who lamely insisted the shooting was an accident. Read needed a posse to arrest her assailants but his would-be supporters were now refusing to join out of fear of Regulator retaliation. In the end, he was able to muster a group of sixty men—a fraction of the strength of the Regulators—some of who were actually outlaws seeking shelter from the Regulators. Notwithstanding, with his small posse, Read proceeded to make the first arrests of ten Regulators.

Unwilling to submit to what they considered Flathead aggression, three hundred Regulators now marched on Metropolis City to rescue their men. At the jailhouse, they were met by Read's inferior force. Anxious to avoid bloodshed, Read agreed to surrender his prisoners on the promise of no retribution. No sooner had he released the prisoners than the Regulators seized several men in Read's posse and handed them over to a contingent of thirty Kentuckians to do as they saw fit. One of the men who resisted was shot at twice but unharmed. But as the Kentuckians were leading him away, one of the Regulators, keen to settle a personal score, rushed him from behind and stabbed him in the back. The wounded man screamed in agony, prompting one of the Regulators, a Methodist minister, to exclaim, "Now they are using them as they should be!" Although the wounded man was innocent, he and several others were hauled off to Paducah. Once there, they were "gone to Arkansas," a phrase implying they had been drowned in the Ohio River and their bodies left to drift downstream toward Arkansas.[11] As for old man Mathis, he too had probably gone to Arkansas for he was never heard from again.

Once again, the Regulators ordered Read and the rest of the posse, including state legislator Enoch Enloe, to leave the county while Judge Scates was threatened with lynching if he ever again held court in Massac. In November, Read fled to Springfield, asking Governor Ford for support in reinstating the erstwhile exiles of Massac, namely himself and the other county officials. Ironically, Ford was with his own militia trying to reinstate the exiled residents of Hancock County. With less than three weeks remaining in his term in office, Ford was reluctant to undertake retaliatory action against the Regulators that his successor was unlikely to support. More to the point, if he called out the militia to protect the

Flatheads, he feared he would be accused of protecting the horse thieves.[12] Instead, he ordered Dr. William J. Gibbs of Johnson County to call up the militia in some of the neighboring counties to protect Read and other county officials, as well as the grand jury and witnesses who had produced warrants against some of the Regulators—what Ford essentially viewed as "the honest part of the community."

Gibbs arrived in Massac County on November 11. After discussing the situation with local officials, he invited Regulators to come before five justices of the peace from five neighboring counties to hear criminal charges against any citizen of Massac they wished to lodge.[13] In investigating charges, neither Regulators nor Flatheads would be permitted to interfere.

Since the Regulators had long since refused to have anything to do with the government—let alone someone like Gibbs who was ignorant of the realities on the ground—the plan was woefully naïve from the start. For the Regulators declined to appear before him, leading Gibbs to the simple-minded conclusion that there were no outlaws in Massac, therefore, all persons were entitled to protection against the Regulators. When Gibbs called up the militia in Union and several other counties, they refused to turn out to protect Flatheads. With their hand inadvertently strengthened, Regulators proceeded to round up more suspected Flatheads.

While Gibbs was floundering in Massac, Governor Ford stepped down on December 8. The new governor, Augustus French, who had once led a group of vigilantes in Edgar County, seemed all but paralyzed by the chaos in Massac. Admittedly, French was handicapped by a dearth of information. French was prepared to send a military force to quell the violence but until he had a better understanding of the chaos in Massac, he felt hamstrung. But after two weeks on the job he had gotten little more than a confusing welter of information about the disturbances— and virtually nothing from Gibbs. "A great number of representations in relation to the disturbance in that county have already reached me and, as might be expected, they embrace almost every conceivable shade of difference," he grumbled in a letter to Captain George Aiken.[14] On December 21, he sacked Gibbs and dispatched Captain Aikin of Franklin County on a "fact-finding mission" to Massac.

While Aiken was setting out for Massac, the Regulators were holding a secret convention of the tri-county (Pope, Massac, and Hardin) Regulators to decide next steps. On December 23, they ordered Read, the county clerk, Judge Scates, and other anti-Regulators to leave within thirty days. Taking his family, Read fled to Springfield, this time to beg for help from the legislature.

With all legally constituted authorities driven from Massac, the Regulators now stepped up their vigilante activities, rounding up and trying a large number of suspected Flatheads. Some were acquitted; those found guilty were whipped, tarred and feathered, and ordered to leave the county. Whether out of approval or fear of the Regulators, more citizens joined the movement, including criminals, bringing the total number of Massac Regulators to over three hundred.

As the turmoil deepened, on December 24, the *Sangamo Journal* appealed to the state legislature for urgent action:

> *From the statements in the St. Louis Republican, and other papers, we are compelled to believe, that in some of the Southern counties of this State all law is abolished, and society is under control of an organized mob. Statements made are of such a character, in our opinion, as to demand the serious and prompt action of the constituted authorities of the State . . . If our laws are lame and do not provide for the emergency of the case, now is the time when the Legislature is in session, to provide by the enactment of suitable laws, an adequate and effectual remedy for the evil.*[15]

Instead of "prompt action," the legislature served up the kind of bureaucratic inertia that could have only reassured the Regulators of the necessity of their actions. The previous day, the House had instructed the judiciary committee to draft a bill to prohibit vigilantism and threats to law enforcement officials, juries, and witnesses. When the bill went to the floor for discussion, objections and counterproposals flew fast and furious. Some wanted to declare martial law, suspend the writ of habeas corpus, and assert the supremacy of the law; others engaged in pettifogging changes in the bill's language. Readings followed motions that were followed by more motions and proposed amendments. Amid the seesaw wrangling, one legislator saw fit to perorate in flowery language on the House floor: "The beautiful and placid waters of the Ohio have been tinged with the blood of American citizens who have been mercilessly scourged and tortured whilst crying in vain for the protection of our laws."[16]

Admittedly, few legislators could say with any certainty exactly what was going on in Massac. It wasn't until January 11 that Governor French shared Aikens's report and only then after a formal request by the House. To ensure an impartial account of the situation, Aikens had visited taverns and stores, speaking only to men who professed to be on neither side. Despite his sound methodology, his anodyne conclusion offered little grist for a plan of action: "[T]he Regulators as well as the Flatheads had in their ranks both good men and rogues." The only other thing he could say with any certainty was that people of Massac were "sick and tired of the difficulties, and anxious to see them at an end."[17]

By January, no decision on the bill had been reached. Thus far, there had been thirty extrajudicial hangings in Massac alone. Both Houses of the legislature continued to debate the Massac issue, encumbered by partisan prejudices and rivalry between the two legislative bodies. On January 6, the Senate referred a bill amended by the House to the Judiciary Committee. Five days later, the Judiciary Committee reported, recommending Senate concurrence of certain of the House amendments and nonconcurrence of others. Citing legal technicalities, some legislators noted that neither could a supreme court judge sit in a circuit court while the Supreme Court was in session nor could a circuit court judge preside over a trial held outside his district. Others denounced as unconstitutional denying the defense the right of a change in venue. Several legislators wanted to call up the federal militia because the state had virtually no money to fund its own. A few thought the entire proposal smacked of a military tribunal and called on the existing civil courts to handle the problem. Others proposed abolishing Massac County altogether and restoring it to its original status within Johnson and Pope Counties. Around these dubious recommendations swirled the fundamental concern of whether and how to use force to suppress force.

As debate over the bill lingered on, on January 11, Judge Scates resigned as associate justice, apparently giving up hope of ever again presiding in a Massac court. A week later, the House informed the Senate that it would delete one amendment but refused to compromise on the others. Thus deadlocked, it was ordered that a committee of two each from the Senate and House attempt to reach a compromise.

As the legislature dithered, in late January, residents of nearby Franklin County, which had been unaffected by the conflict, sent a letter to Governor French urging him to take action.

> *The unfortunate difficulties in Massac county continue unabated: the party called "Regulators," not only killing, whipping, and torturing, in every way possible, men, but are engaged in tearing down houses, over the heads of defenseless women and children, turning them adrift in the inclemency of weather, unprotected; insulting and abusing them; trampling under their feet all law and order, and the dearest and best right of citizens . . . we have lost all confidence in the Legislature passing any law to restore order, and punish the guilty . . . if the Legislature is disposed to spend weeks in making "bucomb" speeches while the cries of innocent women and children fill the air with their lamentations of distress.*
>
> *We call upon the Executive of Illinois to take the "responsibility," and with any necessary force to put down the insurrection, punish the guilty, and protect the interests of the innocent; and that he be earnestly requested to act* immediately *and* promptly.[18]

Unless the state authorities acted immediately, the letter added, signatories would "take responsibility into our own hands . . . let the consequences be what they may." However well-intentioned the Franklin residents, the threat by a county thus far untouched by the crisis could only widen it.

On February 27, the bill finally passed into law. The "Act to Suppress Riots and Regulating Companies and Maintain the Supremacy of the Law" established district courts in each Illinois circuit and authorized the governor to order a special session when a crime was committed by ten persons or more.[19] To ensure a fair trial, juries were to be composed of an equal number of jurors from each county in the circuit. William A. Denning was nominated to serve as judge of the Third District comprising Pope, Johnson, and Massac Counties. The bill also authorized Sheriff Read to empanel a grand jury of twenty-four men and a traverse jury of forty-eight who had not taken any part in the disturbances. To assist the Sheriff, $10,000 was earmarked to allow the governor to call up the militia. Penalty for unlawful imprisonment, trial, punishment, or threats of banishment—which essentially defined Regulator activities—was from one to three years. The law was in force for two years from the date of its passage.

Meanwhile, fighting had worsened in Massac. When the district court law was passed, Judge Sloan, one of the original Pope County Regulators, tried to convince the Massac Regulators to disband now that the state was against them. But Regulators dismissed Sloan as little more than a Flathead stooge. Regulators had even taken to stopping passengers to see if they were agents of the governor. At least two unlucky travelers were whipped and one tarred and feathered. Sheriff Read complained, "[T]he Regulators are assembled nearly all the time and doing and carrying on the same as before the law was passed."

In late March, Governor French issued a proclamation ordering Judge Denning to hold session for the trial of Regulators in Massac. Clearly, it was a vote of support for Read and the other state officers among the Flatheads, if not the Flatheads themselves. On April 10, a militia of ninety armed men arrived in Metropolis and began making arrests. Seventeen Regulators were taken into custody and driven to Benton seventy-five miles north to face trial. When arraigned on charges that included breaking the peace and the assault on Mrs. Mathis, they were denied bail and packed into a tiny room in a tavern under heavy guard. As the time of the trial drew near, a dozen more Regulators turned themselves in and were incarcerated in another of the cramped tavern rooms where they were neither allowed bail nor visitors.

Although the Regulators were willing to stand trial, they wanted to do it in their own county where they felt they would be exonerated of any wrongdoing. They maintained they were essentially fighting outlaws even though, unlike their Pope counterparts, they were administering summary justice. When the court of inquiry met on April 17, an armed mob of over a hundred Regulators surrounded the courthouse and threatened to throw Denning out if he empaneled a jury that did not suit them. After reviewing the cases, Denning discharged several Regulators. Before they were released, he ordered them to pay the cost of their incarceration at $2.62 per week, a dollar more than the actual costs incurred.

The trial began on Thursday, April 22. Because bail had been set so high, three days were taken up in arranging bail so that when the court adjourned on Saturday evening it had accomplished nothing else. The following Monday, the session resumed to face a challenge from an unlikely quarter. Arguing for the defense, former Judge Scates, who until now had been a sworn enemy of the Regulators, pointed out that because the offenses had been committed in Massac County, the defendants had a constitutional right to be tried there and not in Benton. Just why Scates would be arguing on behalf of the defendants wasn't all that surprising. As a judge he had consistently condemned the Regulators for acting outside the law. He was now arguing on similar grounds out of his conviction that the provisions in the special law were unconstitutional. Skeptics argued that wealthy Regulators had paid handsomely for Scates to represent them. Whatever his motives, Denning denied the motion on the grounds that it would defeat the legislature's purpose in passing the law in the first place. Scates countered that the state constitution prohibited ex post facto laws. In other words, the Regulators could not be tried for crimes committed *before* the passage of the special law. Essentially, Denning's final ruling was that the accused would be tried by the district court as that was now the law. Nine days of more motions and maneuverings followed when the court adjourned until May 24. During the last week of May, the court was able to obtain twenty convictions for assault, rioting, and other offenses. On June 1, believing his mission complete in effectively curbing regulating, Denning adjourned.

In fact, though regulating had subsided in Pope County, the convictions had done nothing to discourage regulating in Massac and Johnson Counties—either on the part of the Regulators or the Flatheads. Both sides continued to arrest suspects (or opponents), whip or tar and feather them, and order them from the country.

One of the reasons behind the resurgent fighting was that over summer, the Lynn gang had returned to Massac. This time, the Regulators were seeking the Lynns for murdering a man who had prosecuted their father, Cheatham Lynn, for stealing a black worker from his farm. The Lynns had also taken part in a Flathead assault on Regulator Andrew Douglass, whom they accused of arson. After Douglass was acquitted, the Lynns beat a confession out of him implicating two Regulators in the fire. Before they could be properly arrested, the Lynns and other Flatheads captured the two Regulators and beat them senseless.

When Massac constable David Edwards, armed with an official warrant, tried to arrest Daniel Lynn and his associates, Regulators and Flatheads turned out in force to take sides. In an effort to avert bloodshed, Enoch Enloe struck an agreement with Edwards and the Regulators that he would turn Lynn over on July 28 at Cheatham Lynn's place. In the meantime, the suspects would be guarded by twelve men, six of whom were Flatheads. On the appointed day, when Edwards came to take custody of Lynn and several others, he was confronted by twenty armed Flatheads who refused to release them. Retreating to town, Edwards returned with a posse of seventy armed men. Forming a defensive line in front of the house, the Flatheads dared the men to attack. When Edwards's men were within a hundred yards of the house, the Flatheads fired and absconded. There were several casualties on both sides including Enoch's son, Daniel. After the battle, the Flatheads went to Judge Denning, requesting he call on the governor to send the militia. The entire incident underscored the fact that there still was no recognized legal authority in the county, prompting *The Daily Journal* to conclude sententiously, "One of the parties will have to leave the country."[20]

Many other newspapers now began to weigh in on the chronic violence. The *Cairo Delta* charged Denning with being in secret alliance with the rioters (i.e., the Flatheads).[21] The accusation prompted Massac's *Metropolitan* to characterize the charge as being "so monstrously false as to need no refutation at our hands," adding caustically that the author "had better embark on another profession."[22] The *Peoria Democratic Press* urged the governor to hold a special session of the circuit court—at a cost of around $13,000 or about 4 percent of the annual state revenue, an idea the *Illinois Journal* dismissed as costly and unnecessary.[23] A military force could keep the peace but quite possibly only as long as it was on the ground, making it an open-ended risk for a state that was just getting its financial feet on the ground after years of crippling debt. Once boots were on the ground, no one could predict just how long they would stay, or once removed, whether violence would return. In Hancock County alone, Illinois had spent a staggering $140,000 to quell the Mormon riots. Yet, without holding lawbreakers on both sides accountable, the cycle of violence would only continue. Armed bodies of men were still encamped in the county and still bidding defiance to the law.

With no recognized legal authority in Massac, stalwart Read was reelected Sheriff for a third term in August 1849. Just how bad things still were was revealed in separate affidavits sent to the legislature by Read, the court clerk, the constable, and the acting justice of the peace. In them, they stated it was impossible to enforce the laws or processes of the court.[24] Since military action would be costly and statutorily could not bring offenders to justice, on October 22, Governor French called a special session of the legislature to amend the Constitution to establish district courts. Once again, the old law made the rounds in the chambers and the judiciary committees, though this time it was hustled through in ten days, passing both chambers on November 3, 1849.

Yet, whether the district court ever met to hear Flathead–Regulator cases is uncertain, as no record of them exists.[25] Even more mysterious, within a year, the violence and lawlessness suddenly subsided.[26] While Flatheads and Regulators continued to be factions in Massac political society, which occasioned minor disputes well into the 1850s, the War itself had ended. No one knows how many people were killed, driven from their homes, or mistreated. Some residents say bitter feelings over the injustices and wrongs committed lasted for generations.

As to why the War ended when it did will never be known with any certainty. Perhaps the district courts had held trials and succeeded in restoring law and order and respect for institutions of justice. Or perhaps, after five long years of lawlessness and anarchy, people had simply become exhausted. Or perhaps, just perhaps, it was because that year, with a population of nearly a million, Illinois had quietly, imperceptibly, passed from being a wooly frontier to a wholly settled state.[27] As the frontier moved westward, so too did the banditti.

# Notes

*Prologue*
1 Eliza W. Farnham, *Life in Prairieland* (New York: Harper & Brothers, 1846), p. vi.
2 Ibid., p. 301.
3 Ibid., p. 304.
4 John Locke, *The Works of John Locke*, Vol 2 (London: John Pemberton, 1727), p. 219.
5 Ibid., p. 226.
6 Richard Maxwell Brown, *Strain of Violence, Historical Studies of American Violence and Vigilantism* (New York: Oxford University Press, 1975), p. 98.
7 Locke, *Works of John Locke*, Vol 2, p. 162.

*Chapter 1*
1 Black Hawk, *Life of Ma-ka-tai-me-she-kia-kiak or Black Hawk* (Boston, MA: Russell, Odiorne, and Metcalf, 1834), p. 69.
2 Ibid., p. 271.
3 William Cullen Bryant, *Letter of a Traveller: Notes of Things Seen in Europe and North America* (London: Richard Bentley, 1850), p. 149.
4 Christiana Holmes Tillson, *A Woman's Story of Pioneer Illinois* (Chicago, IL: R.R. Donnelley, 1919), p. 23.
5 Though no record exists in county or state records of Driscoll's birth, it appears on https://www.geni.com/ people/Johnson-John-Driscoll-or-Driskel along with other particulars of his family. Accessed July 15, 2016.
6 "Building of the National Road," *Gale Encyclopedia of U.S. Economic History*. Encyclopedia.com. Retrieved May 11, 2017.
7 Ben Douglass, *History of Wayne County, Ohio: From the Days of the Pioneers and Settlers to the Present Time* (Indianapolis, IN: Robert Douglass, 1878), p. 726.
8 Ibid., p. 396.
9 Abraham J. Baughman, *History of Richland County, Ohio, from 1808 to 1908*, Vol 1 (Chicago, IL: S.J. Clarke, 1908), p. 344.
10 Abraham J. Baughman, *History of Ashland County, Ohio* (Chicago, IL: S.J. Clarke, 1909), p. 118.

*Chapter 2*
1 Achille Murat, *The United States of North America* (London: Effingham Wilson, 1833), p. 66.
2 H.F. Kett, *The History of Ogle County, Illinois* (Chicago, IL: H.F. Kett, 1878), p. 355.
3 William Cullen Bryant, *Letters of a Traveller: Notes of Things Seen in Europe and America* (London: Richard Bentley, 1850), p. 65.

4 Joseph N. Balestier, *The Annals of Chicago: A Lecture* (Chicago: Fergus Printing, 1876), p. 44.

5 Lynn Glaser, *Counterfeiting in America: The History to an American Way of Wealth* (New York: Crown, 1968), p. 17.

6 *History of Winnebago County* (Chicago, IL: H.F. Kett, 1877), p. 264.


## Chapter 3

1 John Dean Caton, *The Early Bench and Bar of Illinois* (Chicago, IL: Legal News Company, 1893), p. 54.

2 H.F. Kett, *The History of Ogle County, Illinois* (Chicago, IL: H.F. Kett, 1878), p. 356.

3 Ibid., p. 356.

4 Ibid., p. 359.

5 Ibid., p. 359–360.

6 Ibid., p. 361.

7 Charles A. Church, *Past and Present of the City of Rockford and Winnebago County, Illinois* (Chicago, IL: S.J. Clarke, 1905), p. 42.

8 Kett, *History of Ogle County*, p. 363.

9 Ibid., p. 366.


## Chapter 4

1 Thomas Ford, *A History of Illinois, 1818–1847*, Milo Quaife, ed., Vol 1 (Chicago, IL: Lakeside Press, 1945), p. xv.

2 Newton Bateman and Paul Selby, eds., *Historical Encyclopedia of Illinois*, Vol 2 (Chicago, IL: Munsell, 1909), p. 451.

3 H.F. Kett, *The History of Ogle County, Illinois* (Chicago, IL: H.F. Kett, 1878), p. 369; *The Sangamo Journal*, July 16, 1841.

4 *Peoria Register*, July 9, 1841.

5 *Ottawa Free Trader*, July 9, 1841.

6 *Galena Gazette*, July 3, 1841.

7 Lewis M. Gross, *Past and Present of DeKalb County, Illinois*, Vol 1 (Chicago, IL: Pioneer, 1907), p. 71.

8 Ibid., p. 72.

9 Kett, *History of Ogle County*, pp. 344–345.

10 Rodney O. Davis, "Judge Ford and the Regulators: 1841–1842," Unpublished paper, p. 11.

11 Kett, *History of Ogle County*, p. 376.

12 John Dean Caton, *The Early Bench and Bar of Illinois* (Chicago, IL: Legal News Company, 1893), pp. 97–98.

13 *Peoria Register*, October 1, 1841.

14 Caton, *Early Bench and Bar of Illinois*, p. 99.

15 *Ottawa Free Trader*, October 1, 1841.

16 *Chicago Democrat*, August 3, 1842.

## Chapter 5

1 H.F. Kett, *The History of Ogle County, Illinois* (Chicago, IL: H.F. Kett, 1878), p. 372.
2 Ibid, p. 372.
3 Edward Bonney, *The Banditti of The Prairies: A Tale of The Mississippi Valley* (Chicago, IL: D.B. Cooke, 1856), p. 12.
4 Ibid, p. 14.
5 Charles A. Church, *History of Rockford and Winnebago County, Illinois: From the First Settlement in 1834 to the Civil War* (Rockford, IL: New England Society, 1900), p. 186.
6 Ibid., p. 180.

## Chapter 6

1 Thomas Ford, *A History of Illinois*, Vol 2, p. 293.
2 Kenneth H. Winn, *Exiles in a Land of Liberty: Mormons in America, 1836–1846* (Chapel Hill, NC: University of North Carolina Press, 1992), p. 130–131.
3 George Q. Cannon, *Church Encyclopedia, Book I,* (Salt Lake City, UT: Andrew Jackson 1889), p. 488.
4 John D. Lee, *The Mormon Menace: The Confessions of John D. Lee, Danite* (St. Louis, MO: Bryan, Brand, 1877), p. 108.
5 Ford, *History of Illinois*, p. 265.
6 Robert Flanders, *Nauvoo: Kingdom on the Mississippi* (Champaign, IL: University of Illinois, 1975), p. 99.
7 Ibid., p. 266.
8 Truman G. Madsen, *Joseph Smith, the Prophet* (Salt Lake City, UT: Bookcraft, 1989), p. 112.
9 Ibid., p. 320.
10 B.H. Roberts, ed., *History of the Church*, Vol 7 (Salt Lake City, UT: Deseret Book, 1962), p. 123.
11 Ford, *History of Illinois*, p. 332.
12 Keith Huntress, "Governor Ford and the Murderers of Joseph Smith," *Dialogue: A Journal of Mormon Thought*, Vol 4, 1969, p. 10.
13 J.M. Reid, *Sketches and Anecdotes of the Old Settlers and the New Comers, the Mormon Bandits and Danite Band* (Keokuk, IA: R.B. Ogden, 1877), p. 37.
14 Ibid., p. 40.
15 Edward Bonney, *The Banditti of the Prairies: A Tale of the Mississippi Valley* (Chicago, IL: D.B. Cooke, 1856), pp. 25–26.
16 Reid, *Sketches and Anecdotes of the Old Settlers*, p. 40.
17 Some observers believe Bonney exaggerated his role in the capture of Miller's killers, but his account of the investigation accords with other known facts of the case. J.M. Reid believed Bonney played an instrumental role in the capture of the attackers.
18 Bonney, *Banditti of the Prairies*, p. 17.

19 Bill Shepard, "The Notorious Hodges Brothers: Solving the Mystery of Their Destruction at Nauvoo," *John Whitmer Historical Association Journal*, Vol 26, 2006, p. 281.
20 Ibid., p. 263.
21 Bill Shepard, "Stealing at Mormon Nauvoo," *Whitmer Historical Association Journal*, Vol 23, 2003, p. 98.
22 Bonney, *Banditti of the Prairies*, p. 33.
23 Ibid., pp. 6–7.
24 Ibid., pp. 55–56.
25 Shepard, "The Notorious Hodges Brothers," p. 269.
26 Shepard, "Stealing at Mormon Nauvoo," p. 100.
27 Shepard, "The Notorious Hodges Brothers," p. 270.
28 Reid, *Sketches and Anecdotes of the Old Settlers*, p. 42.
29 Ibid., p. 43.
30 "An Old Time Letter Discovered Telling on the Hodges Tragedy," *Burlington Hawk Eye*, January 25, 1914, p. 1.
31 Shepard, "The Notorious Hodges Brothers," p. 274.
32 Reid, *Sketches and Anecdotes of the Old Settlers*, pp. 46–47.
33 Ibid., pp. 50–51.

## Chapter 7

1 *The History of Jackson County, Iowa* (Chicago, IL: Western Historical Company, 1879), p. 358.
2 Susan K. Lucke, *The Bellevue War: Mandate of Justice or Murder by Mob?* (Ames, IA: McMillen, 2002), p. 44.
3 Ibid., pp. 38–39.
4 Ibid., pp. 360–361.
5 Ibid., p. 366.
6 Ibid., p. 372.
7 *The Bellevue Leader*, May 12, 1875.
8 Lucke, *The Bellevue War*, p. 380.
9 *The Bellevue Leader*, August 11, 1875.

## Chapter 8

1 *The Bellevue Leader*, October 27, 1875.
2 *The History of Jackson County, Iowa* (Chicago, IL: Western Historical Company, 1879), p. 383.
3 Ibid., p. 383.
4 Ibid., p. 390.
5 Ibid., p. 395.
6 Ibid., p. 399.

## Chapter 9

1 Benjamin F. Gue, *History of Iowa from the Earliest Times to the Beginning of the Twentieth Century*, Vol 4 (New York: Century History, 1903), pp. 67–86.

2 Black Hawk, *Life of Ma-ka-tai-me-she-kia-kiak or Black Hawk* (Boston, MA: Russell, Odiorne, and Metcalf, 1834), p. 151.

3 Edward Bonney, *The Banditti of the Prairies: A Tale of the Mississippi Valley* (Chicago, IL: D.B. Cooke, 1856), p. 48.

4 Ibid., p. 50.

5 Ibid., p. 189.

6 J.M. Reid, *Sketches and Anecdotes of the Old Settlers and the New Comers, the Mormon Bandits and Danite Band* (Keokuk, IA: R.B. Ogden, 1877), p. 44.

7 Bonney, *Banditti of the Prairies*, p. 52.

8 Ibid., p. 64.

## Chapter 10

1 Edward Bonney, *The Banditti of the Prairies: A Tale of the Mississippi Valley* (Chicago, IL: D.B. Cooke, 1856), p. 104.

2 Ibid., p. 160.

3 J.M. Reid, *Sketches and Anecdotes of the Old Settlers and the New Comers, the Mormon Bandits and Danite Band* (Keokuk, IA: R.B. Ogden, 1877), p. 45.

## Chapter 11

1 Edward Bonney, *The Banditti of the Prairies: A Tale of the Mississippi Valley* (Chicago, IL: D.B. Cooke, 1856), p. 162.

2 "The Murder at Rock Island," *New York Sun,* October 27, 1845.

3 "Outrages in Nauvoo," *Warsaw Signal,* October 29, 1845.

4 Bonney, *Banditti of the Prairies*, p. 189.

5 Ibid., p. 34.

6 *The Davenport Gazette*, October 30, 1845.

7 Ibid.

8 Bonney, *Banditti of the Prairies*, p. 176.

9 Gayle A. McCoy, *A Clearing in the Forest* (Rock Island: IL: John M. Brown Memorial Museum, 1980), p. 67.

10 Bonney, *Banditti of the Prairies*, p. 179.

11 Ibid., pp. 180–181.

12 Ibid., pp. 186–187.

## Chapter 12

1 Otto A. Rothert, *The Outlaws of Cave-in-Rock* (Cleveland, OH: Arthur H. Clark, 1924), p. 25.

2 Clarence Walworth Alvord, *The Illinois Country, 1673–1818*, Vol 1 (Springfield, IL: Illinois Centennial Commission, 1920), p. 368.

3 Alexander C. Finley, *The History of Russellville and Logan County, Kentucky*. Vol 1 (Logan County, KY: O.C. Rhea, 1878), p. 17.
4 *History of Union County, Kentucky* (Evansville, IN: Courier, 1886), p. 377.
5 Ibid., p. 379.
6 Paul Wellman, *Spawn of Evil: The Invisible Empire of Soulless Men Which for a Generation Held the Nation in a Spell of Terror* (New York: Doubleday, 1964), p. 43.
7 Ibid., p. 45.
8 William D. Snively and Louanna Furbee, *Satan's Ferryman: A True Tale of the Old Frontier* (New York: F. Unger, 1968), p. 40.
9 Maria R. Audubon, *Audubon and His Journals*, Vol 2 (New York: Scribner's, 1897), p. 232.
10 See Wellman, *Spawn of Evil*.
11 Otto Rothert believed they were brothers, though, according to Fred Rosen, they were cousins, an assertion further supported by their considerable physical differences. See Fred Rosen, *Historical Atlas of American Crime* (New York: Facts on File, 2005), p. 33.
12 Rosen, *Historical Atlas of American Crime*, p. 33.
13 Rothert, *Outlaws of Cave-in-Rock*, p. 61.
14 Edmund L. Starling, *The History of Henderson County, Kentucky* (Henderson, KY: n.p., 1887), p. 26.
15 Ibid., p. 525.
16 William B. Allen, *A History of Kentucky* (Green County, KY: Bradley and Gilbert, 1872), p. 415.
17 Rothert confuses Wilson with Samuel Mason. Wilson arrived at the Cave fully a decade after Mason had left.
18 Judge James Hall, *Sketches of History, Life, and Manners, in the West*, Vol 2 (Philadelphia, PA: Harrison Hall, 1835), p. 90.
19 Ibid., p. 89.
20 Rothert, *Outlaws of Cave-in-Rock*, pp. 284–285.
21 Snively and Furbee, *Satan's Ferryman*, p. 90.
22 Ibid., pp. 174–175.
23 Ibid., p. 317.

*Chapter 13*
1 *The Sangamo Journal*, November 16, 1846.
2 O.J. Page, *History of Massac County* (Metropolis, IL: n.p., 1900), pp. 168–169.
3 Page, *History of Massac County*, p. 160.
4 *The Louisville Journal*, August 31, 1846.
5 James A. Rose, "The Rose Manuscript" (Carbondale, IL: Southern Illinois University, 1951), pp. 8–9.
6 Thomas Ford, *History of Illinois*, Milo Quaife, ed., Vol 2 (Chicago, IL: Lakeside Press, 1945), p. 438.

7 Nicole Etcheson. "Good Men and Notorious Rogues: Vigilantism in Massac County, Illinois, 1846–1850," in *Lethal Imagination: Violence and Brutality in American History*, Michael A. Bellesiles, ed. (New York: NYU Press, 1999), p. 150.

8 Ford, *History of Illinois*, Vol 2, p. 347.

9 Rose, "The Rose Manuscript," p. 59.

10 *The Sangamo Journal*, October 29, 1846.

11 Ford, *History of Illinois*, p. 444.

12 Ibid., p. 441.

13 *Illinois State Register*, November 27, 1846.

14 *Governor's Record of Letters*, December 21, 1846.

15 *The Sangamo Journal*, December 24, 1845.

16 Remarks of Mr. Marshall Hamilton, *Illinois State Register*, Springfield, January 15, 1847.

17 Rose, "The Rose Manuscript," p. 149.

18 Rose, "The Rose Manuscript," pp. 178–179.

19 Ibid., p. 198.

20 *The Daily Journal*, August 7, 1849.

21 *The Cairo Delta*, September 5, 1849.

22 *The Metropolitan*, September 6, 1849.

23 Rose, "The RoseManuscript," pp. 238–239.

24 Ibid., pp. 252–254.

25 Etcheson, "Good Men and Notorious Rogues," p. 162.

26 Ibid, p. 162.

27 See James E. Davis, *Frontier Illinois* (Bloomington, IN: Indiana University Press, 1998).

# Bibliography

*Primary Sources*

*Books*

Audubon, Maria R. *Audubon and His Journals.* Vol 2. New York: Scribner's, 1897.

Balestier, Joseph N. *The Annals of Chicago: A Lecture.* Chicago, IL: Fergus Printing, 1876.

Black, Hawk. *Life of Ma-ka-tai-me-she-kia-kiak or Black Hawk.* Boston, MA: Russell, Odiorne, and Metcalf, 1834.

Bonney, Edward. *The Banditti of the Prairies: A Tale of the Mississippi Valley.* Chicago, IL: D.B. Cooke, 1856.

Bryant, William Cullen. *Letters of a Traveller: Notes of Things Seen in Europe and America.* London: Richard Bentley, 1850.

Caton, John Dean. *The Early Bench and Bar of Illinois.* Chicago, IL: Legal News Company, 1893.

Farnham, Eliza W. *Life in Prairieland.* New York: Harper & Brothers, 1846.

Ford, Thomas. *A History of Illinois, 1818–1847.* Milo Quaife, ed. Vols 1–2. Chicago, IL: Lakeside Press, 1945.

Hall, James. *Sketches of History, Life, and Manners, in the West.* Vol 2. Philadelphia, PA: Harrison Hall, 1835.

Lee, John D. *The Mormon Menace: The Confessions of John D. Lee, Danite.* St. Louis, MO: Bryan, Brand, 1877.

Locke, John. *The Works of John Locke.* London: John Pemberton, 1727.

Murat, Achille. *The United States of North America.* London: Effingham Wilson, 1833.

Reid, J.M. *Sketches and Anecdotes of the Old Settlers and the New Comers, the Mormon Bandits and Danite Band.* Keokuk, IA: R.B. Ogden, 1877.

Rose, James A. *The Rose Manuscript.* Carbondale, IL: Southern Illinois University, 1951.

Tillson, Christiana Holmes. *A Woman's Story of Pioneer Illinois.* Chicago, IL: R.R. Donnelley, 1919.

Woods, John. *Two Years' Residence in the Settlement on the English Prairie in the Illinois Country.* London: Longman, 1822.

*Newspapers*

*The Bellevue Leader*
*Burlington Hawk Eye*
*The Cairo Delta*
*Chicago Democrat*
*The Daily Journal*
*The Davenport Gazette*
*Galena Gazette*
*Illinois State Register*

*The Louisville Journal*
*The Metropolitan*
*Peoria Register*
*The Sangamo Journal*
*Ottawa Free Trader*


*Secondary Sources*

*Books*

Allen, William B. *A History of Kentucky.* Green County, KY: Bradley and Gilbert, 1872.

Alvord, Clarence Walworth. *The Illinois Country, 1673–1818.* Vol 1. Springfield, IL: Illinois Centennial Commission, 1920.

Bateman, Newton, and Paul Selby, eds. *Historical Encyclopedia of Illinois.* Vol 2. Chicago, IL: Munsell, 1909.

Baughman, Abraham J. *History of Ashland County, Ohio.* Chicago, IL: S.J. Clarke, 1909.

———. *History of Richland County, Ohio, from 1808 to 1908. 2 Vols.* Chicago, IL: S.J. Clarke, 1908.

Brown, Richard Maxwell. *Strain of Violence: Historical Studies of American Vigilantes and Violence.* New York: Oxford University Press, 1975.

Brumbaugh, Alice Louise. "The Regulator Movement in Illinois." Master's thesis, University of Illinois, 1927.

Cannon, George Q. *Church Encyclopedia, Book I.* Salt Lake City, UT: Andrew Jenson, 1889.

———. *The Life of Joseph Smith, the Prophet.* Salt Lake City, UT: Juvenile Instructor Office, 1888.

Church, Charles A. *History of Rockford and Winnebago County, Illinois: From the First Settlement in 1834 to the Civil War.* Rockford, IL: New England Society, 1900.

———. *Past and Present of the City of Rockford and Winnebago County, Illinois.* Chicago, IL: S.J. Clarke, 1905.

Davis, James E. *Frontier Illinois.* Bloomington, IN: Indiana University Press, 1998.

Douglass, Ben. *History of Wayne County, Ohio: From the Days of the Pioneers and Settlers to the Present Time.* Indianapolis, IN: Robert Douglass, 1878.

Downer, Harry E. *History of Davenport and Scott County Iowa.* Chicago, IL: S.J. Clarke, 1910.

Finley, Alexander C. *The History of Russellville and Logan County, Kentucky.* Vol 1. Logan County, KY: O.C. Rhea, 1878.

Flanders, Robert. *Nauvoo: Kingdom on the Mississippi.* Champaign, IL: University of Illinois, 1975.

Glaser, Lynn. *Counterfeiting in America: The History of an American Way to Wealth.* New York: Crown, 1968.

Gregg, Theodore. *History of Hancock County, Illinois.* Chicago, IL: Charles C. Chapman, 1880.

Gross, Lewis M. *Past and Present of DeKalb County, Illinois.* Vol 1. Chicago, IL: Pioneer, 1907.

Gue, Benjamin F. *History of Iowa from the Earliest Times to the Beginning of the Twentieth Century*. Vol 4. New York: Century History, 1903.

*The History of Jackson County, Iowa*. Chicago, IL: Western Historical Company, 1879.

*The History of Lee County, Iowa*. Chicago, IL: Western Historical Company, 1879.

*The History of Pike County*. Chicago, IL: Charles C. Chapman, 1880.

*History of Union County, Kentucky*. Evansville, IN: Courier, 1886.

*The History of Wayne County*. Indianapolis, IN: B.F. Bowen, 1910.

*The History of Winnebago County, Illinois*. Chicago, IL: H.F. Kett, 1877.

Jordan, Philip D. *Frontier Law and Order: Ten Essays*. Lincoln, NE: University of Nebraska Press, 1979.

Kaufmann, Horace G., and Rebecca H., eds. *Historical Encyclopedia of Illinois and History of Ogle County*. Vol 2. Chicago, IL: Munsell, 1909.

Kett, H.F. *The History of Ogle County, Illinois*. Chicago, IL: H.F. Kett, 1878.

———. *History of Winnebago County*. Chicago, IL: H.F. Kett, 1877.

Lucke, Susan K. *The Bellevue War: Mandate of Justice or Murder by Mob?* Ames, IA: McMillen, 2002.

Madsen, Truman G. *Joseph Smith, the Prophet*. Salt Lake City, UT: Bookcraft, 1989.

May, George. *History of Massac County, Illinois*. Galesburg, IL: Wagoner, 1955.

McCoy, Gayle A. *A Clearing in the Forest*. Rock Island, IL: John M. Brown Memorial Museum, 1980.

Ogle County American Revolution Bicentennial Commission. *History of Ogle County 1976*. Oregon, IL: The Commission, 1976.

Page, O.J. *History of Massac County*. Metropolis, IL: n.p., 1900.

Pease, Theodore. *The Frontier State: 1818–1848*. Chicago, IL: A.C. McClurg, 1919.

Quaife, Milo M. *Chicago's Highways, Old and New, from Indian Trail to Motor Road*. Chicago, IL: D.F. Keller, 1923.

Roberts, B.H., ed. *History of the Church*. Salt Lake City, UT: Deseret Book, 1962.

Rose, James A. "The Regulators and Flatheads in Southern Illinois." Springfield: Publications of the Illinois State Historical Library. No 11: 108–121, January 1906.

Rosen, Fred. *Historical Atlas of American Crime*. New York: Facts on File, 2005.

Rothert, Otto A. *The Outlaws of Cave-in-Rock*. Cleveland, OH: Arthur H. Clark, 1924.

Smith, Thomas Marshall. *Legends of the War of Independence and of the Earlier Settlements in the West*. Louisville, KY: J.F. Brennan, 1855.

Snively, William D., and Louanna Furbee. *Satan's Ferryman: A True Tale of the Old Frontier*. New York: F. Unger, 1968.

Starling, Edmund L. *The History of Henderson County, Kentucky*. Henderson, KY: n.p., 1887.

Wellman, Paul. *Spawn of Evil: The Invisible Empire of Soulless Men Which for a Generation Held the Nation in a Spell of Terror*. New York: Doubleday, 1964.

Winn, Kenneth H. *Exiles in a Land of Liberty: Mormons in America, 1836–1846*. Chapel Hill, NC: University of North Carolina Press, 1992.

*Articles*

Ander, O. Fritiof. "Law and Lawlessness in Rock Island Prior to 1850." *Journal of the Illinois State Historical Society.* Vol 52, No 4: 526–543, Winter 1959.

Bodenhamer, David. "Law and Disorder on the Early Frontier: Marion County, Indiana 1823–1850." *Western Historical Quarterly.* Vol 10, No 3: 323–336, July 1979.

Etcheson, Nicole. "Good Men and Notorious Rogues: Vigilantism in Massac County, Illinois, 1846–1850." In Michael A. Bellesiles, ed. *Lethal Imagination: Violence and Brutality in American History.* New York: NYU Press, 1999.

Grimstead, David. "Ne d'hier: American Vigilantism, Communal Rebirth and Political Traditions." https://discoverarchive.vanderbilt.edu, 1992.

Huntress, Keith. "Governor Ford and the Murderers of Joseph Smith." *Dialogue: A Journal of Mormon Thought.* Vol 4: 1–13, 1969.

Jones, Robert Huhn. "Three Days of Violence, the Regulators of the Rock River Valley." *Journal of the Illinois State Historical Society (1908–1984).* Vol 59, No 2: 131–142, Summer 1966.

Parish, John C. "White Beads for Hanging." *The Palimpsest.* State Historical Society of Iowa. Vol 1: 9–28, 1920.

Reed, Doris M. "Edward Bonney, Detective." *Indiana University Bookman.* No 2, 1957.

Shepard, Bill. "The Notorious Hodges Brothers: Solving the Mystery of Their Destruction at Nauvoo." *John Whitmer Historical Association Journal.* Vol 26: 250–286, 2006.

———. "Stealing at Mormon Nauvoo." *Whitmer Historical Association Journal.* Vol 23: 91–110, 2003.

*Papers*

Davis, Rodney. "Judge Ford and the Regulators: 1841–1842." Illinois State Historical Society unpublished paper.

Rose, James A. "The Rose Manuscript: The War between the Flatheads and The Regulators, Massac and Adjoining Counties, 1846–1851." Transcribed by Roy Vail Jordan. The Illinois State Historical Society.

# INDEX

# About the Author

Ken Lizzio is a professor of anthropology, having taught at Winthrop and James Madison Universities. He is the author of *Embattled Saints: My Year with the Sufis or Afghanistan*, an ethnography of an Islamic mystical brotherhood, which won the IBPA's 2015 Ben Franklin Silver Award, and *Forty-Niner: The Extraordinary Gold Rush Odyssey of Joseph Goldsborough Bruff*. Having an abiding interest in the American frontier, he is currently at work on a book about a father and son's struggle against slavery from "bleeding Kansas" to the Civil War.